Books by Sam Moskowitz

Author:

EXPLORERS OF THE INFINITE: SHAPERS
    OF SCIENCE FICTION

THE IMMORTAL STORM: A HISTORY OF
    SCIENCE FICTION FANDOM

Editor:

EDITOR'S CHOICE IN SCIENCE FICTION

LIFE EVERLASTING, AND OTHER TALES OF SCIENCE,
    FANTASY AND HORROR BY DAVID H. KELLER, M.D.

GREAT RAILROAD STORIES OF THE WORLD

THE COMING OF THE ROBOTS

EXPLORING OTHER WORLDS

A MARTIAN ODYSSEY AND OTHERS
    BY STANLEY G. WEINBAUM

SAM MOSKOWITZ

Explorers

of the Infinite

SHAPERS

OF

SCIENCE

FICTION

HYPERION PRESS, INC.
WESTPORT, CONNECTICUT

Library of Congress Cataloging in Publication Data

Moskowitz, Samuel.
    Explorers of the infinite: shapers of science
fiction.

    Reprint of the ed. published by World Pub.
Co., Cleveland.
    1.   Science fiction--History and criticism.
I.   Title.
[PN3448.S45M65   1973]   809.3'876   73-15068
ISBN 0-88355-130-6
ISBN 0-88355-159-4 (pbk.)

Published in 1963
by The World Publishing Company, Cleveland, Ohio
Copyright © 1963, 1959, 1958, 1957 by Sam Moskowitz.
Copyright © 1960 by Ziff-Davis Publishing Co.
"How Science Fiction Got Its Name," copyright © 1957
by Fantasy House, Ind. for *The Magazine of Fantasy and
Science Fiction.* Reprinted by permission of Sam Moskowitz.

Portions of this book have appeared in *Amazing Stories,
Fantastic Science Fiction, The Magazine of Fantasy and
Science Fiction, Science Fiction Times,* and *Satellite
Science Fiction.*

Hyperion reprint edition 1974

Library of Congress Catalogue Number 73-15068

ISBN 0-88355-130-6 (cloth ed.)

ISBN 0-88355-159-4 (paper ed.)

Printed in the United States of America

NEH

CONTENTS

CONTENTS

INTRODUCTION

An adequate definition of science fiction as it exists can best be phrased: "Science fiction is a branch of fantasy identifiable by the fact that it eases the 'willing suspension of disbelief' on the part of its readers by utilizing an atmosphere of scientific credibility for its imaginative speculations in physical science, space, time, social science, and philosophy."

The term "science fiction" was coined in 1929 by Hugo Gernsback, the father of the modern genre. It was Gernsback who established *Amazing Stories*, the world's first science fiction periodical, in April 1926.

The form itself can with logic be traced back to the ancient "travel tales" preserved in the Mediterranean basin long before Christ. The most famous of these is Homer's *Odyssey*, a mixture of fiction, myth, and fact which attempted to maintain an "atmosphere of scientific credibility" consistent with the limited knowledge of the time. As man began to grasp the true nature of the cosmos, the scope of the travel tale was extended to include the moon, the sun, the planets, and the stars.

Many of the so-called utopias, while basically intended to present "unpopular" political, sociological, or philosophical views, are technically works of science fiction. Plato, early in the fourth century B.C., laid the groundwork for such presentations when he included his ideas on Atlantis in *Timaeus* and *Critias*. The popularization of the term comes from Thomas More's *Utopia* (literally, the word means No Place), issued in 1515-16. The science fiction satire, of which *Gulliver's Travels* (1726) by Jonathan Swift is the best-known example, was an outgrowth of the utopia, as are the more modern "utopias in reverse," such as Aldous Huxley's *Brave New World* (1932) and *1984* (1949) by George Orwell.

Greater emphasis upon the more scientific aspects of the stories was a natural development of technical and intellectual progress, beginning in the seventeenth century with *Somnium* by famous scientist Johannes Kepler, published in Latin in 1634, to be followed by *The Man in the Moone* (1638) by Bishop Francis Godwin, *Voyage to the Moon* (1650) by Cyrano de Bergerac, with development through the techniques of Edgar Allan Poe and Jules Verne, which eventually became the tools for today's more sophisticated efforts.

The last major ingredients of science fiction as we know it today were elements of the psychological and philosophical incorporated within such spine-chillers as *Frankenstein* (1818) by Mary Wollstonecraft Shelley and Robert Louis Stevenson's *The Strange Case of Dr. Jekyll and Mr. Hyde* (1888); with an occasional flavoring of Freud, these elements still quench the emotional and literary thirsts of the present.

Science fiction is not a prime mover in our current society, but it does play a role. It is a symptom both of civilization's progress and of the desire for progress. Its study by scholars of centuries to come may give them a much finer insight into the attitudes, hopes, fears, aspirations, and direction of thinking of twentieth-century man than an entire library of best-sellers.

For thirty-five years copies of periodicals devoted entirely to science fiction have been found on our newsstands. Today an adequate selection is present in hard covers, and a generous sampling in paper-bound books. Almost weekly the motion picture theaters offer new films in this vein, usually stressing horror and aimed at the younger element but nevertheless significant inasmuch as these fantasies are explained through scientific and not supernatural means. Television has also found a place for science fiction. Nothing comparable to the western or the gangster show, nevertheless the science fiction TV scripts fall into the acceptable part of the entertainment pattern of that media. "Comic strips" and "comic books," more accurately "adventure strips" and "picture adventure story books," include now, as they have ever since their inception, a liberal scattering of science fiction themes.

Science fiction plays a part even in the cold war. The Soviet Union regards science fiction as an important means of stimulating creative thinking among its scientists, and its writers are openly urged to be more boldly imaginative in the presentation of their concepts, to soar to the limits of their fancies and not to cling to the safe and the certain.

Its appeal to youth was underscored by Hugo Gernsback in a talk delivered at the Massachusetts Institute of Technology on October 21, 1960:

> It has been said that the space age belongs to the young. Equally true is the fact—it has always been a fact since its inception—*that science fiction is the domain of youth.* The gifted young mind often has the faculty of an uninhibited, intuitive, forceful imagination that can soar and ferret out secrets of nature.

To youth, science fiction today is not only a means for expressing advanced scientific ideas but one of the few remaining outlets of social protest.

No definitive history of science fiction has yet been written, nor does this book make any claim to comprehensiveness. However, it does claim to present the framework of such a history through emphasis upon the contributions of major molders of the form from the beginnings of man's literature up until 1940, with but a brief look beyond.

The men and women who shaped the direction of modern science fiction were by no standards ordinary people or hack writers. By any measure they were among the most colorful and nonconformist literary figures of their times, and a few of them were among the greatest. The appraisals in the chapters that follow focus on the contribution made by these authors to the development of science fiction. As background the book supplies insights regarding their contemporaries. It regards their efforts in the perspective of the total impact of science fiction on all media: television, moving pictures, radio, comics, magazine fiction, paperback books, as well as to the major literary currents.

For some of these writers, the profiles in this book are the first serious studies ever done which are concerned explicitly with their prophetic fiction, including writers of the rank of A. Conan Doyle, Karel Čapek, and Philip Wylie. H. G. Wells, Edgar Allan Poe, and Jules Verne have frequently been evaluated as prognosticators, without regard to where they belonged in the history of the type. There have been a number of books on the life of Mary Wollstonecraft Shelley, all of them written with the idea of casting light upon her husband, Percy Bysshe Shelley, ignoring completely the quite obvious fact that Shelley's poetry is all but unknown to the masses but Frankenstein is a household word.

Cyrano de Bergerac's accomplishments as a pioneer in science fiction will come as a surprise to many who still regard him as Edmond Rostand's fantasy, and a view of Edward Everett Hale as a science fiction writer makes possible a new insight into his interests. The sketch of Fitz-James O'Brien shows how, in at least one instance, science fiction influenced the mainstream.

Each of the other authors discussed is a bona fide member of Science Fiction's Hall of Fame, a particular type of literary immortality, as real, enduring, and satisfying as that of James J. Corbett in boxing, Ty Cobb in baseball, or Bobby Jones in golf.

I wish to express acknowledgment for their prior researches, among others to Thomas S. Gardner, Allan Howard, and Vernell Coriell, whose own researches into the life and works of Edgar Rice Burroughs simplified my research task, and to C. B. Hyde, who made sure I dotted my *i*'s and crossed my *t*'s.

The very real part an editor plays in making a manuscript into a book is often overlooked. That is why I feel it imperative to underscore my indebtedness to Jerome Fried, managing editor of The World Publishing Company, for the extraordinary dedication of his editorial skills not only to the rhetorical nuances of the manuscript, but also as an authority in his own right on science fiction, in back-checking the references in the book with an enthusiast's zeal and a scholar's devotion.

SAM MOSKOWITZ

Newark, N. J.
January 1963

1
CYRANO DE BERGERAC:
SWORDSMAN OF SPACE

Physicist and dreamer . . . these,
Rhymer, musician, fighter an it please,
And sailor of aerial seas
Swordsman whose parry was attack
Lover, lacking all love's keys;
Here he lies, this Hercules
Savinien Cyrano Bergerac,
All and nothing. Rest in Peace.
                                    —EDMOND ROSTAND

Cyrano de Bergerac collapses only minutes after he has revealed to the beautiful Roxane that it was he and not Christian who had written those inspired love letters to her. The
secret that has eaten like a slow malignancy at his happiness
and well-being for more than fourteen years is at last known.

The fact that Roxane now realizes that she really loved the
great spirit who had teamed his wit and facile pen with the
handsome figure of Christian, to win vicariously the love of a
woman whom he dared not woo, fearing that the ugliness of
his gigantic nose would lead to a rebuff, provides small com-

fort to Cyrano, for now he is dying. His oldest and dearest friend, Henry Le Bret, arrives at the nunnery garden, prompted by a premonition that Cyrano has met with foul play.

Tenderly as a mother, Le Bret bends over the prone figure of Cyrano, and then, indicating the moonlight filtering through the branches of a tree, sobs, "Thy other love!"

Cyrano, smiling and addressing the moon, says: "Welcome, fair friend above!" Then, ignoring Roxane's lament, "I loved but once, and twice I lose my love," he whispers to Le Bret, "I'll journey to that moonland opaline, unhampered—eh, Le Bret?—by a machine."

"What are you saying?" Roxane asks, thinking Cyrano is delirious.

He replies, "I shall have one prize. They'll let me have the moon for paradise. In yonder sphere, we shall hold converse high, Galileo, and Socrates and I."

The quoted lines are from Edmond Rostand's masterpiece, *Cyrano de Bergerac*, written in 1897, a play that has charmed and thrilled millions on the stage and as a motion picture. Of that play, Jay B. Hubbell, and John O. Beaty, in their book *An Introduction to Drama*, say:

> "On the stage the sharp contrast between extreme ugliness and greatness of soul is startlingly effective. Cyrano, however, is, for all his charm, a bundle of fine points for the actor rather than a living man like Hamlet or Falstaff. And yet on the stage the play is so effective that we are swept off our feet and our critical faculties are paralyzed. *Cyrano*, if not a great tragedy, is, in spite of its faults, one of the best of contemporary plays."

Yet the irony of it is that Hamlet and Falstaff were fictional characters, woven out of whole cloth by their author, but Cyrano was real. Cyrano de Bergerac really lived! Some poetic license on the part of Rostand aside, the play is built on fact.

Cyrano de Bergerac was a very famous seventeenth-century Frenchman indeed. He was not only the greatest fencer of his time, but a poet, playwright, philosopher, and an acolyte of science. And he was endowed with a nose virtually as monstrous—though not quite as large—as the one in the play and was inordinately sensitive about it. And while the audience may, between snifflings, regard the quoted references to the moon in Rostand's play as a bit of colorful trimming to adorn a romance, they are in reality an acknowledgment of de Bergerac's role as the greatest science fiction writer of his century!

His most famous work, A Voyage to the Moon, went into nine editions in France and was twice translated into English between the years 1650 and 1687. Previous to its publication it was extensively circulated in manuscript, and read by many of de Bergerac's more distinguished contemporaries.

Unlike other romancers, utopians, and satirists of the period, who wrote occasional works of primitive science fiction as a convenient means of forwarding a particular political or social concept, de Bergerac persisted in his literary endeavors and wrote a sequel entitled A Voyage to the Sun. The story, though apparently incomplete, was no mere fragment, for it exceeded in length A Voyage to the Moon. A third science fiction novel, The Story of the Spark, is referred to in contemporary writings, but the manuscript was stolen and has never been found.

Cyrano de Bergerac was baptized Savinien de Cyrano II, March 6, 1619. The fifth of six children of Abel de Cyrano, he was born on his father's estate near Paris. Though his father was an educated man and moderately well off, he was not of noble birth. On the contrary, Cyrano's grandfather had made his fortune as a fish merchant.

At a country private school, Cyrano met Henry Le Bret, who was to become his lifelong friend. Personality conflicts with his instructor resulted in Cyrano's transfer to the Collège de Beauvais in Paris. This was literally jumping from the frying pan into the fire since the headmaster at Paris proved even more insufferable to a boy of Cyrano's precocious temperament than the rural private-school tutor, for both men believed that the rod was a more effective road to learning than reason. What was worse, he quite brutally exercised that conviction.

Cyrano completed his studies at Beauvais in 1637 and one year later, at the age of nineteen, entered the Gascon guard, which was commanded by M. de Carbon de Casteljaloux. The Gascon guard was famous for the noblemen in its ranks and Cyrano's membership in that select corps gave the erroneous impression that he was born to honor, a misconception which Cyrano did nothing to discourage. Actually, it was his remarkable ability as a swordsman that caused the unit to overlook his background and accept him on merit.

The truth about Cyrano's swordsmanship is more fantastic than the fiction in Rostand's play. On one occasion a poet friend, the Chevalier de Lignières, came running to Cyrano pleading for help. It seemed that Lignières had spread some off-color talk concerning a ranking lord of the area. Learning that the lord had hired a group of men to waylay and teach him the error of his ways, he dared not go home. De Bergerac courageously decided to see his friend safely to his door. They were attacked by one hundred swordsmen. The battle raged while Lignières cowered in a doorway. In what must surely have been one of the great sword battles of all times, Cyrano killed two of the attackers, wounded seven, and routed the rest. Then he nonchalantly escorted his friend home.

Such a story would be dismissed as a fantastic exaggeration were it not for the fact that it was substantiated by two witnesses of such reliability that historians have accepted it without question. The witnesses were M. de Cuigy, son of an Advocate of the Parliament of Paris, and Mestre de Camp of the Prince de Conti's regiment.

Also on historical record is the fact that Cyrano fought dozens of duels at real and imagined slights to his nose. There is no question that Cyrano had a proboscis of truly majestic proportions. Though it was not as grotesque as the one utilized by Jose Ferrer in the motion picture version of the play, the four known portraits of Cyrano reveal it as being incontestably an immense beak, and this despite the fact that the portrait painters must certainly have made some attempt to minimize its proportions.

Cyrano himself said of it: "This veridic nose arrives everywhere a quarter of an hour before its master. Ten shoemakers, good round fat ones too, go and sit down to work under it out of the rain."

Cyrano could say such things about himself and have it construed as wit, but woe to the unwary acquaintance who so much as *looked* too hard at his nose. Duels inspired by his nose were responsible for Cyrano's killing at least ten men and wounding undoubtedly many more.

Not only human beings, but at least one poor ape died as a result of de Bergerac's nose. Trained for the performance, just previous to his arrival an ape was dressed like Cyrano, and given a sword and an artificial nose of heroic size by Brioché, a man who ran a marionette theater near Pont-Neuf. The ape was ordinarily used as a means of attracting attention to Brioché's show, and was billed under the name of Fagotin. When Cyrano appeared and viewed this parody of himself, he unsheathed his sword and, driving the crowd right and left, ran the ape through. The owner of the marionette show sued Cyrano for damages. Regaling the authorities with the dubious logic that since all this happened within the theater, the realm of art, Cyrano succeeded in getting the case dropped by offering to pay in the "coin of the realm," and proceeded to write a poem immortalizing the unfortunate ape. At least, so the story goes.

That Cyrano could be a bully as well as a gallant is best illustrated by his feud with Montfleury, an exceedingly fat actor of the period who was also a playwright. On one occasion, Cyrano forced Montfleury to cease acting in a play halfway through the performance and forbade him to appear again for a month on pain of death. When the actor did appear two days later, Cyrano once again drove him from the stage. The booing and hissing of the audience resulted in

Cyrano's challenging all present to a duel. No one took him up on it.

It was only after Cyrano had been severely wounded in military combat several times that he turned seriously to the arts. He was wounded once when a musket ball passed through his body and again when his throat was cut by a sword.

His period of serious writing commences in 1643. Ironically, it is the relatively quiet period from this date to 1653 which is the least known portion of his fantastic life. While he bombastically and colorfully flaunted his swordsmanship, there always seemed to be someone to record his achievements, but when he settled down to serious writing, only his own works, some of them posthumously mutilated, spoke for him.

A *Voyage to the Moon* is the work for which he is best known today, but one of his plays, the poetic tragedy *Agrippina,* still has substantial support as an outstanding work of the French theater. Curtis Hidden Page says of *The Death of Agrippina* that it "is worthy not only to be ranked with the best dramas of his contemporaries except Corneille, but even to be at least compared with Corneille's better work (except perhaps for *The Cid* and *Polyeucte*)."

Richard Aldington, another student of Cyrano de Bergerac, agrees with Page: "*The Death of Agrippina* has been compared favorably with Corneille's minor tragedies. . . . The play is well written and impressive."

Probably, even if de Bergerac had not written his famous interplanetary stories, he would have earned a minor place in the classical drama of France. Basically his stylistic quality was far above that of Lucian, Francis Godwin, Johannes Kepler, and other writers of the interplanetary voyage who preceded him.

A *Voyage to the Moon* and A *Voyage to the Sun* occupy a special place in the history of science fiction, even though they are not the first interplanetaries ever written nor the first in which a machine is constructed to carry its passengers to another world nor the first to use science fiction as a medium for contemporary satire.

True, they blend all of these, but their real importance lies in their prodigious effort to free science fiction from its previous burden of utopianism and superstition. Cyrano wrestles with the unknown wherever he encounters it. He attempts to side-step nothing. Cyrano avers there is a logical reason for everything, and he tries to give it.

Cyrano's personal struggle, as expressed in A Voyage to the Moon, is the struggle of his times. Not too long out of the Dark Ages, the world was slowly freeing itself from an appalling concretion of superstition and ignorance. With the mystical as well as theological truths of his age literally whipped into him in the course of his education, de Bergerac now swung to the other extreme, became a freethinker, and attempted to make reason prevail.

There are places where Cyrano obviously is unaware that he has substituted mythology for fact. There are times when his careful scientific explanations fall apart on close examination, and he lapses into the prejudices and misconceptions of his time. But for the most part his instincts were correct and he frequently arrived at the right answers, despite gaps in his knowledge or error in his method.

When the final history of space travel is written, Cyrano de Bergerac will have to be enshrined as the first man to think of rockets as a propellant for a space vehicle. In A Voyage to the Moon, de Bergerac's hero spends weeks experimenting on a spaceship, several models failing to get off the ground. Success crowns his efforts when some Canadians tie rockets to his space shell and he is fired aloft.

High in the atmosphere, the rockets give out, but fortunately Cyrano has rubbed himself with bone marrow, to ease the bruises of a previously unsuccessful flight. It was popularly believed in Cyrano's time that the moon sucked up bone marrow, and thus our hero is carried by this method through space, ultimately to land on the moon.

The moon turns out to be inhabited by humanoid creatures that go about on all fours. It is interesting to note that Cyrano makes a point of the light gravitational pull of the moon, by relating how the inhabitants are able to "fan" themselves through the air.

In his two novels, Cyrano makes seven different suggestions for defying gravity to reach the moon: *all seven* are mentioned in Rostand's play.

In addition to detailed descriptions of rocketry and the moon's affinity for bone marrow we have the following:

> One way was to stand naked in the sunshine, in a harness thickly studded with glass phials, each filled with morning dew. The sun in drawing up the dew, you see, could not have helped drawing me up too!
>
> Or else, mechanic as well as artificer, I could have fashioned a giant grasshopper, with steel joints, which, impelled by successive explosions of saltpeter, would have hopped with me to the azure meadows where graze the starry flocks. [This comes fairly close to conceiving an internal combustion engine.]
>
> Since smoke by its nature ascends, I could have blown into an appropriate globe a sufficient quantity to ascend with me. [Fellow Frenchmen, the Montgolfier brothers, made this prophetic—June 5, 1783—ascending in the first balloon.]
>
> Or else, I could have placed myself upon an iron plate, have taken a magnet of suitable size, and thrown it in the air! That way is a very good one! The magnet flies upward, the iron instantly after; the magnet no sooner overtaken than you fling it up again . . . the rest is clear! You can go upward indefinitely. [In descending upon the moon, Cyrano would occasionally throw the magnet up to break the speed of descent. He had its problems well thought out.]
>
> Draw wind into a vacuum—keep it tight—rarefy them, by glowing mirrors, pressed icosahedron-wise within a chest. [This method Cyrano used to go to the sun, forcing the expanded air out in a ramjet principle.]

After reaching the moon, Cyrano very clearly and definitely establishes the fact that the earth and the other planets revolve around the sun and that the sun is the center of the solar system. Lest the reader of the twentieth century regard this as a rather elementary observation, is should be noted that only sixteen years before Cyrano made this statement, Galileo, on his knees before the Inquisition, recanted the "heresy" that his telescope had confirmed.

Cyrano observes that the fixed stars are other suns with planets about them and offers the opinion that the universe is infinite. This latter view, of course, is no longer held by the majority of modern astrophysicists.

Earth was created, as were the other planets, by fragments thrown off from the sun as it cooled, thought Cyrano. It even seemed likely that the sunspots were new planets in formation.

In one of his experiments, Cyrano uses a parachute to descend safely to earth, an idea he possibly obtained from reading Leonardo da Vinci.

On the moon, Cyrano meets creatures who are able to alter their forms at will, a device tremendously popular in science fiction in recent years. These moon-dwellers visited earth in prehistoric ages and gave rise to the stories of mythological monsters and pagan gods that have been passed down to us.

He discovers that these people are actually from the sun and are capable of living thousands of years by transferring their intelligences to new bodies when the old ones wear out.

On the moon, the people eat by inhaling the vapors of food. They have embraced the concept—previously unheard of in Cyrano's time—of going to doctors to *keep well* and taking preventive medicines, instead of waiting until they are ill.

Certainly the most advanced and astonishing theories in his book are those concerning atoms. Cyrano insists that the entire world is composed of infinitesimal bits of matter called "atoms" and that these make up all known elements. He points out that earth, water, fire, and air are merely different arrangements and densities of the same atomic matter. These thoughts may not have been original with him, but are most enlightened for the period.

The origin of life on our planet was a matter of chance, Cyrano feels. In his opinion, in the vastness of the universe infinite combinations of conditions were capable of occurring, and on this planet the chemical and climatic conditions accidentally created life forms.

Before the appearance of de Bergerac's moon story, a volume entitled *The Man in the Moon: or a Discourse of a Voyage Thither*, by Domingo Gonsales, was published in 1638. The book was written by an Anglican bishop, Francis Godwin, and as part of the story his hero, Domingo Gonsales, travels to the moon, with birds serving as the motive power for a contraption he has built. Cyrano, in his book, meets Gonsales on the moon, an acknowledgment of his debt to the earlier imaginative writer.

Of course, Cyrano de Bergerac's wide reading was the source of most of the ideas he expounds and he quite honestly gives credit where credit is due. He praises Girolamo Cardan, an Italian mathematician who gained a great reputation during the sixteenth century; Johannes Kepler, the German scientist whose moon story *Somnium* appeared first in 1634; Tommaso Campanella, the Italian author of a classic utopia, *The City of the Sun*, who is one of the characters in de Bergerac's *A Voyage to the Sun*; Gassendi, who deplored the concepts of Aristotle and Descartes—there is a story extant that Cyrano forced his way into the lectures of this man at sword point, so anxious was he to absorb his theories—and literally dozens of others, including Pythagoras, Epicurus, Democritus, Lucian, Sorel, Copernicus, Rabelais, Rehault, Tritheim, and Nostradamus.

The ideas of all these men and many more profoundly influenced Cyrano's thinking and references to them abound in such profusion in his two interplanetary novels that it is small wonder that Marjorie Nicholson, in her scholarly work *Voyages to the Moon*, appraises Cyrano's works as "the most brilliant of all seventeenth century parodies of the cosmic voyage."

Cyrano's careful description of a machine on the moon

that records and plays back voices, written in 1648, and his prediction of radiant bulbs providing artificial light on the moon belong in the category of first-rate prognostication. Because of the numerous and carefully worked out scientific opinions, theories, and extrapolations included in Cyrano's *Voyages*, we are sometimes inclined to lose sight of the fact that they are also biting satires, appraising the beliefs, customs, and laws of mankind as well as the possibilities of future invention.

Cyrano de Bergerac was opposed to organized religion, believing that it was responsible for more evils than it cured. Strangely, for a man himself a firebrand and master swordsman, he did not believe that physical force in itself proved anything, and he scoffed at the concept of courage, attributing it to men too brutal and ignorant to understand danger or the consequences of their acts. Cyrano deplored "Momism" centuries before Philip Wylie thought of the term and caustically castigates mothers and fathers who establish an emotional despotism over their children, making selfish demands merely because they sired and bore them. De Bergerac was firmly convinced that a great many illnesses were psychosomatic, laying stress on the fact that witch doctors were often able to effect cures in cases which had baffled the greatest of medical practitioners.

Amidst all this philosophy, the scientific marvels never ceased to come, and the cities of Cyrano's moon had some houses on wheels which by a combination of bellows and sails were moved at will about earth's satellite to take advantage of climatic changes. The homes that were stationary rested on giant screws and in the winter dropped into immense underground cellars, protected from the harsh weather above. A *Voyage to the Moon*, despite its flaws, was the most soundly scientific science fiction story of the period.

In narrative flow it is episodic and uneven, chopped into segments of action, science, philosophy, sociology. But it contains at least one description that is as beautiful and poetic as anything in seventeenth century pastoral writing.

A *Voyage to the Moon* depended for its effects upon the presentation of ideas which must have been real shockers in the seventeenth century. It is in every sense of the term the first "thought-variant" science fiction tale in history. It is intended to instruct, but above all else it demands that the reader think for himself.

The sequel, A *Voyage to the Sun*, begins as a straight action adventure on earth, where Cyrano evades chastisement for the views expressed in his first book. About one third of the way through the story, Cyrano carefully constructs a space-ship from a six-by-three-foot box "closed so exactly that not a single grain of air could slip in except through two openings." The box has, on its summit, a globe formed of crystal.

> The vessel was expressly made with several angles, in the shape of an icosahedron, so that as each facet was convex and concave my globe produced the effect of a burning mirror. . . . I have told you that the sun beat vigorously upon my concave mirrors, and uniting its rays in the middle of the globe drove out with ardor through the upper vent the air inside; the globe became a vacuum and, since Nature abhors a vacuum, she made it draw up air through the lower opening to fill itself. . . . I should continue to rise, because the ether became wind through the furious speed with which it rushed through to prevent a vacuum and consequently was bound to force up my machine continually.

For steering his vessel, Cyrano attached a sail!

Out in space, Cyrano calls attention to the difficulty of telling the difference between "up" and "down" in the inter-planetary void, an observation extraordinary for his period.

He dwells ingeniously on possible life-tolerance variations in solar temperature and actually lands on one of the sun-spots, which turns out to be a cooled area, much like our earth.

On the sun, Cyrano indulges in some of his most savage satire, comparing human beings in a most unfavorable light to birds and to animals.

A *Voyage to the Sun*, first published in 1662 as *The Comic*

History of the States and Empires of the Sun, some years after Cyrano's death, is never brought to a finish, but breaks off abruptly. On whether or not the break was intentional there are two schools of thought. The outstanding de Bergerac scholar, Richard Aldington, who was responsible for the first complete English translation of the unexpurgated manuscript of *A Voyage to the Moon,* raises strong doubts about whether Cyrano de Bergerac deliberately closed the manuscript in that manner.

Other scholars point to the first authorized edition of A *Voyage to the Moon,* published in 1657, soon after Cyrano's death—an edition was published without permission in 1650 —where Cyrano apparently added an addendum which does not appear in the manuscript. It reads:

> But foreseeing, that it will put an end to all my Studies, and Travels; that I may be as good as my word to the Council of the World; I have begg'd of Monsieur Le Bret, my dearest and most constant Friend, that he would publish them with the *History of the Republick of the Sun,* that of the *Spark,* and some other Pieces of my Composing, if those who have Stolen them from us restore them to him, as I earnestly adjure them to do.

The addition, translated by A. Lovell, A.M., in 1687— whose edition was the best in English until Richard Aldington's in 1923, and the first in English also to include A *Voyage to the Sun*—indicates that Cyrano refers to the *Sun* as a completed work. It is possible that the ending may be with *The Story of the Spark,* the third of Cyrano's science fiction satires, if the stolen manuscript is ever located.

Ironically, though Cyrano's best friend was Henry Le Bret and though he made Le Bret his literary executor, Le Bret, a staunch pillar of the Church, dared not publish the *Voyages* in their original form, containing as they did atheistic matter as well as scientific speculation contrary to contemporary theological tenets. He therefore hacked away some of Cyrano's most brilliant literary ripostes and toned down others until they made no sense. Many contemporaries referred to Cyrano as a "madman" because the Cosmic Voyages often appeared disjointed, never dreaming that censorship was the culprit. Fortunately, the original manuscript of A Voyage to the Moon survived, but this is not the case with its sequel, A Voyage to the Sun, and we now have no way of telling what was excised from that work unless the original manuscript is someday uncovered.

Cyrano's influence was monumental. Scores of authors imitated him. Tom d'Urfey's work, Wonders in the Sun or the Kingdom of the Birds, published in London in 1706 and used as the basis of an opera, is a direct steal from Cyrano, even to the use of his characters. But the most important author influenced by Cyrano de Bergerac was unquestionably Jonathan Swift, author of Gulliver's Travels.

Swift's biographers have never attempted to side-step his debt to Cyrano. As early as 1754, Samuel Derrick dedicated a new translation into English of A Voyage to the Moon . . . A Comical Romance to the Earl of Orrery, author of Remarks on the Life and Writings of Jonathan Swift, and gave as his reason "your Lordship's mentioning this work in your Life of Swift" as the inspiration for Gulliver's Travels.

Literally dozens of instances of borrowing from Cyrano can be detected in Gulliver's Travels. The most obvious are the Houyhnhnms, in which Swift put men in a very poor light by comparing them to birds and beasts, and a passage in Chapter 6 of Voyage to Lilliput beginning with "Their notions relating to the duties of parents and children differ extremely from ours," and ending with ". . . when they come to the age of twenty moons, at which time they are supposed to have some rudiments of docility," which is a direct re-phrasing of Cyrano's views on "Momism" and the relationship of children to their parents.

In brief sections, the slashing satire contained in de Bergerac's works is every bit as powerful and effective as Swift's, but the quality is not sustained. Nevertheless, had Swift not arrived on the scene, completely eclipsing Cyrano with his satirical genius and evenness of style, the latter might well be more commonly read and referred to today.

Commenting upon the manner in which a great French playwright, Molière, adapted material from Cyrano's play, *The Pedant Outwitted*, for the two best scenes of *Les Fourberies de Scapin*, Curtis Hidden Page concluded: "Real genius is, finally, the essential thing, which Cyrano once more just missed attaining—missed just by the lack of that simplicity, perhaps. But exaggeration, sometimes carried to the burlesque, is the essential trait which makes him what he is; and we cannot wish it away."

It seems almost as if it were not genius which Cyrano lacked but the discipline essential to its full germination. His emotional temperament combined with his fierce independence stood in the way.

He died in his middle thirties, possibly as the result of injuries received from a beam dropped on his head by his enemies. During the latter years of his life, he was sustained by the patronage of the Duc d'Arpajon, but lost favor when the heretical nature of the material in his play, *The Death of Agrippina*, became the scandal of Paris. Ailing from his "accident," he was cared for at the home of Regnault des Bois-Clairs, a friend of Le Bret, where three sisters from a convent labored ceaselessly to restore his faith in religion. They ultimately claimed success and de Bergerac was buried as a Catholic.

The works and even the life of Cyrano de Bergerac might have been permanently relegated to scholarly obscurity had it not been for Edmond Rostand's play. Its first showing in 1897 created an instantaneous revival of interest. Not only did new editions of Cyrano's works appear in both France and England shortly thereafter but works of fiction such as *Captain Satan*, by Louis Gallet, based factually on the life of the great-nosed gallant, gained popular favor.

Through Rostand's play, the world added to its gallery of legendary heroes the heroically pathetic figure of Cyrano de Bergerac, Cyrano of the ready wit, the poetic phrase, the flashing sword, the titanic nose, and the crushingly hopeless love. Audiences revel in the drama, never knowing that such a man truly lived and breathed, never knowing the prophetic role he played in man's coming conquest of space.

His epitaph is simply and poetically framed beneath a seventeenth-century engraving from an original portrait of Cyrano by Zacharie Heince:

> All weary with the earth too soon
> I took my flight into the skies,
> Beholding there the sun and moon
> Where now the Gods confront my eyes.

2
THE SONS OF
FRANKENSTEIN

The most important woman contributor to nineteenth-century science fiction—a field only meagerly graced by the writings of the so-called gentler sex—was Mary Wollstone-craft Shelley, author of the scientific horror classic *Franken-stein*. That novel marked the decline of the widely popular Gothic horror story school of writers and also paved the way for a transition from superstition and legend to a firm foundation of science as the basic ingredient of successful fantastic literature.

In the realm of science fiction, *Frankenstein* was, in addition, the first story to amalgamate skillfully the previously isolated forms in the field, such as the travel tale, the fiction-disguised utopian prophecy, and the almost factual science story. It thus influenced a chain of distinguished authors from Edgar Allan Poe to Nathaniel Hawthorne, Fitz-James

O'Brien, Jules Verne, Ambrose Bierce, and so on to the greatest science fiction writer of them all, H. G. Wells, and through Wells the whole vast field of mid-twentieth-century science fiction.

The earliest approach to science fiction was the travel tale, and in that particular realm Homer's *Odyssey* has never been surpassed. In an era when the "entire world" was thought to be confined to the Mediterranean basin, and when all that was known of the stars had been fitted into the framework of Greek mythology, a pack donkey or a sailing ship was every bit as good a device as a spaceship for locating strange and bizarre civilizations and boldly seeking out fantastic adventures on the rim of the world.

Authors of that period were able, because of paucity of geographical knowledge and the lack of scientific information, to permit their fancies to rove at will. The authors and titles of dozens of ancient, scroll-inscribed adventures are known, even today, and there is no telling how many more have been erased by the slow passage of time.

Nearly as old as the travel tale is the still very much alive, creatively imaginative form of science fiction known as the future utopia. Such stories were usually careful voicings of the author's discontent with the state of the world in which he found himself, taking the reader on a tour of an ideally constructed civilization closer to his heart's desire.

Some of these stories were exceedingly satiric in tone and, though they often incorporated elements of the travel tale, were differentiated sharply from the latter by the fact that intellectual concepts, rather than a desire to entertain, dominated the thinking of almost all utopian-minded writers. Outstanding utopias are *The Republic* and *Critias* by Plato, *Utopia* by Thomas More—the Latin work by an English scholar which gave its name to the entire genre—*The New Atlantis* by Francis Bacon, and *The Common-Wealth of Oceana* (1656) by James Harrington.

The third major category, in which extrapolation from present knowledge in the physical and social sciences is very much in evidence, was the last type to arrive on the scene. Before 1800, science stories received scant attention, the two major examples of fiction stressing scientific theory being *Somnium: or the Astronomy of the Moon* by Johannes Kepler, first published in 1634, and *A Voyage to the Moon* by Cyrano de Bergerac, first published in 1650.

The old travel tale was primarily looked upon as a literature of escape. The prophetic utopia was a literature of political and social reform through philosophical as well as material change. The science story was a kind of experiment in public education through sugar-coated science on the level of the fireside journal. Before Mary Shelley, these three forms tended to be very sharply differentiated. *Frankenstein* proved that it was possible to blend and enrich them with a single compelling purpose in mind—to turn out a work of fiction that was entertaining as well as thought-provoking.

Frankenstein; or, The Modern Prometheus was first published in three volumes by Lackington, Hughes, Harding, Mayor & Jones; Finsbury Square, London, on March 11, 1818. At the time the novel appeared, Mary Shelley was twenty, but she had begun writing the story sometime during May 1816, when she was only eighteen.

The work was an immediate sensation. Though horrified by its subject matter, the critical journals of the day unanimously lauded the excellence of its writing and the forthrightness of its execution. *The Edinburgh Magazine and Literary Miscellany* for March 1818 said in part: "There never was a wilder story imagined; yet, like most of the fiction of this age, it has an air of reality attached to it, by being connected to the favorite projects and passions of the times."

Blackwood's Edinburgh Magazine for March 1818 said:

> Upon the whole, the work impresses us with the high idea of the author's original genius and happy power of expression. We shall be delighted to hear that he had aspired to *paullo majora*; and in the meantime, congratulate our readers upon a novel which excites new reflections and untried sources of emotion.

Frankenstein was published anonymously and was universally believed to be the work of a man, most informed guesses attributing it to Percy Bysshe Shelley, probably because he had written an introduction to the volume. The appearance of a second novel by Mary Shelley in 1823, a nonfantasy titled *Valperga*, helped to dispel these misconceptions. In *Blackwood's Edinburgh Magazine* for March 1823, a reviewer confessed:

> *Frankenstein*, at the time of its appearance, we certainly did not suspect to be the work of a female hand. The name of Shelley was whispered, and we did not hesitate to attribute the book to Mr. Shelley himself. Soon, however, we were set right. We learned that *Frankenstein* was written by Mrs. Shelley; and then we most undoubtedly said to ourselves, "For a man it was excellent, but for a woman .t was wonderful."

What sort of upbringing could inspire a teen-age girl to write a novel that even today is generally regarded as the single greatest novel in the horror story tradition ever written? Mary Wollstonecraft Shelley's life is even more fantastic than her monstrous creation. She was born August 30, 1797 at the Polygon, Somers Town, England, her mother, Mary Wollstonecraft, dying only ten days after her birth.

Her father, William Godwin, has been referred to as a second-rate Samuel Johnson with proper table manners. In his day he was very well known as the head of a movement of freethinkers.

Though trained for the clergy he believed firmly in free love, atheism, and anarchy. He preached that the proper use of logic and reason could solve all of man's problems. He was opposed to the intrusion of emotions into the fabric of the orderly life, and denounced the age's obsession with selfish materialism and accumulation of wealth.

The works which established Godwin's reputation were *An Inquiry Concerning Political Justice*, published in 1793, and *Things As They Are: or, The Adventures of Caleb Wil-*

liams, which first appeared in 1794. *Things As They Are* was fiction and of the Gothic school, for all its directness of writing, even though it carried a pronounced social message. It was Godwin's intent to expose the abuses that can arise from concentration of too much power in the hands of a few, and the ordeals undergone by Caleb Williams, persecuted by a wealthy man against whom he has gained evidence of murder, forthrightly and savagely illustrate that point.

In most of his thinking, Godwin was an uncompromising critic of things as they were. He also wrote a novel of science fantasy entitled *St. Leon, A Tale of the 16th Century*, which appeared in 1791. This novel is a fable of immortality, whose lead character, St. Leon, brews and drinks an elixir of life and wanders, deathless, throughout the world, inadvertently bringing sorrow and tribulation to everyone he encounters.

The theme, derived from the legend of the Wandering Jew, was hoary with age even when Godwin wrote it, but the introduction of an alchemical rather than a supernatural means of extending life was new to the Gothic tale. It was a harbinger of the definite break that his daughter Mary was to make with the Gothic tradition in her novel *Frankenstein*. Critics generally credit St. Leon with specific influence on the writing of three famous Gothic novels: *Melmoth the Wanderer* by Charles Robert Maturin; *St. Irvyne; or, the Rosicrucian* (1811) by Percy Bysshe Shelley, and *A Strange Story* by Lord Bulwer-Lytton.

Mary's mother had been every bit as determined a free-thinker as her husband. After having lived for several years as the mistress of an American named Gilbert Imlay, she found herself cast off, with an illegitimate child. She met Godwin in 1796 and married him in March 1797. They kept their marriage a secret, fearing ridicule as hypocrites.

Mrs. Godwin was also a prominent author in her own right. Before her marriage she had published a pamphlet entitled *Thoughts on the Education of Daughters*, a novel called *Mary*, and *Original Stories from Real Life*. She became most renowned for her book *Vindication of the Rights of Woman*. The title is self-explanatory.

Because her father was famous, the young girl met many literary figures who visited the household, not the least of whom was Charles Lamb and, most important, the poet Percy Bysshe Shelley, who was first introduced to Mary on May 5, 1814. Shelley, though only twenty-two at the time, had already established a reputation for poetry that was described as the essence of sweetness, beauty, and spirituality. A youthful atheist, he shared many of Godwin's views.

Though still married to his first wife, Harriet Westbrook, Shelley induced Mary to run off with him on July 28, 1814, accompanied by her liberal-minded stepsister, Claire.

After Shelley's wife committed suicide in 1816 the union with Mary was legalized. The stimulating company of Shelley's circle of friends soon prepared her for the writing of *Frankenstein*. Among Shelley's closest acquaintances and companions was Lord Byron.

Since the three were prone to read ghost stories to one another, together with a friend of Byron's, an Italian physician named John William Polidori, it was decided to have a contest in which Mary Wollstonecraft Shelley, Percy Bysshe Shelley, Lord Byron, and John William Polidori would compete to see who could write the most paralyzing novel of horror.

All but Mary Shelley began at once to work on their novels. Both Shelley and Byron lost interest before getting very far; the fragment that Byron completed was tacked on to the end of the book in which his long poem, *Mazeppa*, was published in London in 1817, and it was appropriately titled A *Fragment*. A young man solicits the friendship of a wealthy individual "of considerable fortune and ancient family." They journey together on the continent, but the younger man finds that his companion is steadily declining in strength, for no obvious reason. The older man dies in a long-untended graveyard in Smyrna, Greece, after exacting a promise that his youthful companion will tell no one of his death for a year. The story does not go beyond the burial, but its direction seems to indicate that it would have been a tale of vampirism.

Dr. Polidori doggedly kept at it and eventually produced a long short story titled *The Vampyre; a Tale*, issued in 1819 in London. Apparently Byron and Polidori proceeded from the same plot, for in *The Vampyre* a youth strikes up the acquaintanceship of a nobleman, whom he accompanies upon a trip which takes them to Greece. They separate after a disagreement, but are reunited when the youth has a traumatic experience involving a girl killed by a vampire and the nobleman appears to nurse him back to health. During their further travels the nobleman is shot by bandits and before his death exacts a promise that the youth will not reveal his death for a year. This oath later prevents the youth from warning his sister of danger when the nobleman apparently returns from the dead, marries her, and sucks the life from her veins. Polidori's brief tale initially enjoyed a good sale, largely due to a preface and afterword concerning Lord Byron which led readers to believe the book had been written by him.

Mary Shelley for days could not even think of an idea. Finally, after listening in on a philosophical discussion between her husband and Lord Byron regarding the nature of life, she experienced a vivid dream in which she saw a scientific student create artificial life in a laboratory. She realized she had her story and proceeded to write it.

The theme is by now almost universally familiar. A young scientist, Victor Frankenstein, pieces together a humanlike creature from parts obtained from slaughterhouses and graveyards and infuses it with life by scientific means. When he sees his monstrous creation begin to move, he becomes frightened at what he has accomplished and flees.

The monster wanders away, eventually is embittered by the persecution and loneliness he is subjected to because of his appearance, and finally searches out the young Frankenstein, from whom he exacts a promise to make a female companion for him. The monster promises he will then go with her to some far-off place, forever beyond the sight of man.

Nearing success in creating a female, Frankenstein is filled with doubts as to the wisdom of his project, and wrestles with his conscience:

> But now, for the first time, the wickedness of my promise burst upon me; I shuddered to think that future ages might curse me as their pest, whose selfishness had not hesitated to buy its own peace at the price, perhaps of the existence of the whole human race.

Frankenstein impulsively destroys the uncompleted body of the female he has been constructing. The monster, who observes this action, waits his chance for revenge, which he obtains by murdering Frankenstein's fiancée on their wedding night. Frankenstein then dedicates his life to searching out and destroying the monster. But after years of chasing a seeming phantom, Frankenstein dies in the cabin of a ship in the far north, without fulfilling his purpose.

The monster enters the cabin through a window, and confronted by a friend of Frankenstein's, expresses supreme remorse at the tragedy he brought into the life of his creator. When he leaves, he promises to destroy himself, thereby ending his own personal agony as well as fulfilling Frankenstein's desire for vengeance.

This oblivion was purely rhetorical. Frankenstein's monster was destined for immortality. Nearly a century and a half later a number of editions of *Frankenstein* are still in print, both hard- and soft-cover. Though the style and technique are dated, the story still retains a grandiose element of horror, as well as many almost poetic passages which sustain its life as a literary work.

Beyond its appeal as an early example of literary art in the realm of scientific horror, *Frankenstein* has a visual shock appeal surpassed by few stories, both as a play and motion picture. Five years after the story first appeared as a book, *Presumption; or the Fate of Frankenstein* appeared on the

London stage. The play was a smash hit and the same year found two other companies presenting serious versions and three more offering burlesques of the story.

Part of the original success of *Presumption* as a play was attributed to the superior acting ability of T. P. Cooke, an outstanding performer of the early part of the nineteenth century, whose name became synonymous with the role of Frankenstein's monster. At least fifteen stage versions of Mary Shelley's famous book have appeared in England, France, and the United States, two of them within the past thirty-three years.

The motion picture history of the book bids fair to outdo that of the stage in number of versions and far outdistances it as a money-maker. Boris Karloff was catapulted to a fame that has eclipsed that of T. P. Cooke in the role of the monster when the film *Frankenstein* was first released in 1932. Its success was nothing short of fabulous and it was soon followed by *The Bride of Frankenstein*. (Here note should be taken of the transference of the name from maker to monster, for the "bride" was to be the monster's companion, not the scientist's. The impact on readers' or audiences' minds of the character of the monster has made *him* Frankenstein, and thus it has generally been, popularly, though the pedantic still insist on "Frankenstein's monster.")

The first two films on the Frankenstein theme were rooted in incidents in Mary Shelley's book, but the clamor for more films to show necessitated original stories as vehicles, and there followed at spasmodic intervals the lesser known sequels *Son of Frankenstein* and *Ghost of Frankenstein*. As with the earlier stage history, burlesques began to appear on the screen and there were *Frankenstein Meets the Wolf Man*, *Abbott and Costello Meet Frankenstein*, and *House of Frankenstein*. There was also the strange take-off on juvenile delinquency, *I Was a Teenage Frankenstein*.

The Curse of Frankenstein, a more recent release, returns to the original story pattern. Forrest J. Ackerman, the authority on fantasy films, reports that the title *Frankenstein from Space* has been registered, insuring the monster's survival into the space age.

When Mary Shelley wrote *Frankenstein*, the high tide of the Gothic novel was abating and the flood of the romantic period in British literature had already begun. What Mary Shelley did was to salvage the themes of the supernormal and the horrific from that literature, which are best epitomized by Matthew Gregory Lewis's *The Monk*, Horace Walpole's *The Castle of Otranto*, and Ann Radcliffe's *The Mysteries of Udolpho*, and perpetuate their thrills by applying the light of scientific rationality.

The superiority of her method is attested by the present-day appeal of the three great landmarks in Gothic fiction mentioned above. Even the fast-moving, sex-charged *Monk* is revived only as a collector's item, whereas the comparatively more dated and slower novel, *Frankenstein*, is still popularly read.

Mary Shelley wrote many other novels, short stories, and works of nonfiction, but they have been obscured by the fame of *Frankenstein*. Of greatest interest to readers of science fiction is her very long novel *The Last Man*, first published by Colburn in London in three volumes during 1826. A reprint appeared the same year in Paris.

By this time Mary Shelley's life had undergone a great change. Her husband, Percy Shelley, had drowned in a small boat with two friends on July 8, 1822. Mary had lost four of five children and now only one son, Percy Florence, survived. Shelley's love had been anything but torrid toward the last and he had been involved in at least one blatant extramarital affair. Mary, holding tight to the memory of what had been good in her marriage, fanned into enduring constancy the flame of her love for Percy Bysshe as a beacon to his memory.

She never remarried, though other worthy suitors desired her, including John Howard Payne, author of "Home Sweet Home." One of the principal characters in her book *The Last Man* is unquestionably Percy Bysshe Shelley—another is Lord

Byron—and this work describes many of the European scenes she visited with him.

Biographers have poetically described the wanderings of Verney in *The Last Man* as an allegorical symbol of the twenty-nine years that Mary Shelley was to spend as a lost spirit in a world become a desert, now that her husband was gone. Perhaps this was so. Perhaps as women tend to forget the pain of childbirth they also gloss over the sordid where affairs of the heart are concerned.

The action of *The Last Man* begins in the year 2092, when a plague strikes Constantinople. It quickly spreads over Europe and a small group of survivors assembles in Paris, where they debate trivialities until a recurrence of the invisible death kills all except one man. Verney is left amid a world desolate of humanity and sardonic in the vibrant green of a new spring. He wanders down through Italy and finally sets sail in a skiff to scour the coast lines of the earth for survivors. Though the story is laid in the future, its principal innovation is passenger balloon service.

The Last Man, although it enjoyed a fair sale in a number of countries, did not help Mary's reputation. The critics were hard on it. To a man they condemned its long-winded tediousness and its almost terrifying descriptions of the deadly disease slowly decimating the populations of the earth. Their criticisms degenerated into personal, satiric jibes at Mary Shelley which hurt her popularity so badly that her publisher accepted her next novel only after she agreed to a considerably reduced advance.

Yet *The Last Man* is now generally regarded as the second best of her works. Though it is pedestrian in pace and excessively wordy, it possesses a phraseology that is often poetic, and finely drawn characterization. Mrs. Shelley's relation of the final agonies of the plague is a masterpiece of horror in literature.

This story proves that Mary Wollstonecraft Shelley had an abiding interest in those concepts which we today label science fiction. It is true that *The Last Man* theme was old when she wrote it; a very popular novel, *The Last Man or Omegarus and Syderia: A Romance in Futurity*, was published by Dutton in London in two volumes in 1805. Nevertheless *The Last Man* proved that her youthful venture into science fiction in *Frankenstein* was no mere coincidence.

Mary Shelley also wrote a number of short stories, most of which were collected in *Tales and Stories*, edited by Richard Garnett and published by William Paterson & Co., London, in 1891. Two of the stories in this book are fantasies. The first, *Transformation*, originally published in the annual *Keepsake* for 1831, tells of a young wastrel who, fleeing from the problems of his excesses, meets, floating into shore atop a sea chest, "a misshapen dwarf with squinting eyes, distorted features and body deformed, till it became a horror to behold." This dwarf, who has supernatural powers, offers to swap the sea chest filled with jewels for the use of the young man's body for a short time.

The young man, after some thought, agrees to the proposal. When the strange creature does not return at the allotted time, the young man, now in the dwarf's grotesque frame, goes searching and finds this creature wooing his girl. Convinced that the dwarf will not keep his promise, he engages himself in combat, is run through, stabs his antagonist in return, and awakes to find himself once again in his own body.

The second tale, *The Mortal Immortal*, originally published in the *Keepsake* for 1834, appears to have been inspired by William Godwin's book, *St. Leon*, and deals with an alchemist's helper who, by chance, drinks an elixir of immortality. The problems he encounters when he later marries and his wife grows old while he remains young are excellently handled. At the story's end, his wife has died and he plans a venture—not revealed—which may cause his death. If the theme had not been done so many, many times since in just the same way, and if surprise endings had not come into vogue, this story might be rated, even today, as above average in interest.

What we know of Mary Wollstonecraft Shelley is today

preserved in her letters, which were kept primarily for the light they shed on her famous husband and only secondarily because she was the author of the great horror novel, *Frankenstein*. Yet, future students of the history of science fiction may be grateful that, because of this circumstance, the motivating factors are apparent in the life of the woman who wrote the novel which truly began an unbroken chain of science fiction development.

3

THE PROPHETIC
EDGAR ALLAN POE

That science fiction would develop and eventually grow into an important literary force was inevitable as scientific invention and technology began to make gargantuan strides during the early part of the nineteenth century. The mood of the period reflected the pride of man in his progress, and the fascination which the newly created marvels exercised over him took the form of an overwhelming curiosity as to where all this would lead and what was to come next.

Edgar Allan Poe, with his supremely logical and brilliant mind, became the leading proponent of the science fiction tale in the first half of the nineteenth century. The literature owes to his influence an enduring debt, quite on a par with the recognition accorded him for his contributions to detective and mystery fiction and to the art of the short story.

Basically, Poe's science fiction stories can be divided into two major categories. The first, including such tales as *Ms. Found in a Bottle*, *A Descent into the Maelström*, and *A Tale of the Ragged Mountains*, comprises artistic science fiction in which the mood or effect is primary and the scientific rationality serves merely to strengthen the aesthetic aspect.

In the other group, examples of which are *Mellonta Tauta*, *Hans Phaall—A Tale*, and *The Thousand-and-Second Tale of Scheherazade*, the idea was paramount and the style was modulated to provide an atmospheric background which would remain unobtrusive, and not take the spotlight from the scientific concept.

Poe's greatest reputation and certainly his most magnificent tales and poems have been built around themes stressing psychological horror. It is not surprising, therefore, that many readers tend to think of him as a horror story writer, with a decided penchant for ghosts.

They forget that not a single Poe story ever contained a supernatural ghost, and the angels which on rare occasions appear, merely play the role of sardonic storytellers. Poe abhorred mysticism in almost any form, including the notion of a deity in religion. If he was not an atheist, his published statements, taken at their most conservative, reveal a militant agnostic.

His classic tales of terror, *The Fall of the House of Usher*, *The Tell-Tale Heart*, *The Black Cat*, and *William Wilson*, are actually coolly based on abnormal psychology and contain many elements which the modern writer, inspired by Sigmund Freud, mines for rich literary ore. Poe, through his own tormenting problems, knew that ultimate damnation lies in the distortions of a man's own inner consciousness and not in any supernatural event.

That he was skeptical of anything at odds with cold, dispassionate logic was made abundantly clear by his brilliant exposé of Johann Nepomuk Maelzel, a German visiting America, who brought with him an elaborate mechanism which he claimed could play chess automatically. This device had duped Europeans since its invention by Baron von Kempelen of Hungary in 1769. The machine would play a chess game with anyone. It was not infallible; at times it would even lose a game. But what angered Poe was the fact that its showman, Maelzel, claimed that the entire operation was automatic.

With nothing to go on except the manner in which the game was conducted, Poe, in his remarkable essay *Maelzel's Chess-Player*, published in the April 1836 issue of *The Southern Literary Messenger*, successfully exposed the machine as a fraud, manipulated by a concealed man. In that essay we get a clear picture of the superlatively logical mind that conceived C. Auguste Dupin, forerunner of Sherlock Holmes, and cleverly constructed and unraveled cryptograms in the popular tale of lost treasure *The Gold Bug*.

His brilliance in that respect demonstrates that there was nothing inconsistent in his writing spine-chillers on the one hand and legitimate science fiction on the other. That his epics of fear had, for the most part, a greater literary impact was more accidental than otherwise, for Poe might have achieved fame as a philosopher or a mathematician without writing a single line of imaginative fiction.

But the writing of science fiction did not occupy merely a youthful phase of Poe's writing career, to be later set aside for more "mature" subject matter, as was the case with H. G. Wells. Originally, Poe attempted to make his reputation as a poet, seriously turning to prose in 1832 when five of his short stories, including his very first, *Metzengerstein*, appeared in *The Philadelphia Saturday Courier*.

His first published science fiction story was *Ms. Found in a Bottle*, which won a fifty-dollar first prize in a contest sponsored by *The Baltimore Saturday Visitor*, appearing in the issue of that periodical for October 19, 1833. From that time until his death in 1849, in which year he published *Von Kempelen and His Discovery* and *Mellonta Tauta*, science fiction tales were a regular part of his literary production.

Edgar Allan Poe was born in Boston, January 19, 1809, son of an English actress, Elizabeth Arnold Hopkins, and an Irish actor, David Poe. There was a brother and a sister, and all three of the children had to be supported by the mother, whom the father deserted while Edgar was still an infant.

When Mrs. Poe died in Richmond, Virginia, in 1811, the children were adopted by well-to-do families of that city. Edgar was given a home by a successful merchant, John Allan, from whom he took his middle name.

Poe received good elementary schooling and was then sent to the University of Virginia, where his immoderate gambling eventually resulted in his removal. Admission to West Point, obtained through the influence of his father, ended in his being court-martialed for neglect of duty. Upon resigning from the U.S. Military Academy, in March, 1831, he redoubled his efforts to get his poetry published and began the first of his many short stories.

The Baltimore Saturday Visitor prize for *Ms. Found in a Bottle* brought him immediate, gratifying recognition. The judges of the contest, J. H. B. Latrobe, John P. Kennedy, and Dr. James H. Miller, indicate, in letters and records they have left behind, that they were well aware that they had discovered a writer of extraordinary talent. Latrobe, in later describing the reactions of the judges during the reading of six of Poe's short stories submitted to the contest under the heading of *Tales of the Folio Club,* said:

> There was genius in everything they listened to; there was no uncertain grammar, no feeble phraseology, no ill-placed punctuation, no worn truisms, no strong thought elaborated into weakness. Logic and imagination were combined in rare consistency. . . . There was an analysis of complicated facts —an unravelling of circumstantial knowledge that charmed . . . a pure classic diction that delighted all three.

After the reading, there was a considerable discussion as to whether to select *Ms. Found in a Bottle* or *A Descent into the Maelström* as the winner. *Ms. Found in a Bottle* is the story of an old-time freighter blasted apart by a sudden tropical storm and slowly sinking.

> At a terrific height directly above us, and upon the very verge of the precipitous descent, hovered a gigantic ship of perhaps four thousand tons. Although upreared upon the summit of a wave more than a hundred times her own altitude, her apparent size still exceeded that of any ship of the line or East Indiaman in existence.

The ghostly ship collides with the wreckage and the impact throws the narrator to safety on her deck. The mystery vessel is manned by a crew of incredibly ancient mariners, who pay scant attention to the new arrival. Though in almost the final stages of senility, the captain and the crew appear to be attempting to thwart some inescapable doom.

It soon becomes evident that the vessel is inexorably drawn across the seas by a powerful current or undertow. This river of the sea races like "a tide which, howling and shrieking by the white ice, thunders on to the southward with a velocity like the headlong dashing of a cataract. . . ." Rushing through "stupendous ramparts of ice, towering away into the desolate sky, and looking like the walls of the universe" the ship is sucked into a whirlpool of waters rushing toward the center of the earth.

While the atmosphere of the story owes a debt to the legend of the Flying Dutchman, the ending undoubtedly was inspired by a theory circulated by Captain John Cleves Symmes of Hamilton, Ohio, beginning in 1818. Symmes believed that the earth was hollow and that there were openings to the interior at both poles. He even estimated the size of the entrances to be four thousand miles in diameter at the North Pole and six thousand at the South. Each opening, he claimed, was enclosed in a circle of ice.

A work of science fiction titled *Symzonia* and credited to Captain Adam Seaborn (possibly a pseudonym of Symmes) appeared in 1820, based on Symmes's theory and involving strange animals, a lost civilization, and much adventure at the earth's center.

That Poe was acquainted with the concept of the hollow earth may be drawn from the postscript to *Ms. Found in a Bottle*, which referred to his not having become familiar "with the maps of Mercator, in which the ocean is represented as rushing, by four mouths, into the (northern) Polar Gulf, to be absorbed into the bowels of the earth; the Pole itself being represented by a black rock, towering to a prodigious height," until "many years" after its publication. What raises a question about the verity of this statement is that he gives the date of *first* printing as 1831, two years before it actually appeared.

It has been pointed out that *Ms. Found in a Bottle* reads like the prelude to a longer story dealing with the earth's center. Similar observations have been made concerning *The Narrative of Arthur Gordon Pym of Nantucket*, which might conceivably have become a tale of a hollow earth, with an ending very similar to *A Descent into the Maelström*. Poe's mention of the earth's North Pole as concave in appearance in *Hans Phaall—A Tale*, affords further substantiation that he was familiar with Symmes's theories.

Poe hovered on the brink of new adventures many times and always drew back. All of the tales which seem to have something in common with Symmes are, in a real sense, unfinished. The impression, in each of them, is that for reasons best known to himself the author preferred to leave the story hanging.

Perhaps the most imaginative of Poe's science fiction stories, *Hans Phaall—A Tale*, was in the process of creation at the very time *Ms. Found in a Bottle* was published. Thrilled by the selection of his story as a prize winner, Poe called upon the three judges individually to thank them.

The account of his visit to Latrobe is recorded:

> I asked him whether he was then occupied with any literary labor. He replied that he was then engaged on *A Voyage to the Moon*, and at once went into a somewhat learned dis-

quisition upon the laws of gravity, the height of the earth's atmosphere, and capacities of balloons . . . presently, speaking in the first person, he began the voyage . . . leaving the earth and becoming more and more animated, he described his sensations as he climbed higher and higher . . . where the moon's attraction overcame that of the earth, there was a sudden *bouleversement* of the car and great confusion among the tenants.

By this time the speaker had become so excited, spoke so rapidly, gesticulating much, that when the turn upside-down took place, and he clapped his hands and stamped with his foot by way of emphasis, I was carried along with him. . . .

That Poe was extraordinarily enthusiastic about the writing of his "moon" story is undeniable. His preoccupation with science fiction was not a literary accident. Neither was it an outgrowth of financial necessity. It was undeniably what he wanted to write.

A very good case has been made for A *Voyage to the Moon* by Joseph Atterley, published in 1827, as one of the prime movers in arousing Poe's interest in writing a moon story. Joseph Atterley was actually a pen name of Professor George Tucker, chairman of the faculty of the University of Virginia, which Poe had attended in 1826–27. Tucker's novel is of historical interest on another count, since it is one of the earliest stories using what has come to be known as antimatter or, in science fiction terminology, "contraterrene matter," as a means of space navigation.

To accomplish his space voyage Poe used a balloon. Despite this, the story was far from being unscientific. He paved the way for the use of the balloon by presenting the theory that the sun's atmosphere extended beyond Venus into the orbit of the earth in a somewhat attenuated form. As theoretical evidence, he offered the shortening intervals between arrivals of Encke's comet, which could not be satisfactorily explained by the science of his day, but which he surmised might be due to the fact that there was more resistance to movement in space than was commonly supposed.

The narrative itself is documentary. It is similar in technique to *Destination Moon*, the motion picture made from Robert A. Heinlein's script, which graphically describes the mechanics of space flight in a completely realistic and believable fashion.

At the very end of his tale, Poe turns increasingly facetious and intimates that the entire thing is a hoax, but not before a city of "ugly little people" is discovered on the moon. The impression is strongly conveyed that the story was never truly finished and was quickly tidied up to facilitate a sale. Nevertheless, it is, in the main, deadly serious, scientific, and well done.

Hans Phaall—A Tale appeared in *The Southern Literary Messenger* for June 1835, only a few months before another moon story which was destined to create a national sensation. *The New York Sun*, during the months of August and September 1835, carried what it claimed to be a completely authenticated news story titled *Discoveries in the Moon Lately Made at the Cape of Good Hope*.

This story, which today is known as *The Moon Hoax*, was perpetrated by Richard Adams Locke and purported to be a report of the discoveries made by Sir John Herschel at his observatory on the Cape of Good Hope with the aid of a newly constructed telescope. The readers were completely taken in and other papers, including the *Journal of Commerce*, reprinted the account. The excitement reached such proportions that the author, fearing unforeseen and unpleasant reactions when the hoax was finally discovered, voluntarily confessed before he could be exposed.

Poe was furious, largely because he believed the idea had been lifted from his own moon story. In a letter, dated September 11, 1835, to his Baltimore benefactor, John P. Kennedy (one of the judges who had awarded first prize to *Ms. Found in a Bottle*), he wrote:

> Have you seen the "Discoveries in the Moon"? Do you not think it altogether suggested by Hans Phaall? It is very singular, but when I first proposed writing a tale concerning the

Moon, the idea of *Telescopic discoveries* suggested itself to me—but I afterwards abandoned it. I had however spoken of it freely, and from many little incidents and apparently trivial remarks in those *Discoveries* I am convinced that the idea was stolen from myself.

When *Hans Phaall* was later incorporated in a book, Poe added a footnote pointing out that his story enjoyed prior appearance to *The Moon Hoax*. In his footnote, he mentioned that New York papers had reprinted his story side by side with Locke's to ascertain if they were written by the same person. Though he refers to the "very celebrated and very beautiful 'Moon Story'" by Locke, in a review which he wrote shortly after the appearance of the hoax, he figuratively cut the story to shreds, both scientifically and artistically.

There is speculation that the real cause of Poe's anger was that he planned a sequel to *Hans Phaall*. Possibly that was the original motive behind the abrupt ending of the Poe story, and Locke's hoax destroyed his opportunity to add to it.

The longest story Poe ever wrote, actually a novel in length, was *The Narrative of Arthur Gordon Pym of Nantucket*, originally serialized in a magazine edited by Poe, *The Southern Literary Messenger*, January-February 1837, and later completed for hard-cover publication.

Commencing as a bloodcurdling action adventure on the high seas, the story becomes a science fiction tale as a lost race is discovered on islands near the South Pole. The sequence of events closely follows those of Seaborn's *Symzonia* and the tale becomes more fantastic as it evolves, with the discovery of hitherto unknown aquatic creatures and water which is "veined" and peculiarly alive.

As the ill-fated ship journeys closer, the area near the South Pole seems to warm up, strange white creatures go drifting by, a peculiar ash falls continually from the sky, and in the distance can be dimly seen through the vapor a "limitless cataract, rolling silently into the sea from some immense and far-distant rampart in the heaven. The gigantic curtain ranged along the whole extent of the southern horizon. It emitted no sound."

Overhead

> gigantic and pallidly white birds flew continuously now from beyond the veil, and their scream was the eternal *Tekeli-li* . . . there arose in our pathway a shrouded human figure, very far larger in proportions than any dweller among men. And the hue of the skin was of the perfect whiteness of the snow.

There the story ends, and what might have come next has fascinated readers for over a century, none more so than Jules Verne, who wrote a sequel, *The Sphinx of the Ice-Fields*, and H. P. Lovecraft, who in a sense also wrote a sequel in *At the Mountains of Madness*. Lovecraft's novel of the exploration among the remains of an advanced and ancient civilization beneath the ice of the Antarctic closes with the repetition of a single, mad word of all too obvious source: "Tekeli-li . . . Tekeli-li!"

Poe's *The Conversation of Eiros and Charmion*, first published in *Burton's Gentleman's Magazine* for December 1839 is of singular literary significance. A comet, passing through the earth's atmosphere, alters its chemistry so that all life perishes. This being the case, the story is necessarily told by two spirits in the hereafter. But the fact that the earth had never before been wiped out in fiction, in quite this astronomical and scientifically sound fashion, cannot be minimized.

It is a striking commentary upon the attitude of American publishers toward native authors in Poe's time that one of his most powerful stories, the gripping A *Descent into the Maelström*, which we know to have been in manuscript form as early as 1833, had to go begging until 1841, when *Graham's Lady's and Gentleman's Magazine* for May of that year published it. Dramatic poetry in prose, this tale moves along with the speed of a modern thriller, recounting the adventures of two brothers, fishing off Norway, who are sucked down into an immense whirlpool off the coast.

They descend for many miles, accompanied by a myriad objects which the maelstrom has also captured. The tale is powerfully related, with scrupulous attention to scientific accuracy. Through the use of known natural principles, one of the brothers saves himself and returns to the surface, while the other perishes.

Those who have read Jules Verne's *Twenty Thousand Leagues Under the Sea* must certainly have recognized *A Descent* as the genesis of a similar incident in which Captain Nemo and his marvelous submarine, *The Nautilus*, steer into virtually the same whirlpool off the coast of Norway.

A Tale of the Ragged Mountains, appearing first in *Godey's Lady's Book* for April 1844, has, strangely enough, not been one of the author's frequently reprinted stories, though it certainly ranks among his better works. Under the effects of morphine, the protagonist, while strolling through the Ragged Mountains, which Poe knew well, since they were only a short distance from the University of Virginia which he attended, suddenly finds himself transported into the past and becomes involved in a battle between the British and the natives of old India.

Though there is an element of the contrived, the tale is cleverly told and the writing is sheer delight.

At almost the same time, April 13, 1844, *The New York Sun* published a sensational extra with headlines that read:

ASTOUNDING NEWS BY EXPRESS, VIA NORFOLK! THE ATLANTIC CROSSED IN THREE DAYS! SIGNAL TRIUMPH OF MR. MONCK MASON'S FLYING MACHINE!

The same Poe who had shredded Richard Adams Locke for his moon hoax had descended to an almost identical trick, which was to become known as *The Balloon-Hoax*. Poe was determined to give the readers of the *Sun* their money's worth. The technical construction of the balloon was described in a faultless scientific manner. A reprint of the balloon's journal was published along with interpolations by one of the passengers, Mr. Harrison Ainsworth. For a brief time the hoax was believed, brought Poe a few dollars, and focused the public spotlight upon him and his brand of craftsmanship. Since the Atlantic was not to be traversed by a gasfilled flying machine for almost one hundred years after the appearance of Poe's story, this fabrication qualifies as science fiction for the time of its appearance.

Hypnotism or mesmerism was, in Poe's time, of as questionable a nature as flying saucers are today. Reputable scientists frequently looked upon it as a form of quackery. Though few were more skeptical of the existence of anything of an occult or mystical nature than Poe, he evidently was fascinated by the possibilities of hypnotism, because he utilized it as a device in many of his stories. *Mesmeric Revelation*, which appeared in *Columbian Lady's and Gentleman's Magazine* for August 1844, used a hypnotized man as a means of projecting Poe's views on the nature of God and the universe, including the concept of the "universal mind" (all elements in the universe combined into a thinking whole), which later formed one of the primary bases of Olaf Stapledon's philosophical fantasy, *The Star Maker*.

The theme of hypnotism was employed again in *The Facts in the Case of M. Valdemar*, which appeared in *The American Review* for December 1845. In this tale, an experiment is conducted to see how long hypnotism may prolong the life of a dying man. Though the body dies, through posthypnotic suggestion the unfortunate Mr. Valdemar, who is the subject of the experiment, continues to communicate. When after *seven months* the "dead" man is snapped out of his hypnotic trance, his body dissolves into "a nearly liquid mass of loathsome—of detestable putridity." As a work of fiction this is a much more effective scientific horror tale than its predecessor, *Mesmeric Revelation*.

Though he was preoccupied with mesmerism, Poe had by no means discarded his interest in the more physical sciences. *The Thousand-and-Second Tale of Scheherazade* purported to be the further adventures of the *Arabian Nights*, and related the *real* fate of the marvelous fabricator, Scheherazade.

Not satisfied with her past triumphs, Scheherazade continues the adventures of Sinbad, who now encounters giant ocean-going steamships with thousands of passengers and every conceivable luxury aboard, railroad trains, wireless telegraphy, calculating machines, chess-playing robots, teletypes, printing presses, methods of converting baser metals into gold, ultraviolet rays, galvanic batteries, electricity, photography, the astronomical paradoxes of light, and other modern miracles. The king, Scheherazade's husband, had been perfectly willing to believe all the previous relatively reasonable adventures of Sinbad, but now he feels certain that Scheherazade is pulling his leg and not even being very subtle about it, so he has her choked to death. This story was introduced to the public by *Godey's Lady's Book* in its issue for February 1845.

Closely akin to it in mood and presentation is the tale *Some Words with a Mummy*, which followed only two months later in *The American Review* for April 1845. A mummy is brought to life and the achievements of the "modern world" are compared to those of ancient Egypt, with the nod going consistently to the latter until it comes to patent medicines, where the mummy, embarrassed, decides to be rewrapped and returned to his sarcophagus.

A distinct element of humor pervades it. The fame of Poe's terror tales and the misery and suffering which attended his life have understandably given the impression that his demeanor and thought were eternally grim and devoid of hope. Actually, he wrote a substantial number of tales of pure humor and a jocular note is present in many of his works. Apart from tales intended to be satiric or facetious, Poe also wrote things like *The Angel of the Odd—an Extravaganza*, in *Columbian Lady's and Gentleman's Magazine*, October 1844, which reads like and could easily have served as a model for a quite funny vaudeville skit, replete with phonetic German accents, bottles bouncing off craniums, and loss of breeches. This story includes, as part of the plot, the use of a man-carrying balloon, which emphasizes again Poe's fascination with flying.

The Sphinx, presented to the world by *Arthur's Ladies' Magazine*, January 1846, tells of a man who, from the window of his cottage, sees a monstrous winged creature ascending a hill. The hideous thing, relative to the trees it passes, is estimated as being larger than a warship and bears markings like a death's-head on its back. When its eerie call penetrates the room, the observer faints. Later, he finds that he has been viewing a Death's-head Sphinx, a moth crawling up a spider's thread on the window, right in the line of vision, so that it appeared to be superimposed on the landscape. This insect is capable of issuing a "melancholy kind of cry." While little more than an incident, the story is nonetheless masterfully told.

The year of his death, 1849, found Poe still very much occupied with the writing of science fiction. *Mellonta Tauta* appeared in *Godey's Lady's Book* for February 1849. The story was laid in the year 2848 and told in the form of a letter to a friend written by a lady taking a transatlantic trip on a powered passenger balloon, traveling at the rate of 100 miles per hour. Some of the marvels of that future date included telegraph wires floating on the surface of the ocean and railroad trains traveling 300 miles per hour on fifty-foot-gauge tracks. Creatures on the moon and their civilization are observed through telescopes and the story ends with antiquarians excavating on the site of old New York a plaque for a monument in memory of George Washington upon the anniversary of the surrender of Lord Cornwallis. No one is quite sure who these gentlemen were and just what was implied by the surrender of Cornwallis.

Poe, in this story, presents his concept of a finite universe so balanced that it revolves around a common center of gravity.

Mellonta Tauta appears to have been written to create interest in a new theory of the universe propounded by Poe in his controversial essay *Eureka, a Prose Poem*, first published in book form by George Putnam in 1848. This nonfiction work was the basis of a number of dramatic lectures delivered by Poe and he believed it to be his supreme masterpiece.

Literary researchers and critics alike have either ignored it or viewed it askance. Some feel it represents the product of a mind no longer rational, others contend that it indicates intellectual strength and the grasp of advanced theories which have since received acceptance, while a third school maintains that the ideas should be ignored and that it should be considered on its literary merits alone.

One of the theories in *Eureka* is the concept that all matter sprang from nothing and that there is a process resembling that of "continuous creation" of matter. Another is that there is an "equable irradiation" of matter through a "limited" space and that the number of stars and their extent is finite, not infinite.

Poe also believed that matter is attracted to matter and not to one common point in the universe and therefore that gravitation indicated a tendency of all things to return into their original unity: that the universe began from nothing and would return to nothing.

That further, space and time are one, and matter is only attraction and repulsion:

> a finally consolidated globe of globes, being but *one* particle, would be without attraction, i.e., gravitation; the existence of such a globe presupposes the expulsion of the separative ether which we know to exist between the particles as at present diffused:—thus the final globe would be matter without attraction and repulsion: but these *are* matter:—then the final globe would be matter without matter:—i.e., no matter at all:—it must disappear. Thus Unity is *nothingness*.

The last science fiction story of Poe's to see print was *Von Kempelen and His Discovery*, presented in *The Flag of Our Union* for April 14, 1849, involving the successful transmutation of lead into gold by the title character.

The full range of Poe's influence upon science fiction is incalculable, but his greatest contribution to the advancement of the genre was the precept that every departure from norm must be logically explained *scientifically*. This made it easy for the reader to attain a willing suspension of disbelief and to accept the unusual.

The greatest writers in the history of the field owe a profound debt to his method: "that everything must be scientifically logical"; and in some cases an even stronger one to his inspired techniques of narration.

The details of Poe's tortured life would not be believable or acceptable in fiction. The bouts with alcohol and drugs as temporary respite from his plight, the strange circumstances of the marriage to his 14-year-old, tubercular cousin, and his own grievous personality faults conceal a man who was essentially a hard-working, willing, self-sacrificing writer and husband.

It is reported that the night of his death, October 7, 1849, in Baltimore at the age of 40, the corridors of the hospital rang for hours with his cries of "Reynolds! Reynolds! Oh, Reynolds!" Reynolds was a man interested in Antarctic exploration who was thought to have influenced the writing of *The Narrative of Arthur Gordon Pym*. Truly, this time Poe was being carried by a relentless current toward a roaring cataract which poured ceaselessly into a fathomless chasm, while white figures hovered nearby and the screams of "Tekeli-li . . . Tekeli-li!" achieved their ultimate meaning.

4

THE FABULOUS FANTAST—
FITZ-JAMES O'BRIEN

Any serious student of American letters asked to name the half-dozen writers of the nineteenth century who exerted the greatest influence upon the development of the American short story would be most unlikely to omit Fitz-James O'Brien. And he would have to admit that O'Brien's high standing as a practitioner of the short story was earned primarily on the basis of the science fiction he wrote, secondarily on his works of fantasy and horror; and on his other works, not at all.

His most famous story, *The Diamond Lens*, became the literary sensation of the year, when it appeared in the *Atlantic Monthly* for January 1858. The story deals with a young microbiologist, who, in his thirst for knowledge, is frustrated by the limitations of his glass. To find a way of constructing a superior one, he consults, through a medium, the spirit of Leeuwenhoek, the father of microscopy. Informed that he needs a diamond of 140 carats in order to construct a finer instrument, he obtains such a stone by killing a close friend who owns one.

Through a special lens ground from the diamond, he views in a drop of water a microscopic world of surpassing beauty. In that tiny cosmos, his attention is drawn to a humanlike female creature he names Animula. He falls hopelessly, despairingly in love with the small unattainable woman, whose grace and delicacy make the most accomplished women dancers of the ballet appear gross and clumsy by comparison.

Though the drop of water containing the fantastic, minute world was coated with oil of turpentine to insure its protection, it gradually evaporates. Helpless to do anything about it, the young scientist watches his beloved Animula shrivel and die.

Shattered by the experience, he loses the will to work and spends the rest of his life on charity. Occasionally he is invited to lecture at optical societies, where his theories are always regarded as good for a laugh.

The tale carries the reader along with such verve, displays such a richness of imagination, and engenders so high an interest that it is little wonder that the editor of *Atlantic* felt that he could claim sole credit for publishing an original work of fiction which was destined to change the entire direction of American short-story writing.

This claim was not completely without substance, for though O'Brien did not write with the brilliant economy of means and accomplished style of Edgar Allan Poe, he did add an effective note of credibility to his stories by placing them in the familiar setting of the New York City of his day. The result was the beginning of a trend which the famous critic, Arthur Hobson Quinn, in his book *American Fiction* termed "the transition to realism." That O'Brien was able to contribute to and profoundly influence a trend toward realism with stories of scientific extrapolation is impressive evidence of his originality and literary skill.

Fitz-James O'Brien was not to be permitted to enjoy the plaudits of the critics for long. No sooner had *The Diamond Lens* achieved wide popular recognition, than O'Brien was accused of having derived the theme of his story from an unpublished manuscript by William North, entitled *Microcosmus*. Since North was dead and the manuscript in question was not found among his effects, the accusation could not readily be confirmed or disputed. As a result, O'Brien found himself trying to stamp out rumors that were springing up everywhere like prairie fires.

Finally, Dr. Alfred H. Guernsey, editor of *Harper's*, came to O'Brien's defense by publicly stating that he had read North's manuscript, which had previously been submitted to him and rejected, and that there was not the remotest similarity in the handling of the theme of the microscopic world by the two authors. North's manuscript never was found, so the science fiction world lost a story of historical interest, if not of significant literary importance.

Fitz-James O'Brien was born in Ireland on December 31, 1828, the son of a well-to-do lawyer. Even during his youth his stories and poems were published in Irish, Scottish, and British magazines. He squandered an inheritance of eight thousand pounds in two and one half years. Following an unsuccessful attempt to run off with the wife of an English officer, he fled to the United States. He arrived in December 1852, and within a few short months succeeded in placing poems and stories in several American publications.

His earliest reputation rested largely on his somewhat flowery poetry and for some years his verse was lavishly praised by the critics of the period. When William Winter put together the first hard-cover volume of his work—it was published by James R. Osgood and Co. of Boston in 1881 under the title of *The Poems and Stories of Fitz-James*

O'Brien—the poetry was placed ahead of the fiction and occupied nearly half the book.

But in the second collection of O'Brien's work, under the title *The Diamond Lens and Other Stories,* published in 1885 by Charles Scribner's Sons, New York, *all* of the poems were omitted.

In the United States, O'Brien lived the life of a true Bohemian, almost as if he considered Bohemianism inseparable from the literary accomplishments of a true man of letters. He never married, or worried where his next dollar was coming from, and he played literary God to the aspiring writers of his coterie. He was welcome in the better social as well as literary circles.

His literary career in the United States lasted only ten years, however. When the Civil War broke out, he enlisted in the Union army and was wounded in one of the earliest skirmishes. His wound became infected and he died shortly after an operation in which part of his left arm and shoulder bone were removed. The date of his death was April 6, 1862. O'Brien, then a lieutenant, was only thirty-three years old.

While *The Diamond Lens* derived much of its form from Poe and Hawthorne, *The Wondersmith,* another highly admired short story, which first appeared in the *Atlantic Monthly* for October 1859, was patterned after the style of E. T. A. Hoffmann. The tale is a superbly atmospheric blend of science and fantasy, so individualistic that it remains unique of its type in American literature.

The use of wooden manikins which can perform many of the actions of a human being makes this tale historically important as one of the earliest robot stories. What no one has mentioned until now is the debt A. Merritt's classic horror fantasy *Burn Witch Burn!* owes to this story. Not only the basic plot, but the devices in Merritt's novel—the fiendish, soulless devil dolls; the evil mover behind the scenes; the tiny, needlelike weapons dipped in poison employed by the dolls; the malevolent eyes of the manikins—are all so similar

to those in *The Wondersmith* as to make coincidence unlikely.

In *The Wondersmith*, there is a truly memorable scene of
a battle between the "Lilliputian assassins" and two caged,
talking Mino birds. During a battle, in which the Mino birds
have inflicted heavy casualties on their murderous adversaries,
they are outflanked:

> Quick as lightning the Mino turned to repel this assault, but
> all too late; two slender quivering threads of steel crossed in
> his poor body, and he staggered into a corner of the cage.
> His white eyes closed, then opened; a shiver passed over his
> body, beginning at his shoulder-tips and dying off in the ex-
> treme tips of the wings; he gasped as if for air, and then, with
> a convulsive shudder, which ruffled all his feathers, croaked
> out feebly his little speech. "What'll you take?" Instantly
> from the opposite corner came the old response, still feebler
> than the question—a mere gurgle, as it were, of "Brandy and
> water." Then all was silent. The Mino birds were dead.

Earlier the same year, the March issue of *Harper's New
Monthly Magazine* had carried O'Brien's story *What Was
It? A Mystery*, which is a well-conceived, almost documentary
account of a man who is attacked by an invisible creature
and who, after a terrific battle, subdues it. A plaster cast is
made of the mysterious thing, which reveals a humanlike
form with a hideous face. The creature refuses to eat any
food set before it and starves to death, carrying its mystery to
the grave with it.

Chronologically, this story precedes Guy de Maupassant's
The Horla and Ambrose Bierce's *The Damned Thing*, both
with very similar plots. There is strong internal evidence that
Bierce drew heavily upon the idea and techniques of presentation of *What Was It?* in composing his own story. Since
there is no bibliographical record of O'Brien's story being
translated into French, it is doubtful that de Maupassant was
actually influenced by O'Brien. It is more likely that the invisible creature in *The Horla* was de Maupassant's symboliza-

tion of the mental twilight he knew was approaching and which eventually did engulf him completely.

Probably the least known of all of O'Brien's science fiction stories is *How I Overcame My Gravity*. This story may have been his last piece of fiction to appear in print. It was published anonymously more than two years after his death in the May 1864 issue of *Harper's New Monthly Magazine*, and was never reprinted until *Satellite Science Fiction* resurrected it for its June 1958 number.

While it is marred by the use of a dream ending, a plot technique virtually taboo in modern science fiction, the skillfully written story has historical importance in suggesting the gyroscopic principle as a possible antigravity method and in advancing the theory that a weightless object hurled hard enough by a catapult might travel away from the earth forever.

Had O'Brien dared go just a little further in this line of reasoning, he might have preceded Edward Everett Hale by a few years as the first human being to suggest, in either factual writing or fiction, the concept of an artificial earth satellite. As it was, O'Brien might very well have sparked Hale's thinking along such lines, since both were contributors to the same periodicals during the same period and it is more than likely that Hale read most of O'Brien's output.

Another Hale—Edward Everett Hale's sister, Lucretia Peabody—has involved the name of Fitz-James O'Brien in a literary mystery that still has not been solved to everyone's complete satisfaction. A set of books, published in 1884 as *Stories by American Authors*, carries as the lead story in Volume 3 a tale entitled *The Spider's Eye*. This story, originally published anonymously (as were most stories of that period), first appeared in *Putnam's Monthly Magazine* for July 1856, and dealt with the possibility of reading people's thoughts through acoustics.

The entire plan and development of the story and even

some of the phrases seem typically O'Brien's, and a pattern can be demonstrated in the plotting which shows a similarity to that of *The Diamond Lens*, which appeared two years later. When the story was included in *Stories by American Authors*, O'Brien was given credit for authorship both on the front binding cloth and inside the book. However, a second edition of the set, published in 1898, attributes the story to Lucretia P. Hale, who made her reputation writing charming juveniles such as *The Peterkin Papers* and books on crocheting like *Faggots for the Fireside*.

Were it not that Lucretia P. Hale wrote at least one other fantasy, which appears to be incontestably her own, the story in question could probably be listed without challenge as one of O'Brien's. It is a story whose imagination and execution would bring him no discredit.

The fact is that Lucretia P. Hale had published under her own name, in both *Atlantic Tales* (a collection of stories from *Atlantic Monthly*, in which it had appeared anonymously) and in a separate book, *Queen of the Red Chessboard*, a fantasy bearing the last mentioned title. In its original, anonymous publication, in the February 1858 issue of *Atlantic Monthly*, only a month after the appearance in that same magazine of O'Brien's smash success, *The Diamond Lens*, *Queen of the Red Chessboard*, judged by its adroit writing and perfect short story form, could easily have been mistaken for a work of the transplanted Irish author.

The story is a fantasy of a chess queen who turns into a real woman and is followed into the real world by the White Prince, who has held her prisoner on the chessboard. Though given the chance of marrying a real human being and remaining free, she chooses to return to the chessboard as a prisoner of her White Prince.

One passage remarkably approaches the basic idea of O'Brien's *The Diamond Lens*: "Is all this beauty around you created merely for you—and the other insects about us? I have no doubt it is filled with invisible life."

This fantasy demonstrates that Lucretia Hale was quite capable of writing a short story of the caliber of *The Spider's Eye*. It seems probable that, when it was decided to include the story in the book, an understandable mistake was made and the work was ascribed to O'Brien. The error was undoubtedly spotted by Miss Hale, who probably saw to it that a correction was made in the second edition.

Perhaps this airing of the controversy may have a salutary effect and result in the unearthing of other stories of a similar nature by Miss Hale, so that she will, in some future appraisal of American fantasy writers, at least be considered.

The Golden Ingot (1858) by Fitz-James O'Brien may ring familiarly to some, since it was adapted to television only a few years back. It tells of an old scientist who is searching for a way to turn baser metals into gold and believes he has succeeded when one morning he finds a gold ingot in his crucible. He dies of a stroke upon learning that his daughter, in order to make him happy, has saved her money and secretly purchased a gold ingot. While almost a bit too direct and bare, and containing a note of the overmelodramatic, the story is nevertheless an effective one.

Among the better-known fantasies of Fitz-James O'Brien is *The Lost Room* (1858), which tells of a man who leaves his room on an errand, then returns to find it filled with strangers, and the furniture changed. Unable to prove it is his room, he tosses dice for it and loses. He is ejected. When he tries to regain entrance there is only a blank wall and he never again finds his room. This story has inspired the writing of dozens of similar others on the theme. Despite some not-too-convincing dialogue on the part of the lead character, the overall effect of an evil and usurping power is powerful and memorable.

One of O'Brien's most charming and delightful fantasies is *The Dragon Fang Possessed by the Conjurer Piou-Lu* (1856). In modern times, only Frank Owen among Western writers has come as close to capturing the complete essence and mood of Chinese storytelling. This tale of a Chinese conjurer is strikingly successful and truly outstanding.

If there was any factor that characterized O'Brien's talent, it was his professional versatility. This is aptly displayed by his mastery of the standard ghost story gambit in *The Pot of Tulips* (1855). In that story the ghost of a man who hid evidence of his wealth, so that a child he thought was not his own would fail to inherit his property, returns from the grave to remedy his error by pointing out the hiding place of his legacy. It is a good story of its kind, strongly reminiscent of another great Irish fantast, Sheridan Le Fanu.

A beautifully wrought weird prose pastel by O'Brien, *The Child Who Loved a Grave*, was not reprinted after its original anonymous publication in *Harper's New Monthly Magazine* for April 1861 until Groff Conklin included it in his paperback anthology *The Graveyard Reader*, published by Ballantine Books in 1958. It tells of the unhappy son of drunken and bickering parents who forms an attachment for the quiet grave of a child. He gains solace by spending time there. When it develops that the grave belongs to a member of nobility, it is dug up and the remains removed overseas. Deprived of his only source of comfort, the boy, before going to bed that night, tells his father that he is going to die and begs that he be buried in the newly opened grave. The next morning the father finds him dead.

O'Brien wrote a remarkable surrealistic fantasy in *From Hand to Mouth*, originally serialized in *The New York Picayune* during 1858. Disembodied eyes, ears, hands, and mouths fill a hotel room in this story, which, though skillfully composed, loses the reader with situations so complex that not even the author could figure them out, for he never finished the last installment.

The publisher of the weekly, Frank H. Bellew, finally completed the story himself. Despite this, *From Hand to Mouth* was twice reprinted in book form, once in 1868 in *Good Stories* and again in *Famous Stories*, issued in 1880. In any form, it remains a collector's item. Despite its faults, the writing of *From Hand to Mouth* is sheer delight and the light handling of surrealistic nightmarish imagination compares favorably with Lewis Carroll.

Other stories by Fitz-James O'Brien, worth mentioning for their elements of the supernatural or horror, are *The Bohemian* (1885), which employs hypnotism to induce extrasensory perception. Though the devices of the story are dated, a number of passages are sheer poetry. *Jubal, the Ringer* (1858) concerns a bell ringer who employs a flock of bats to loosen the plaster binding the stones of his belfry, then utilizes the acoustical vibrations of his bell to bring the stones crashing down into the church, killing himself and the woman he loves (who is marrying another), together with the marriage procession. A *Terrible Night* (1856) is a suspense story in which a man kills his best friend as a result of a fear-induced nightmare. The wife in *Mother of Pearl* (1860) kills her child and attempts to kill her husband while under the influence of narcotics.

Many American critics agree that Fitz-James O'Brien made a signal contribution to the art of short-story writing by "the addition of a Defoe-like verisimilitude to the Poe-like tale of terror." Among them are Henry Seidel Canby, who in his excellent critical work *The Short Story in English* lists the three most important influences of the 1850s and '60s in the short story as Fitz-James O'Brien, Edward Everett Hale, and Bret Harte; and Edward J. O'Brien, late editor of the famed O'Brien's best short-story collections of the year, who stated: "Fitz-James O'Brien was the most distinguished short story teller between Edgar Allan Poe and Bret Harte."

O'Brien's failing, in the long-term literary view, was that he was *too* talented, too versatile, and too conscious of what the market of his period preferred.* O'Brien was a true pro-

---

*A comprehensive picture of the life and writings of Fitz-James O'Brien, including his poetry and non-fantasy, appears in Francis Wolle's biography and bibliography, *Fitz-James O'Brien* (University of Colorado, 1944), a work of top-rank scholarship.

fessional—whether in story, essay, poem, song, play, or critique, he could usually strike the mood of the times and give the editors and the public just what they wanted. Making a sale was not his problem. As a result, if O'Brien's standing among American authors depended upon his general fiction and verse, anything more than a footnote in a general history of literature would have been an act of courtesy.

Only when he turned to science fiction or fantasy did he begin to display the full force of his truly outstanding talents. At such times his interest in the subject matter compelled him to write with his mind on the story instead of on the editor or the public. Though his output of such work was small, the quality is truly remarkable and its influence is still visible in today's science fiction and fantasy.

5

AROUND THE WORLDS
WITH JULES VERNE

Jules Verne was by no means the earliest of science fiction
writers, and it cannot be said that his ideas were particularly
original or his literary gifts in any way exceptional. But he was
the first author to develop consciously and consistently an
approach to the genre which turned it into a specialized form
of literature, quite distinct from fantasy, the Gothic horror
tale, the fictional political utopia, or the imaginatively em-
broidered travel tale.

Other writers, many of greater literary stature, had utilized
virtually every major idea that was later to appear in Verne's
books. But only a very few had made the effort to explain
every departure from the familiar and the known on a consistently logical basis. Usually writers asked the reader to
accept too much on faith and were impatient to get on with
their major purpose, which more often than not was a satire,

a political utopia, a hoax, or a preachment rather than a bona fide narrative. If the stories of Verne's predecessors also entertained, it was almost inadvertently, since to write a tale of entertainment was rarely a part of their original plan.

In a period when popular entertainment was far more limited than it is today and life frightfully hard for the masses, the fiction of Jules Verne provided an escape which took his readers far from the uneventfulness of their daily lives—to such unlikely and romantic places as the South Pole, beneath the sea, out into space, into the bowels of the earth, or aloft in balloons to stratospheric heights.

These voyages were invariably accomplished with such carefully detailed adherence to or expansion of known scientific facts that they never failed to produce a complete, and willing, suspension of disbelief. And because their main purpose was to entertain, thrilling situation followed thrilling situation with such absolute persuasiveness that the readers were kept enthralled to the very end.

Before he adopted the formula which was to bring him such brilliant success, Jules Verne—born February 8, 1828, son of a distinguished lawyer in Nantes, France—had been unable to gain any substantial recognition for his literary gifts. At the age of thirty-five he had succeeded only in putting off for an indefinite period the practice of law, for which he had been trained. He had turned instead to the writing of plays—including two libretti for operas—and even collaborated with Alexandre Dumas in a humorous comedy in verse. Though a number of his plays were produced, they won little favor with the dramatic critics of the period.

However, the publication of a short story in 1852, *Master Zacharius*, convinced Verne's father that his son had real literary ability. Verne's father, a devoutly religious Catholic, was especially pleased because the story, which dealt with the changes which nineteenth-century science was bringing to the orderly and logical development of man's thinking, seemed, symbolically at least, to lean strongly in the direction of religion. This story has since appeared in America as *The*

Watches' Soul in a one-volume collection of short stories titled *Dr. Ox, and Other Stories*, (J. R. Osgood, Boston, 1874). It was later reprinted in the December 1933 issue of *Amazing Stories.*

There followed a prolonged subsidy of his son by the elder Verne, a situation which, paradoxically enough, proved uncomfortable to Jules, since as the years passed it became increasingly burdensome for him to justify his father's confidence.

The works of Edgar Allan Poe provided Jules Verne with his initial inspiration.

Verne read Poe avidly and, by his own admission, with tremendous admiration. He was impressed by the precise, scientific details which Poe introduced into even his horror tales. Poe's plots, characters, and settings seemed to him not only original but inspired. He never tired of rereading the tales of a scientific nature.

Yet his decision to adopt the methods of Poe resulted in a great inner struggle for Verne, for his early religious training made him see a conflict where none perhaps existed and to look upon Poe's approach as too materialistic. In an essay written shortly after the publication of his first successful science fiction story, *Five Weeks in a Balloon*, Verne wrote of Poe:

> . . . in spite of their other-worldly and superhuman beauty, *Tales of the Grotesque* remain materialistic in their conclusions. One is never aware of the intervention of Providence. Poe even seems unwilling to admit of its existence, and claims to explain everything by physical laws which, at a pinch, he is even ready to invent. One fails to detect in him an atom of that faith which his unceasing contemplation of the supernatural should have endowed him.

Verne's actions obviously contradicted his criticism for he overrode his emotional conflict by utilizing Poe's *Balloon-Hoax* as the model for his own remarkable and completely scientific story, *Five Weeks in a Balloon*, which first appeared in 1863, nearly twenty years after Poe's effort. Thirty-four years later, in 1897, Verne was still so much a disciple that he wrote a sequel to Poe's *The Narrative of Arthur Gordon Pym*, *The Sphinx of the Ice-Fields*.

Though in mood and style there was no great similarity between Verne and Poe, in their approach to the mysterious and the unknown they were very close indeed. The influence of Poe is seen throughout the whole range of Verne's works. His *Mathias Sandorf* (1885) contains episodes of hypnotism deeply suggestive of Poe's *The Facts in the Case of M. Valdemar*. Verne's *A Trip from the Earth to the Moon* parallels to a considerable degree Poe's *Hans Phaal—a Tale*.

The maelstrom into which Captain Nemo's submarine, *The Nautilus*, is drawn in *Twenty Thousand Leagues Under the Sea* can be traced to Poe's *A Descent into the Maelström*. The idea of losing a day in the transit of the world, a pivotal plot device in *Round the World in Eighty Days*, is drawn from Poe's *Three Sundays in a Week*, in which a suitor is given the task of producing three Sundays in one week in order to win the hand of the girl he loves. He accomplishes this seemingly impossible task by having two travelers arrive on a Sunday, one from the east, for whom Sunday was yesterday, and the other from the west, for whom Sunday will be tomorrow.

Verne metamorphosed overnight into one of the world's brightest literary stars simply by hitting upon the idea of stressing speculative scientific adventure in full-length novels which placed the strongest possible emphasis upon credibility.

That Verne consciously set up and followed a pattern of writing calculated to win him the greatest possible popularity is nowhere better illustrated than in a letter to a friend at the Paris Stock Exchange, shortly after he completed *Five Weeks in a Balloon*: "I have just written a novel in a new form," he wrote, "one that is entirely my own. If it succeeds I will have stumbled upon a gold mine. In that case I shall go on writing and writing without pause. . . ."

Though a thousand-mile balloon voyage may not seem very startling today, in 1863 the mere description of such a voyage took readers as far ahead of the accomplishments of the times as a story about a V-2 rocket converted into an interplanetary spaceship would do today.

If there was the slightest doubt concerning the imaginative uniqueness of Jules Verne, it was dispelled by his second novel, A Journey to the Center of the Earth, which appeared in 1864. There has probably never been a finer novel of subterranean exploration. Verne did not originate the idea of another world at the center of the earth. Symmes and Poe and others had used this concept earlier, and Baron Ludvig Holberg, in the eighteenth century, described a land at the earth's core. Early printings of his novel, called A Journey to the World Under-Ground, occasionally crop up even today. Holberg was strongly influenced by Jonathan Swift and cynically chronicled an underground land where females held the whip hand and males did all the menial work.

Apparently, however, good adventure has proved more popular than social significance, since Verne's novel is still in print and has been made into a motion picture, while Holberg's interesting little book remained a relatively rare collector's item until its recent reprinting in soft covers.

Verne did not rest on his laurels with the publication of A Journey to the Center of the Earth. He followed with a novel even more imaginative, that prototype of the modern bestseller, A Trip from the Earth to the Moon. Published in 1865, this book received an overwhelmingly enthusiastic reception from the French public.

Today, a new 45,000-word novel devoted entirely to the construction of a gun which could fire a projectile around the moon would be greeted by a tremendous yawn on the part of the reading public, particularly if there were no strong human interest to motivate the characters. However, the French of 1865 not only ate it up, but they patiently waited another five years for the book publication of the sequel, A

Tour of the Moon, which described with a great deal of exciting detail the adventures of the space pioneers as they completely encircled the moon and fell back to earth.

Verne would undoubtedly have liked to include an actual landing on the moon. But the method he selected for the firing of a projectile into space—a giant cannon—left no logical means of returning his characters to earth.

Despite the mountain of mathematical data Verne assembled to support his cannon hypothesis, we know today that the muzzle velocity of a cannon-projected shell designed to overcome earth's gravitational pull would produce an acceleration so great that any passengers carried in the projectile would quickly cease to draw breath.

Despite this flaw, among others, the book continues to prove of interest today, and Verne's conjecture of a Space Train, in which a group of space projectiles are linked together like sausages on a string, still intrigues those who read the book.

Additional proof that it was Verne's method of presenting his material that brought him such astounding popular success can be obtained by considering Chrysostom Trueman's book, *A Voyage to the Moon*, published in England one year earlier than Verne's novel. Trueman's narrative is today a literary curiosity, despite the fact that it contained some unusual ideas on the construction of a spaceship, including a mineral-repellent antigravity device, and wood for material calked with tar and air-proofed with sheet metal. It even described a live garden to replenish the oxygen for the voyagers. The opening pages of the novel are written in a graphic, documentary style seventy-five years ahead of its time. But Trueman is fundamentally involved with his peculiar utopian theories, whereas Verne is primarily concerned with narrative suspense and a sense of wonder, and the Trueman novel remains obscure and all but unknown.

Probably Jules Verne's finest book, considered from all standpoints—careful plotting, above-average writing, outstanding characterization, and scientific ideas with a resplendent sweep, ideas which completely outdistance the commonplace—is *Twenty Thousand Leagues Under the Sea*, published the same year as *Tour of the Moon*. Verne has been accused by some critics of weak characterization, but the delineation of Captain Nemo, builder and commander of the marvelous submarine *Nautilus*, is an outstanding literary achievement.

On other occasions Verne has created characters quite unforgettably three-dimensional, notably Phileas Fogg in *Round the World in Eighty Days*, and the title character of *Michael Strogoff*.

Then, too, effective characterization in fiction is not solely confined to people. The unusual phenomena and special effects in science fiction require skillful handling to make them believable. They are the focus of the story. In a sense, they are also major "characters."

After all, in Verne's A *Trip from the Earth to the Moon*, aren't the space gun and the projectile actually the lead characters in the story? Certainly Verne exhausted every effort to depict a space gun effectively. In *A Journey to the Center of the Earth*, the strange land near the core of the earth is the focal point of the book's interest and not the characters. It is a case of the author and the readers being more interested in *what* happens than to *whom* it happens.

Similarly, the love story motif is almost entirely absent from Verne's scientific romances. Until recently this was true of ninety per cent of all science fiction. Readers were more interested in the theme than in the love life of the characters.

That Verne was able to create a three-dimensional character as great as Captain Nemo against the tremendous competition of the marvelous submarine *Nautilus* which competes with Captain Nemo page after page for the reader's attention is the true wonder of *Twenty Thousand Leagues Under the Sea*.

Verne's success as a novelist, paradoxically, brought him

the fame in the theater which had eluded him as a play-wright. Many of his novels were adapted to the stage and turned into theatrical extravaganzas which made his name a household word around the world, including, among others, *Round the World in Eighty Days*, *Michael Strogoff*, and *Mathias Sandorf*.

Success brought also a prying into his background and personal life, resulting in the circulation of many rumors, the most famous of which is the story that Jules Verne was actually a Polish Jew named Jules Olschewitz, who had converted to Catholicism and settled in France. The name Olschewitz apparently is derived from the Polish word *olscha*, meaning alder, and the French word for alder is *vergne*, pronounced *verne*.

Further confusion was added to the situation by the fact that there *was* a Polish Jew named Julien de Verne whose name was well known to a Polish priest in Rome, who thought that Julien and Jules Verne were one and the same and added seeming substance to the assertions.

Despite the fact that Verne could show his birth certificate, which coincided with the records in Nantes, and the fact that many people had known him since his birth as a Catholic, in the anti-Semitic atmosphere that pervaded France at the time, the story persisted and, on at least one occasion, Verne answered the door of his home to be confronted by the allegation, in great and specific detail, by a complete stranger. Verne treated the situation as a joke and even embellished the man's story. However, the rumors reached their height in 1876, and became so annoying that in Verne's interplanetary novel, *Hector Servadac, or Off on a Comet*, published in 1878, the appearance of a Jewish villain, who is made out to be thoroughly despicable and consequently the butt of scarcely complimentary jibes from the pen of Verne, might logically be considered to be Verne's attempt to squelch the Jewish story through the expression of pronouncedly anti-Semitic sentiments, which a true Jew would logically not publicize. For good measure, Verne also took a swipe at Negroes in this novel.

Though *Hector Servadac* is one of Verne's most imaginative efforts—he has a group of characters tour the solar system as far into space as Saturn, riding on a comet—it is also one of his weakest stories of prophecy. In previous novels, Verne had gone to fantastic lengths to make every future development scientifically plausible, but in *Hector Servadac* people are snatched off earth by a comet and returned to earth by methods so weak, obscure, and absurd as to make logical presentation a difficult if not impossible task.

With the entire solar system to explore Verne nevertheless succeeds in turning out a tale which can only be characterized as dull, and more than a little ridiculous. Yet *Hector Servadac* was popular when it was published, probably because it went a great deal further in the realm of interplanetary exploration than Verne's moon stories and helped to satisfy the public's curiosity as to what was "out there."

It can perhaps be taken for granted that every science fiction writer will try his hand at general fiction at some time in his career—if only to prove his ability to turn out a smash hit without the sensational element that science fiction so often seems to thrive on. Noticeably after 1870 and predominantly after 1878, Jules Verne turned his hand to such work. The most successful of these new, novel-length departures was *Round the World in Eighty Days*, which was published in weekly installments (in *Temps* in 1872) and aroused such world-wide interest that wire services flashed the plot to newspapers long before the slow-moving mails of 1873 could bring it to them.

As the book progressed, several major steamship lines promised Verne fabulous sums if in the closing chapters he would consent to send Phileas Fogg across the sea on one of their ships. Verne was said to have refused all such offers. The story was made into a play, which is still produced from time to time. And Mike Todd's motion picture production of this famous novel has become one of the great sensations of the screen.

Other non-science fiction novels also brought Verne critical and popular approval notably *The Great Eastern*, a fictionalized account of his trip to the United States. Two other books —*Michael Strogoff*, a powerful novel of life in czarist Russia, and *Mathias Sandorf*, his longest novel and an ironic take-off on *The Count of Monte Cristo*—were well received and also enjoyed phenomenal acclaim when they were turned into plays.

Following his initial success in 1863, Verne regularly produced at least two novels a year. But after 1878 these were often not science at all, or were science fiction only through the courtesy of a very minor scientific invention or development introduced into the narrative artificially.

The almost clocklike precision with which Verne's novels made their appearance and the relative lack of the fantastic in later years eventually led readers to question whether Verne was still alive, and whether he was actually the author of the many volumes bearing his name. Some of his admirers even made special trips to his home in Nantes to reassure themselves on that score.

During Verne's lifetime, many of his scientific prophecies became invented commonplaces that ceased to astound; praise for his perspicacity in that respect reached its zenith when, in 1898, Simon Lake, builder of the *Argonaut*—the first submarine successfully to operate in the open sea—opened his autobiography with the lines: "Jules Verne was in a sense the director-general of my life."

Not satisfied with having written his version of Dumas' *The Count of Monte Cristo* in *Mathias Sandorf*, and having contrived a sequel to Poe's *The Narrative of Arthur Gordon Pym* in *The Sphinx of the Ice-Fields*, Jules Verne in 1900 paid homage to another writer who had influenced him profoundly, J. R. Wyss. He wrote a sequel to *Swiss Family Robinson* entitled *The Second Fatherland*. His much earlier

Mysterious Island, in which Captain Nemo, his most successful character, appears—almost like Shakespeare's Falstaff, by
public demand, had echoed Daniel Defoe's *Robinson Crusoe.*

Jules Verne retained throughout his life a high regard for
the inventive progressiveness of America and many of his
stories featured American leading characters or American lo-
cales. Just when one might have supposed that the well was
running dry and that Verne had abandoned the world of
probable invention, he produced a short story, *In the Year
2889.* It was as prophetic as any of his earlier books, with a
colorfully detailed description of dozens of advances in the
America of the future, such as moving sidewalks and photo-
printing. What makes this story unique among Verne's writings is the fact that its debut was in America in English,
in the February 1889 issue of *The Forum.* Later in French,
it was published in Europe, with numerous revisions and
alterations.

Jules Verne's last story—a science fiction story written just
before his death in 1905—bore the poetic and provocative
title *The Eternal Adam.* It is actually only a long novelette
and deals with a future in which the continent of Atlantis has
risen again from the sea and is inhabited by men who possess
legends about a great civilization of marvelous scientific advancement—apparently our present era—which had flour-
ished with splendor and then vanished from the earth. And,
amazingly enough, there is in this story a slight uneasiness
about the misuse of science that does not seem at all characteristic of Verne. This feeling, coupled with the passing of
loved ones and the burden of illness in old age, had given
Jules Verne a pessimism he had never expressed in his work
until the very end.

In many respects there is a similarity between the literary
lives of the two greatest of all science fiction writers, Jules
Verne and H. G. Wells. Both became famous in their
younger years by writing science fiction. They turned to gen-

eral fiction in their middle age and finally to science fiction again to express a note of disillusion and near despair, because their shared dream—that the advance of science would automatically mean the creation of a better world—had dissolved in the wakefulness of reality.

At first the general run of sophisticated Continental writers had viewed Jules Verne as a freak, naively overproductive. But as novel followed novel and his fame spread around the world, it was soon realized that he had stumbled upon a new literary form that was not only different but was popular with the masses.

Science fiction novels began to appear with increasing frequency. In England, veritable giants were to rise in the field of science fiction and fantasy, men of the caliber of H. G. Wells, A. Conan Doyle, and H. Rider Haggard. And while France never again produced a titan of Verne's stature, lesser men found a ready market for science fiction in that country.

Some of the imitators were actually disciples and followers of Verne, like Paschal Grousset, who wrote under the pen name of André Laurie and collaborated with Verne on a science fiction novel, *The Wreck of the Cynthia*. In *The Conquest of the Moon*, André Laurie avoided the problem of building a rocket to the moon by dragging the satellite almost down to the surface of the earth with magnets, and was thus enabled to supply readers with a great deal of information about its surface, quite outdistancing Verne in that respect. Laurie's novel was a great success, being reprinted in England and the United States, and was followed by several other science fiction books—*New York to Brest in Seven Hours*, *The Crystal City Under the Sea*, and *The Secret of the Magian*.

An entire series of science fiction novels—at least fourteen in number—were written by Paul D'Ivoi in France at the turn of the century and published as "*voyages excentriques*," paralleling the term which Verne had used, "*voyages extraordinaires*." These volumes were enormous in size, weighing just a little under six pounds. They featured four-color paintings printed on the cloth binding, and had sixty or more line and half-tone drawings, most of them strikingly like the illustrations of the later science fiction artist, Frank R. Paul. One volume, *The Master of the Blue Flag*, contains some excellent illustrations of immense, full-wall television screens called *téléphotes*.

Another writer, embarking on science fiction in what was apparently a series only a little less ostentatious in appearance than that of D'Ivoi, was Georges Price, one of whose novels, *The Star of the Pacific*, dealt with a fantastic four-bowed ship shaped somewhat like a star.

A bull's-eye in the direction of good solid prophecy was made in 1883 by the Frenchman Albert Robida, who wrote, illustrated, and published a book titled *Twentieth Century*. ·In this volume he predicted, with appropriate illustrations, a fantastic number of scientific "miracles" which eventually came to pass, such as television, jet planes, antiaircraft weapons, armored cars, poison gas, germ warfare, submarines, radio, and automats.

In all truth, most of these ideas were not original with Robida, but because of the number of accurate guesses the book is almost as impressive as Hugo Gernsback's fabulous *Ralph 124C41+*.

Clearly derived from Verne was *The Russian Scientist* by G. Le Faure and H. De Graffigny, published in Paris in 1889 in two volumes. The first volume was subtitled *The Moon* and dealt quite appropriately with a trip to the moon in a shell, fired from a gun, much in the manner of Verne's *A Trip from the Earth to the Moon*. However, it goes much further in describing lunar inhabitants and civilization and illustrates space suits in great detail, including handsome models for ladies. The introduction by famed astronomer Camille Flammarion, which links the series with Lucian, Cyrano de Bergerac, and Edgar Allan Poe, gives the effort the stamp of respectability. The second volume is entitled *The Small Planets* and involves a trip to the asteroids.

The desire to explore beyond the moon as exemplified in

The Small Planets was shared by other French writers. One popular work, *Voyage to the Planet Venus* by Charles Guyon, published in Paris in 1892, a greatly detailed excursion of the Evening Star with a comprehensive history of its life and the state of civilization, acknowledges its indebtedness to Jules Verne, whose name appears in the text when the Venusians construct a giant cannon to shoot the explorers back to their home planet.

In America, Frank Tousey, a leading New York publisher, started the *Frank Reade Library* in September 1892—a series of "dime novels" dealing with the adventures of a daring young inventor of mechanical robots, electrical flying devices, submarines, and other marvels.

Jules Verne's example shaped the policies and contributed to the success of the world's first science fiction magazine, published in 1926 by Hugo Gernsback.

The first issue of *Amazing Stories* left no doubt as to the debt it owed to Jules Verne. The cover illustration, painted by Frank R. Paul, depicted an ice-skating scene from Verne's *Off on a Comet* as that body approached the orbit of Saturn. The novel itself was serialized, running as a two-part story.

In his first *Amazing Stories* editorial, Gernsback jubilantly announced: "Exclusive arrangements have already been made with the copyright holders of the entire voluminous works of ALL of Jules Verne's immortal stories. Many of these stories are not as yet known to the general American public. For the first time they will be within easy reach of every reader through *Amazing Stories*."

Though Gernsback did not publish all of Verne's stories, he did use a liberal selection of them, including *A Journey to the Center of the Earth*, *The English at the North Pole*, *The Desert of Ice*, *Dr. Ox's Experiment*, *A Drama in the Air*, *The Purchase of the North Pole*, and the two most popular novels of Verne's later years, *Robur the Conqueror* (1886) and its sequel *The Master of the World* (1904). The latter mark a return to the type of story with which he had won his fame, after a long period during which he had confined himself predominantly to straight adventure stories, only occasionally relieved by the inclusion of a minor gadget or an advanced scientific machine. The Robur stories advocated heavier-than-air flying vessels over dirigibles and the helicopter over the glider plane. It also suggested plastics as a means of getting a light substance as strong as metal for heavier-than-air craft. *The Master of the World* was concerned with the construction of a combination submarine, automobile, and airplane.

Robur, principal character of the two novels, was the most powerful creation of Verne's pen, Captain Nemo excepted. Most significant in the two stories is the contrast in philosophy they display, a period of eighteen years intervening between their publication. *Robur the Conqueror* offers science as the great future hope of man, provided that advances are evolutionary and do not outstrip social progress. *The Master of the World* was written by an old, sick, unhappy Jules Verne, and in it the magnificent Robur slid into madness. It pictured the forces of science as blind, the tool of whoever would use them. Scientific advance was not the solution to man's problems.

Beginning in its first issue and continuing for many years, even after it had passed into other hands, *Amazing Stories* carried on its title page a line drawing of Jules Verne's tombstone at Amiens, depicting Verne raising the lid of his tombstone as a symbol of his immortality. And in connection with the reprinting of Verne's *Measuring a Meridian*, editor T. O'Connor Sloane had Leo Morey do a painting portraying the actual tombstone, which appeared on the cover of the May 1934 issue of *Amazing Stories*.

The dramatic figure of Jules Verne, raising his tombstone and reaching aloft, was more than symbolic. It was prophetic, since in every sense of the word the original trail he pioneered with his remarkable tales continues to be followed, as he figuratively still reaches from the grave and guides the minds of today's editors and writers.

6

THE REAL EARTH
SATELLITE STORY

For the record—once and for all—it was a distinguished and world-famous American author who first conceived an earth satellite.

This small satisfaction remains as comfort to the West after the Russian success in the actual launching of the world's first artificial satellite, Sputnik, Oct. 4, 1957. The announcement by President Dwight D. Eisenhower on July 29, 1955, that the United States planned to send a satellite aloft some time in 1957 or 1958 as part of its contribution to the International Geophysical Year was accepted by most as evidence before the fact of accomplishment. More attention should have been paid to the story on the front page of *The New York Times* the following day, headlined:

RUSSIANS ALREADY STRIVING TO SET UP SPACE SATELLITE.

During the period immediately following, West Germany

and Russia engaged in their own private debate to gain credit for the origin of the idea of an earth satellite. Germans pointed to a slim ninety-two-page volume by the famous theoretician of space travel, Hermann Oberth, whose *The Rocket Into Interplanetary Space* was published in 1923, with a few pages on artificial space satellites tacked on almost as an afterthought. The writing of this book had begun during World War I.

The Russians professed to detect a similarity between Oberth's ideas and those contained in Konstantin Tsiolkovsky's article "The Exploration of Cosmic Space by Jet-Propelled Instruments," published in the Russian magazine *Scientific Survey* in 1903. Tsiolkovsky, a deaf schoolteacher residing in Kaluga, a town one hundred miles outside of Moscow, independently and in almost complete obscurity evolved brilliant theories of rocketry, space stations, and interplanetary travel. The article referred to contained very specific details about space stations. To clinch the matter, evidence was offered that the manuscript was accepted by the magazine in 1898, five years before its publication. It was in this article that the word *Sputnik*, which name the Russians gave to their first earth satellite, was coined by Tsiolkovsky.

Then famed rocketry historian Willy Ley referred to his book *Rockets, Missiles, & Space Travel*, published originally in 1944 and revised in 1957, in which he called attention to the fact that Germany did not have to rest her claims on Oberth alone. German theory of earth stations could be traced back to 1897, when Kurd Lasswitz's best-selling interplanetary novel *On Two Planets* featured several of them as integral parts of the plot. To seal the case tighter there were notes to indicate that Lasswitz began writing the book in November 1895.

The Russians then countered with a stunner. If the Germans wanted to get technical about it, discussion of the possibility of a permanent earth satellite appeared in a volume titled *Fantasies of Earth and Sky*, which the Russians referred to as "a book of science fiction," published by A. N. Goncharov in Moscow in 1895. They even gave the page number, 49, where the reference first appeared and a quotation: "Our imagined satellite will b̃e not unlike the moon, but as near to our planet as we wish; only it will be outside the earth's atmosphere, that is some 300 versts [200 miles] from the earth's surface. With its very small mass, it will constitute an example of a gravity-free medium."

Americans, so confident then that the United States would be the first into space, had felt no urge to investigate the origin of the idea. It is quite probable that, even today, few if any are aware that the claims of Russia and Germany merely serve to underscore the fact that one of the United States' most practical men of letters, Edward Everett Hale, was the first human being to conceive of an artificial earth satellite and to put his thoughts on paper.

Edward Everett Hale (1822-1909), author and clergyman, is probably best known for his short story *The Man Without a Country*. During the nineteenth century his works were universally popular and respected. He was one of the early contributing editors of *The Atlantic Monthly*, where his short novel (approximately 25,000 words in length) *The Brick Moon* was serialized as a three-part story, in October, November, and December 1869. A short sequel, *Life in the Brick Moon*, appeared in *The Atlantic Monthly* for February 1870. These were his final literary efforts for that publication, but they stand as the *first* stories anywhere ever to mention an artificial earth satellite.

The stories have been obscured by time but can scarcely be said to be unknown. The two, combined, saw five editions in book form between 1872 and 1900. In the second volume of *The Life and Letters of Edward Everett Hale*, published in 1917, a full page is devoted to a discussion of *The Brick Moon*. Both were listed in a bibliography titled *Fantasy in the Atlantic Monthly* compiled by Walter Sullivan and appearing in the science fiction fan magazine *Stunning Scientifan* for Fall 1939. A brief synopsis of the stories may be found in J. O. Bailey's *Pilgrims Through Space and Time*, 1947.

The only prior reference to earth satellites worth mentioning is found in *A Journey to the World Under-Ground* by the Danish Ludvig Holberg. This tale was first published in Latin in 1741 and enjoyed an English edition the following year under the pen name of Nicholas Klimius (the lead character of the story). In this novel, the hero discovers a sun and planetary system *inside* the earth, and while falling toward one of the worlds accidentally becomes a human satellite for three days. The science is superb for its day but the entire incident is still pretty far removed from the notion of building and sending into orbit an artificial satellite.

To many it appears strange that an idea as imaginative as that of an earth satellite could emanate from a clergyman. Hale was a Unitarian minister, a liberal, and his sociological and humanist ideas were far in advance of his time. He was one of the really important short story writers of his period and his work was characterized by extraordinary originality in plotting and a stylistic approach which frequently went to the extreme of employing trick typesetting to achieve a special effect. The lengths to which he was willing to go in order to be different sometimes lent an element of the artificial or the contrived to his work, so that his greatest strength was also his greatest weakness. *The Man Without a Country* is probably secure as an American classic, as is his clever *My Double and How He Undid Me*.

In 1899, the collected works of Edward Everett Hale were published by Little, Brown and Company of Boston. *The Brick Moon* was reprinted in Volume Four. Hale prefaced the book with an introduction which secures still further the fact that he was the earliest known person to conceive the idea of an artificial earth satellite. The idea was inspired, he said, by the reading of Richard Adams Locke's famous *Moon Hoax*. Hale went on to say that while he was attending Cambridge

University in 1838 the idea grew from "an old chat, dreams and plans of college days" and was finally written in the working room of his brother Nathan at Union College, Schenectady, N. Y., in 1869, where Nathan held a professorship in English.

However, it is important and interesting to note that *The Brick Moon* appeared in book form in an earlier collection of Hale's stories, titled *His Level Best and Other Stories* and published by Robert Brothers of Boston in 1872. This book was reissued the following year by J. R. Osgood and Company and still another edition was brought out, again by Roberts Brothers, in 1877. A paperback edition of *The Brick Moon* alone appeared at the turn of the century.

Then, as now, astronomers were among the most faithful devotees of science fiction. In 1877, seven years after the appearance of Hale's story in *The Atlantic Monthly*, Asaph Hall, astronomer of the National Observatory, was the first to observe the two moons of Mars. He remembered Hale's story and wrote to the author praising its imaginative brilliance and finally concluding, "The smaller of these two moons is a veritable Brick Moon."

The Brick Moon is a serious story and not an attempt at humor. Many of its scientific ideas are decidedly off base, but others are almost miraculously close to the mark. As fiction, *The Brick Moon* reads easily, but like most of Hale's work, it would have been destined for literary oblivion had it not been so imaginatively prophetic.

The most amazing fact about Hale's story of a space satellite is that until Arthur C. Clarke's *Island in the Sky* in 1953 it was the longest story ever written dealing *only* with the earth satellite theme. For, unlike the authors and scientists who came after him, Hale did not bring in the space station idea as an interesting added thought. He devoted every single word of his story to the subject.

Early in 1869, when the story was written, scientific knowledge regarding the basic essentials of space travel was still in a rudimentary state, even electric power being a novelty.

Therefore, Hale's story should not be judged on the basis of accuracy of scientific detail but solely upon its merits as a prophetic work of fiction.

In Hale's narrative, funds are collected by dedicated men for the purpose of launching an artificial earth satellite large enough to be seen with the naked eye, and to serve as a reliable means of judging the longitude of ships at sea. In 1869 ships were the primary means of transportation, and when they were thrown off course in a storm or rough weather, experienced great difficulty in figuring their longitude. An artificial moon whose distance from earth could be accurately established seemed to be the answer. If the first satellite proved successful, the sponsors of the venture planned to follow it with others.

Explaining the theory on which such a project would be based, Hale used a pea as an example.

> If you drove it so fast and far that when its power of ascent was exhausted, and it began to fall, it should clear the Earth and pass outside the North Pole; if you had given it sufficient power to get half 'round the Earth without touching, that pea would clear the Earth forever. It would continue to rotate about the North Pole, above the Feejee Islands, above the South Pole and Greenwich, forever, with the impulse which first cleared our atmosphere and attraction. If only we could see that pea as it revolved in that convenient orbit, then we could measure the longitude from that, as soon as we knew how high the orbit was, as well as if it were a ring of Saturn.

It was decided to build a globular satellite of brick. Why brick? Because all metals known at the time would have melted under the terrific acceleration the satellite would have to achieve for it to leave earth's surface. Brick would prove far more heat-resistant. The satellite was to be coated with a powdery, rocklike substance which would be melted by atmospheric friction after a short interval and form into a porcelainized protective coating to keep the satellite airtight.

(Ceramic exteriors for existing artificial satellites of our own space age are not unheard of.)

The brick moon was to be thrown aloft by centrifugal force through the use of two flywheels built of oak and pine and hooped with iron. Though we know now that such a method would be out of the question as a means of launching any space missile from the surface of the earth, it actually would work on a small moon or a planetoid of extremely low mass. As late as 1923, Clement Fézandié, author of a series of stories called Doctor Hackensaw's Secrets, actually proposed centrifugal force as a method of space propulsion in an ingenious tale published in *Science and Invention* for November 1920, and called *A Car for the Moon*.

In Hale's story it was decided to throw the brick moon into an orbit about 4,000 miles above the earth. The reason this figure was decided upon was that at any lesser distance the artificial satellite would be in eclipse three hours every night, thus severely limiting its use for navigation.

The brick moon was to be 200 feet in diameter. That size was dictated by the fact that telescopes of the year 1869 could just barely pick out a 250-foot object on the moon and it was felt that a 200-foot artificial satellite, 4,000 miles aloft, should be as readily visible to the naked eye or with ordinary opera glasses.

A second moon was to follow shortly after the first, and for maximum visibility it was decided that one moon would be stabilized on the meridian over Greenwich and the other over New Orleans.

The interior of the brick moon was braced by a series of ten round, hollow balls, each held in place by groined arches, with the space between the balls designed to serve as insulation.

The brick moon was built in a wilderness, but in the vicinity there was sufficient water power to activate the flywheels. The workers started construction from the inside out, utilizing the round inner globes as their sleeping quarters and keeping abundant supplies in storage.

One night, shortly before the completion of the brick moon, it accidentally rolled forward onto the flywheel mechanism and was catapulted into space. Fortunately, at the time, the workmen—and their wives—were all sleeping, relaxed in their hammocks. This saved them from instant death. (The use of hammocks to withstand the pressures of take-off, it might be noted, is scarcely outdated even today.) The brick moon unexpectedly carried with it into space quantities of air and even some soil and plant life.

The satellite immediately established itself in an orbit 5,000 miles above the earth, the departure from the original estimate resulting from the unequal distribution of weight in the moon. The satellite turned on its axis every seven hours. Telescopes could detect objects five feet or more in length on the surface, so communication was easily established. The brick moon's inhabitants simply cut out letters and placed them in view.

The weight of each individual on the brick moon was estimated at three tenths of an ounce. A plan to shoot a man up in an asbestos suit and air helmet was debated, and wisely abandoned, and after careful calculations a bag of supplies was catapulted up. The friction from the atmosphere burned the bag open. A few of the supplies reached the surface of the moon, but most of them went into miniature orbits around the satellite.

The inhabitants found themselves enduring extremes of tropical heat and freezing cold when they walked as much as fifty paces on the surface of the satellite.

The brick moon never returned to earth, but the thirty-seven men and women aboard found ingenious, if improbable, means of raising food and surviving. Their early adjustments were detailed but their ultimate fate was left in doubt.

As a result of recent developments, it seems more than likely that *The Brick Moon* will attain a peculiar literary immortality all its own. Indeed, its fame might conceivably outstrip that of *The Man Without a Country*.

Hale's story, because of the definiteness of its creation of an artificial satellite encircling the earth, and because of its date of publication in 1869, establishes him unquestionably as the first man anywhere in the world to write of an earth satellite or space station.

The Brick Moon was not the only tale of science and fantasy written by Hale. My Visit to Sybaris, published in 1869, the same year as The Brick Moon, is regarded as a historically important "utopia." In it, the life and habits in the "advanced" Italian city of Sybaris are described so as to satirize the mid-nineteenth century and its way of life. Descriptions of "utopian" progressiveness appear in municipal umbrellas for rainy weather, registration of all citizenry, fines for late trains, compulsory marriage (the alternative is exile), and old-age pensions. Generally, Hale sticks so closely to the facts of his time that his book today is considerably dated. The same is true of another borderline fantasy of his, Ten Times One Is Ten, based on the ethical influence of a ghost which suggests the idea for a "Lend-a-Hand" society. (As a direct result of his book, a string of such groups spread their benevolent influence across the nation.)

By an editorial quirk, because this tale is by no stretch of the imagination science fiction, Hale's nostalgic short story of a prank in which he sped up the pendulum of a clock to fool his instructor into letting his class out of school earlier —The Good-Natured Pendulum—was reprinted by the octogenarian editor, T. O'Connor Sloane, in the May 1933 issue of the science fiction magazine Amazing Stories.

Hale is credited with the philological feat of tracing the origin of the name of the state of California to a Spanish work of science fantasy, Deeds of Esplandian, published in 1510. Portions of this tale of swashbuckling adventure, involving the black amazons of the fictional Island of California, who, with their trained, winged griffins invade the Mediterranean basin, smiting Christian and pagan alike, were translated by Hale for The Atlantic Monthly. Later, these translated excerpts were collected along with introductory matter and published as *The Queen of California* in the collection *His Level Best*.

Hale's *Brick Moon* was not the end of artificial satellite stories in the United States, though before the appearance of the next one there was a fascinating import involving the idea of manipulating an existing satellite, the moon itself, for illuminating the cities of earth at night. This was projected by the Frenchman Paschal Grousset, writing under the pen name of André Laurie, in *The Conquest of the Moon*. This book was published in 1889 in London and appeared in France under the title *Sélène Cie* slightly before or at about the same date. Soon it was serialized in America in *The Argosy* in seventeen weekly parts starting in the November 16, 1889 issue and later reprinted in the same magazine as *A Month in the Moon* beginning in the February 1897 issue and running eight installments. Grousset was an acolyte of Jules Verne, having collaborated with him on *The Wreck of the Cynthia*, published in 1885. He went on to write other science fiction stories which proved extremely popular in France and were later reprinted in England.

Grousset's idea of pulling the moon from its orbit by the use of giant magnets and bringing it closer to the earth was scarcely practical and quite out of bounds as a realistic contribution to artificial satellite literature. But the novel is readable, even today.

Lost in a Comet's Tail, a true artificial satellite story, is a short novel printed in the boys' weekly *Frank Reade Library* for December 13, 1895, in which dime-novelist Luis P. Senarens used the earth satellite theme with seeming unawareness of Hale's pioneering effort. A super aircraft, lifted by four giant helicopter blades or "rotors" and equipped with airtight cabins, oxygen equipment, electric heaters, and diving suits which eventually double as space suits, is sucked along in the tail of Verdi's comet and pulled out into the void. The comet eventually explodes, freeing the ship, but it remains "motionless" while the earth revolves beneath. A girl, who is part of the crew, accidentally falls from the aircraft only to float nearby unharmed. Reaction from explosives is considered as a means of breaking the ship's "suspension." Finally another passing comet upsets the balance and permits them to descend safely. This juvenile is a contrast in remarkably good and incredibly bad science, but its appearance was early enough for it to have been a contestant for the priority claimed for Tsiolkovsky if the earlier Hale work had not existed.

Lost in a Comet's Tail! Or, Frank Reade, Jr.'s Strange Adventure With His Air-Ship was reissued in the later color-cover series of dime novels, *Frank Reade Weekly Magazine*, for December 4, 1903, where it was noted by Edward Stratemeyer, famed dime-novel writer, editor, and publisher. Stratemeyer had worked as an editor for Street & Smith, and is said to have completed a number of unfinished Horatio Alger, Jr., manuscripts upon that author's death. He left Street & Smith to start the Rover Boys, a series of low-priced teen-age hardcover books, which was to make him a fortune. He was also responsible for the Motor Boys Series, the famous Tom Swift stories, and the Dave Dashaway and Speedwell Boys adventures. He employed, on regular salary, a group of ghost writers who ground out stories on an assembly-line basis.

One of his more interesting properties was the Great Marvel Series, which was composed entirely of science fiction novels for boys, including trips to the planets. This series was begun in 1900 with *The Wizard of the Sea; Or, A Trip Under the Ocean* and terminated with *By Space Ship to Saturn* in 1935. All these works were published under the house name of Roy Rockwood and were quite obviously derived from Luis Senarens' Frank Reade, Jr., series. The boy inventor of the Great Marvel stories was Jack Darrow, who so impressed a youthful Chicago science fiction fan named Clifford Kornoelje that he assumed the name and signed it to dozens of letters which were published in fantasy magazines during the period 1932 to 1936. The result was a certain type of renown for the latter-day Jack Darrow among devotees of fantastic literature in the thirties.

The sixth book in the Great Marvel Series, *On a Torn-Away World*, initially published in 1913, found boy scientist Jack Darrow building an airplane and flying off to Alaska in search of a rare herb. Underground gases build up near a volcano in the Yukon and their explosion blasts an entire valley, with its adjacent mountain range and ocean coast, into space, where it goes into an orbit around the earth. Jack Darrow and his friends, on this fragment, experience the effects of lighter gravitation. After many adventures, the fragment loses its orbital speed around the earth and falls into the Pacific Ocean. Jack Darrow and his friends are saved by the fact that they happened to be aboard a ship on the short-lived satellite, and the ship floated when the mass sank into the Pacific.

The space station concept in Germany originated with novelist Kurd Lasswitz. The possibility of his having learned of Tsiolkovsky's obscure book (no copy has yet been located in a Western nation) seems remote.

Lasswitz' novel, *On Two Planets*, was a best-seller when it appeared in Germany in 1897. It has been translated into many languages and is still in print in Germany today. It is a straight interplanetary story in which Martians visit the earth only to discover that because of the peculiarities of their anti-gravity space traveling equipment they will be forced to build two space stations above the earth. Interplanetary voyagers land on the station and are shuttled to the earth. The station, as Lasswitz conceived it, is very much like the spoked-wheel stations being designed today.

It is hard to deprive Lasswitz of the credit for popularizing the space station in the German mind. His book remained a standard classic in Germany until the Nazis assumed power, and it is inconceivable that anyone in that country interested in space travel would not have been familiar with it.

In Russia, the all-but-unknown Konstantin Tsiolkovsky, speculating in his 1895 book, *Fantasies of Earth and Sky*, wondered how so huge an object as an artificial satellite could be motivated to attain a speed which would clear the earth's atmosphere and place it in orbit. That year he scientifically worked out a method using rockets but did not succeed in getting it into print until *Science Survey* published *The Exploration of Cosmic Space by Jet-Propelled Instruments*, in 1903. According to Russian sources, the copies of *Science Survey* containing Tsiolkovsky's article were confiscated by the government for censorship reasons having no relation to rocketry or earth satellites. Tsiolkovsky, with great difficulty, managed to obtain but a single copy for his own files. This being the case, Russian intimations that the German Hermann Oberth obtained his idea for the artificial earth satellite from Tsiolkovsky are a logical absurdity, all the more so since Oberth could not read Russian.

Toward the end of World War I, Hermann Oberth began formulating his theories on rocketry, space travel, and earth satellites. These were published in 1923 by R. Oldenbourg of Munich under the title *The Rocket into Interplanetary Space*, a paper-covered book of less than one hundred pages. The lion's share of the expense was absorbed by the author. Only a few pages at the end of the last chapter of the book were devoted to artificial satellites, but Oberth had some new ideas to contribute.

These included the possibility of creating artificial gravity by having two units, fastened by wire ropes, revolving about one another. He created the notion of building a reflecting mirror in space which would gather heat from the sun and redirect it to the surface of the earth, as a means either of heating or of destruction.

Receiving a copy of Oberth's book, the Russians (possibly on notification by Tsiolkovsky himself, who *could* read German) resurrected the obscure essay *The Exploration of Cosmic Space by Jet-Propelled Instruments* and reprinted it with an introduction in *German*, notifying that nation that it was a Soviet scientist who had first done the fundamental work on rocket research. This volume appeared in 1924, a year after Oberth's, under the title *The Rocket into Cosmic Space*, going Oberth one better.

However, while Oberth may have been the greatest mathematical theoretician on the subject of earth satellites, a captain in the Austrian army reserve who was also a graduate engineer, writing under the name of Captain Hermann Noordung, A.D., M.E. (real name: Potocnik), was to become the greatest instrument for popularizing earth satellites in the public mind.

He wrote the first book which, except for some introductory and basic material on the physics of space travel, was primarily devoted to the subject of a space station. It was entitled *Das Problem der Befahrung des Weltraums* (*The Problems of Space Flying*) and was published in Berlin by R. C. Schmidt in 1928. It is a truly remarkable work. Tipping his hat in polite acknowledgment in the general direction of Hermann Oberth, Noordung began to outline, in considerable scientific detail, the most important aspects of building, maintaining, and utilizing an earth satellite.

Noordung did more than explore ideas. He actually established theoretical and practical methods of eating, drinking, heating, air supply, communication, safety, movement outside the station (including the design and substance of space suits), power, light, design, placement of living quarters, methods of observation, and dozens of other vital considerations.

Oberth had figuratively said that a space station was possible—that it would be good to have one and that it would serve useful functions. Noordung went on to relate, in considerable detail, just why a station was practicable, how to go about building one in the most realistic fashion, and the methods to be employed in performing various functions.

Concentrating on detail, Noordung neglected to do much research on the necessary orbit of a space station. This lack was filled in by Count Guido von Pirquet, in a series of articles in the official organ of the German Society for Space Travel, *Die Rakete* (*The Rocket*). Since von Pirquet's articles appeared later in the year than Noordung's book, and since they covered ground which Noordung had neglected—Pirquet was the secretary of the Austrian Society for Space Travel Research and Noordung was also an Austrian—it seems quite probable that Noordung's book inspired Pirquet.

Further, Otto Willi Gail, a member of the German rocket group and an outstanding German science fiction writer, later that same year, published a novel titled *The Stone from the Moon*. Both of Gail's two previous novels had been basic, thoroughgoing, detail-by-detail descriptions of how to get to the moon. Neither had so much as mentioned an earth satellite. But his third novel devoted chapters, in considerable scientific detail, to a space station. It was called Astrofel, and it incorporated a number of Noordung's ideas as well as some further brilliant improvisations of his own.

While all this was happening, back in the United States Hugo Gernsback had left The Experimenter Publishing Company, under whose aegis he had established the first science fiction magazine, *Amazing Stories*, in 1926, and formed the Stellar Publishing Corporation, which launched four new science fiction magazines, *Science Wonder Stories*, *Air Wonder Stories*, *Science Wonder Quarterly*, and *Scientific Detective Monthly*.

Gernsback was looking for something different to attract the attention of the public to his new periodicals. He could read German. He heard of and imported Noordung's book. Francis M. Currier translated the work, which appeared as a three-part serial beginning in the July 1929 issue of *Science Wonder Stories*.

The many black-and-white interiors, from Noordung's book, which illustrated the work are certainly among the first, if not the very first, earth artificial satellite drawings published. On the cover of the August 1929 number, Austrian-born artist Frank R. Paul did a full-color portrayal of the space station as conceived by Noordung. In all probability it was the first picture of a space station to appear in the United States and the first color interpretation of an earth satellite anywhere. Since Paul was a trained mechanic and architectural draftsman as well as an imaginative interpreter of ideas, his rendition was minutely faithful to the scientific description.

Gernsback, imaginatively impressed by the idea of space stations, did not stop there. He then imported Otto Willi Gail's *The Stone from the Moon* and published it complete in the Spring 1930 issue of *Science Wonder Quarterly*. Frank R. Paul again came through with a full-color re-creation of Gail's earth satellite on the cover, in addition to a half-dozen skillful and detailed black-and-white interiors.

Gernsback then went on record with one of his predictions, so many of which have come true. In an editorial in the April 1930 issue of *Air Wonder Stories*, carrying the title *Stations In Space*, Gernsback said, "We may be sure that because of the great importance of such observatories we shall see them in use during the present century."

So the earth satellite was popularized in the United States and made an integral part of science fiction. More than that, Noordung's book became the science primer for space travel writing. Noordung's text offered the fundamentals; and Gail's novel was the example of how informed writers successfully incorporate accurate science to create a more plausible interplanetary story.

David Lasser, then managing editor of Gernsback's science fiction magazines and president of the American Rocket Society, wrote the first book, in popular style, on space travel to appear in English. *The Conquest of Space*; published in 1931 by Hurst & Blackett, London, contained the first serious and extensive factual treatment of earth satellites by an American.

With the impetus provided by Gernsback's enthusiastic and effective promotion, earth satellite stories and stories based upon similar principles became increasingly popular.

Science Wonder Stories and *Air Wonder Stories* combined, to appear as *Wonder Stories*. The January 1931 issue of that magazine carried *Satellite of Doom* by D. D. Sharp, a tale of a ship which establishes an orbit around the earth and has to find a means of breaking that orbit and returning to the surface.

The competing *Amazing Stories* projected the idea of building a space station and then pushing it into an orbit forty-one million miles from the sun in order to generate power for the earth. The veteran science fiction author Murray Leinster wrote that one, *Power Planet*, for the June 1931 issue.

The following month Neil R. Jones had *The Jameson Satellite*, the first of the long-lived Professor Jameson series, in which a man provides that after his death his coffin is to be shot into space in an orbit around the earth.

By 1936, general fiction magazine *Argosy* was publishing *Space Station No. 1* by Manly Wade Wellman, about an artificial refueling station between Mars and Jupiter and space station stories had become a permanent addition to science fiction and world literature.

The artificial earth satellite story never has been very common, yet it has appeared frequently enough to constitute a distinct category of science fiction. Typical of the close-to-the-latest-development group was Fletcher Pratt's *Asylum Satellite*, a long novelette in the October 1951 *Thrilling Wonder Stories*. Though it appeared six years before Russia launched the first Sputnik, it described a space satellite whose crew existed on frozen foods, and which was capable of a variable orbit and of pinpointing missiles with atomic warheads on any place on the globe. Both the United States and Russia had one apiece. A cloak-and-dagger tale of the near future, the story is enhanced by a great deal of believably accurate science.

Much more advanced was the imagination of Jack Vance, whose *Abercrombie Station* in *Thrilling Wonder Stories* for February 1952 postulated a ring of twenty-two pleasure worlds circling the earth, each independently owned and on which, because of the weightlessness of the passengers, a culture of extraordinarily fat people evolves. These people possess entirely different standards of beauty since their fat does not sag unattractively nor interfere with the ease with which they can move about. Here we find self-sufficient earth satellites, almost complete worlds in themselves, able to provide many if not all of their wants.

Hundreds of artificial satellites of every variety circle the earth in Raymond Z. Gallun's *Captive Asteroid*, a tale of a giant pleasure hotel built on a bit of sky rock pulled into orbit around the earth, in *Science Fiction Plus* for April 1953.

Great hotels, stores, eating places, docking arrangements for space ships beyond our solar system, and their incredible aliens are provided in "The Ultimate Earth Satellite," an original painting by Frank R. Paul, which was used on the cover of the December 1957 issue of *Satellite Science Fiction*.

It has taken many years and a very imaginative crew to dress out what Everett Hale outlined so brilliantly in 1869 and 1870. His sequel to *The Brick Moon*, *Life in the Brick Moon* had it all, a wealth of scientific speculation, including the problems of communication, lack of gravitation, sustaining the air supply, raising food and obtaining water, reorganizing the social structure, and receiving supplementary supplies from the earth. An original idea is a very rare thing and Edward Everett Hale is one of the few people to have enjoyed one. It would be a singularly appropriate gesture if the first manned permanent space station were to be called the "Edward Everett Hale."

7

GHOSTS OF PROPHECIES PAST, OR, FRANK READE, JR., AND "FORGOTTEN CHAPTERS IN AMERICAN HISTORY"

The United States has become a nation obsessed with history, as the quantity of magazine articles and books on the Civil War and the winning of the West amply attest. Yet, despite the volume of such material and the many publications and societies dedicated to unearthing Americana, many of the most fascinating and pivotally crucial events in our national background have been overlooked.

By 1890 the Indians rarely dared to make an open mass attack upon a fort or trading post because marshaled against them were armored flying vessels; carried aloft like helicopters. When the savages attacked a fortified position, high tension wires were dropped from the flying boats and hundreds were stunned by the current. If this humane method did not dissuade them, bombs, with electrically timed fuses, were hurled from above, creating havoc in their ranks.

Somehow or other, the role of the electrically powered armored stage coach in taming the bad men of the West has been permitted to slip into oblivion, but it was those vehicles more than any other single factor that restored peace and order to the frontier. The most famous encounter involved two hundred outlaws, led by cold-blooded killer Black Bill, who were routed after a twenty-minute engagement in which all their fire power failed to prevail against a single armored stage!

Much has been made of the U-2 incident in Russia but almost forgotten is an even more dramatic event which occurred in 1892! Two American bicyclists had disappeared without a trace in Russia. A helicopter-type flying ship of an advanced design, possessing four lifting rotors in contrast to the single rotor jobs that undid the Indians, was pressed into search for them. The vessel flew freely and infuriatingly over Russian terrain, but the incident was hushed up despite a deadly engagement with a platoon of Czarist regulars. The two bicyclists were recovered and returned to the American embassy in Turkey. Their real mission has never been made public.

Impressed by the launching of the first earth satellite by the Russians in 1957, few people were aware that the Americans put one into orbit as far back as December 13, 1895. Furthermore, that initial satellite was manned! Calculating that Verdi's comet would make a historically close passage to the earth on that day, scientists outfitted with airtight cabins a high-altitude helicopter, similar in design to the one that had penetrated Russia three years earlier. The size and speed of the comet was so great that the vessel was caught in its tail and dragged into space, finally managing to break loose five hundred miles above the earth. It orbited there for two months, gathering valuable scientific data, before circumstances were right for it to descend.

Similarly, crediting the atomic submarine *Nautilus* with the honor of being the first undersea ship to sail under the polar ice cap ignores the feat of *Ferret*, which powered only by electric engines, successfully completed the trip the week of May 4, 1894. By a singular coincidence, *Ferret* also foreshadowed the later accomplishment of *Skate* in surfacing through the polar ice.

Had the Belgians made a sincere effort to educate the Congolese properly, more of them might have been aware of the role played by the Americans in saving tens of thousands of them from bondage. It was in 1893 that one of the earliest functional tanks, heavily armored with electric guns capable of firing dynamite charges front and back, and possessing great scythelike blades revolving from the hubs of its tremendous wheels, was put into action in central Africa, killing hundreds of slave traders and terminating that evil practice for good.

If you are wondering how you could conceivably have overlooked so many vital points in American history, the answer is probably that you never read the dime novels which were so popular in the latter half of the nineteenth century. Hundreds of "untold chapters in history," similar to the foregoing, appeared in them, seemingly an entire school of literature. Actually, more than 75 per cent of all the hundreds of prophetic dime novels written during that period were the work of a single man—Luis Philip Senarens—concealed beneath the masquerade of "Noname"; and he might have remained anonymous but for a premature report of his death issued on the eve of the hundredth anniversary of the birth of Jules Verne in 1928.

Amazing Stories (itself a prophetic pioneer as the world's first science fiction magazine) eulogized Senarens in its June 1928 issue:

> Ulysses, to conceal his identity from the Cyclops whom he had blinded, called himself "Outis," meaning "no one." The American Jules Verne concealed his name under the title "Noname."
>
> The centennial of the birth of Jules Verne is but a few weeks back of us, and it seems fitting to show at this time that we, too, had a Jules Verne, a man whose industry in turning out reams of copy was as remarkable, as was his ingenuity in evolving the strange machines, prototypes of so much of the present, out of his imagination, though he died unheralded and practically unknown.

It was singularly appropriate that "the American Jules Verne" should die on the threshold of the centennial of the birth of his "inspiration," and neither the protest of the "dead" man nor the widespread newspaper obituaries telling of his actual demise twelve years later, December 26, 1939, in Kings County Hospital, New York, at the age of 76, succeeded in destroying this romantic notion. As late as May 1960, *Dime Novel Round-Up*, "a monthly magazine devoted to the collecting, preservation and literature of the old-time dime and nickel novels, libraries and popular story papers," was still respectfully reporting the year of his death as 1927.

Yet there was a relationship between Luis Philip Senarens and Jules Verne that was palpably real. Jules Verne, in 1881, had written to his American counterpart congratulating him on his logical imagination in carrying on a series of serial novels for boys concerning steam-driven mechanical men and horses. The letter lay unanswered on Lu Senarens' desk. It had been read and reread a dozen times. Many abortive replies had been attempted and discarded because Lu Senarens feared that his longhand might reveal the immaturity of his sixteen years.

In 1881 "dime" novels (most of them sold for five cents)

and boys' serial papers were in great vogue. The great West was still the nation's frontier and tales of action and exploration of that region were the mainstay of the dime novel. Horatio Alger's success stories, built around the frontier of business, were also having their day, but there was another frontier that interested the youth of America—the frontier of science and invention. Inventions that eventually would total 1,300 were pouring forth from Edison's laboratory in Menlo Park, New Jersey, firing the minds of youth with the desire to pursue a scientific career.

From the age of 14, Lu Senarens had been successfully selling novels to Frank Tousey's popular weekly, *Boys of New York*. He was even then already a veteran, his writing career having begun with sales to children's publications two years earlier.

Though he lived in Brooklyn, only a few miles from Tousey's editorial offices in lower Manhattan, he had carefully avoided meeting his publisher in person and would not do so for another two years. Tousey was under the impression that Senarens was a savant who was writing in his spare time for supplementary income. This impression was strengthened by Senarens' skill in carrying on a series of stories concerning Frank Reade, Jr., a teen-age inventor whose achievements overshadowed those of Thomas Edison. The Frank Reade type of story, concerning steam-driven robots, aircraft, and submarines, came to be labeled "invention" stories, because a new device was usually the basis of the plot of each of them, but quite obviously they were the forerunners of what today is designated "science fiction."

Well on his way to becoming the most celebrated writer of "invention" stories in America, which would eventually earn him the title of "the American Jules Verne," Lu Senarens was not the first to write science fiction for the dime-novel publishers, nor did he even create the Frank Reade series, which established his fame.

The very first "invention" or science fiction story for a dime-novel paper, *The Steam Man of the Prairies*, which ap-

peared in August 1868 as No. 45 of *American Novels*, published by Irwin Beadle, was written by Edward F. Ellis,
considered by many the greatest dime-novelist of all time and
probably the most prolific. A graduate of Princeton, he eventually became superintendent of schools in the city of Tren-
ton, New Jersey. His serious contribution was the writing of
fifty volumes of American history.

A fifteen-year-old inventor in Ellis' story builds the Steam
Man of the Prairies on the principle of the steam engine,
with the drive shafts moving mechanical legs up and down.
The careful detail devoted to the construction, operation, and
maintenance of the Steam Man lent the story a remarkably
convincing air.

Predominantly a writer of Western sagas, Ellis quickly
reverted to type, had his robot crated and shipped to the
Western frontier, when it was complemented by a cast of
characters that included a heavily accented Irishman, a top-
hatted Yankee, and a veteran trapper. The mechanism becomes engaged in a series of running fights with the Indians
and emerges triumphant. This ingenious combination of a
strange invention in a Western setting proved irresistible to
the youngsters.*

Ellis had displayed no previous interest in inventions, nor
did he ever again write an "invention" story, even though he
promised a sequel in his "Steam Man" novel, which con-
cludes:

> With the large amount of money realized from his western
> trip, Johnny Brainerd is educating himself at one of the best

* One year later *The Steam Man of the Prairies* was reprinted as No. 14
of *Frank Starr's American Library*; on January 4, 1876, under the title
The Huge Hunter; or, The Steam Man of the Prairies, it was No. 40 in
Beadle's Pocket Novels; October 3, 1882, it was republished again as No.
271 of *Beadle's Half-Dime Library* and this edition went into at least
eleven printings. The end was not yet, for it appeared later as No. 591 in
Beadle's New Dime Novels, January 27, 1885; with the title changed to
Baldy's Boy Partner; or, Young Brainerd's Steam Man as No. 245 of
Beadle's Pocket Library, September 19, 1888. Its last recorded printing
was as No. 1156 of *Beadle's Half-Dime Library*, the title once again *The
Huge Hunter*, in December 1904.

schools in the country. When he shall have completed his
course, it is his intention to construct another steam man
capable of more wonderful performances than the first.

So let our readers and the public generally be on the
lookout.

Ellis' Steam Man is historically important as an early presentation of the mechanical manlike robot in fiction. The
fact that it was also the first science fiction story to appear
in dime novels, and, as such, set off a chain reaction, has led
to much speculation as to what prompted a writer like Ellis,
who had previously employed James Fenimore Cooper as his
model, to select so unusual a theme for a novel.

The mechanical man or robot is rare in American fiction
before Ellis. Fitz-James O'Brien utilized tiny wooden manikins brandishing poisoned swords in *The Wondersmith*, published in October 1859; a bit earlier Nathaniel Hawthorne's
Drowne's Wooden Image tells of the bewilderment of the
townspeople when a woodcarver's "masterpiece," shaped in
the image of a woman, appears to have come to life and
boards a ship. And then there is Poe's fleeting mention of a
chess-playing robot in *The Thousand-and-Second Tale of
Scheherazade* in *Godey's Lady's Book* for February 1845.

It is in the last-mentioned that we find the most likely clue
to the inspiration of *The Steam Man of the Prairies*. In that
story Scheherazade regales her king with the "fiction": "One
of this nation of mighty conjurors created a man out of brass
and wood, and leather, and endowed him with such ingenuity
that he would have beaten at chess, all the race of mankind
with the exception of the great Caliph, Haroun Alraschid."

Poe obtained this idea from a mechanical chess player,
built in the form of a turbaned Turk, which was exhibited in
America by a visiting German named Johann Nepomuk
Maelzel. This robot chess player engaged humans in contests
and, though it did not always win, defied analysis of fraud,
since the interior of the machine was always shown to the
audience before each game. Utilizing only a report on how
the performances were staged, Poe, in his article *Maelzel's*

Chess-Player in the April 1836 issue of *The Southern Literary Messenger* in a partially correct surmise exposed the robot as a fake manipulated by a small man. Because of the limited circulation of that publication and the fact that people wanted to believe, it had little or no effect upon the continuing popularity of Maelzel's chess player, which continued to perform in the major cities of America until 1840. In November of that year, it was placed in the Chinese Museum on Ninth, below Chestnut, in Philadelphia, where, after a few performances, it remained on display until destroyed by fire on July 5, 1854.

A statement which appeared under the heading of "Androides" in the *Edinburgh Encyclopedia* corroborates Poe's analysis. Von Kempelen is quoted as saying the chess player was "a very ordinary piece of mechanism—a *bagatelle* whose effects appeared so marvelous only from the boldness of conception and the fortunate choice of the methods adopted for producing the illusion."

So much publicity and speculation accompanied the automaton chess player in the United States (it later was lengthily written up in *The Book of The First American Chess Congress* by Professor George Allen, published in New York in 1857) that it would be amazing if Edward F. Ellis, an educated man had *not* been aware of its history. In fact, if Ellis had been a chess devotee, he could have read an account of a game this machine played with Napoleon in *Hoyle's Games*, published in 1867, only one year before the publication of *The Steam Man of the Prairies*.

The reprinting of Ellis' novel as *The Huge Hunter; or, The Steam Man of the Prairies* in *Beadle's Pocket Novels*, No. 40, dated January 4, 1876, roused competitor Frank Tousey to action. He called in Brooklyn dime novelist Harry Enton, handed him a copy of the reissue, and asked him to do something like it. The result was *Frank Reade and His Steam Man of the Plains*, which appeared as a serial in Nos. 28 to 36 of *Boys of New York*, February 28 to April 24, 1876. The parallel between that novel and Ellis' was close enough to make any author blush. A boy inventor, in this case Frank Reade, builds a steam-driven mechanical man twelve feet high— topping the Ellis creation by two feet—which can go fifty miles per hour in contrast to the twenty miles per hour Ellis dared to venture. This steam man, too, pulls an ordinary wagon carrying fuel and is manned by Frank Reade and his friend Charley Gorse, and a thickly brogued son of the old sod. The formula of placing the robot in contest with the Indians of the old West again proved sure fire. The readers of *Boys of New York*, then a struggling new paper, went wild with an enthusiasm that continued for most of the thousand issues boasted by that paper before it folded.

A second Frank Reade story followed, *Frank Reade and His Steam Horse*. A steam horse, built like the steam man, again returns to the Western locale, with another bona fide Irishman and many harrowing adventures with Indians. Added to the cast of characters is a contingent of secret-service men and, for general excitement, a race between the steam horse and the steam man, with the former winning.

With the third in the series, *Frank Reade and His Steam Team*, it became evident that Harry Enton was confusing numbers with originality. This observation appears most convincing when we consider the fourth story in the series, *Frank Reade and His Steam Tally-Ho*, for a tally-ho is a carriage pulled by *three* horses; apparently Enton wasn't thinking very big. Enton broke off the series himself when Tousey ran the fourth story under the pen name "Noname." Enton demanded that his own name be used and when Tousey refused went over to another publisher, Norman Munro, where he wrote many of the famed Old Cap Collier stories. With the money he made writing dime novels Enton eventually paid his way through medical school, graduating in 1885 and writing relatively little afterward.

Thus, in 1879, Frank Tousey found himself casting about for someone to carry on the popular Frank Reade series. He selected Luis P. Senarens because of that author's allusions to scientific knowledge in a number of novels previously written for Tousey.

To make a clean break, Lu Senarens retired Frank Reade to a farm (completely run by steam-driven mechanical tools) and made his son, Frank Reade, Jr., the hero of the adventures. The first of the new series was *Frank Reade, Jr., and His Steam Wonder*, dealing with a steam locomotive and caboose constructed to run on roads and over plains instead of on tracks. To Frank Reade, Jr.'s permanent circle of friends he added Pomp, a Negro who had formerly been a slave. Banter between the Irishman and the Negro was to become a stock prop of the series and provide the comic relief.

That Tousey had made no mistake in selecting Senarens for the series was evidenced by the modernization of the story line in *Frank Reade, Jr., and His Electric Boat*. This was quite an imaginative concept for 1880 and Senarens moved the series out of its Western locale and to the Great Lakes. As the stories progressed, he would eventually explore almost every region of the earth and become involved in fantastic episodes, such as the introduction of a giant sea serpent into the adventures on the Great Lakes, which would add zest to the stories.

It was at this point that Jules Verne decided to write a letter of praise to the author of the Frank Reade and Frank Reade, Jr., series. Jules Verne could read English and he had evidently seen a number of the "Noname" stories. It is quite possible that Verne's attention was initially directed to *Boys of New York* when Tousey, in 1879, ran a short novel by an anonymous author titled *A Trip to the Center of the Earth*. The duplication of Verne's earlier classic was obvious in both title and plot. Verne did not know who "Noname" was, but addressed his letter to the publisher, who forwarded it to Senarens. The youthful author was immensely flattered and grateful that so important a literary figure as Jules Verne should condescend to write him, but he need not have been. Verne was doing no more than acknowledging a debt, since he had just finished lifting the basic idea for the Frank Reade series *in toto* and incorporating it in his then current novel, *The Steam House*. Taking the idea of a steam man and a steam horse one step further, Jules Verne used as the basis of his story a steam elephant which carried hunters in India. What makes the entire thing even more interesting—this novel was first serialized in a boys' paper in England, *The Union Jack*, running serially from No. 41, October 7, 1880, to No. 76, June 6, 1881!

This was the period of the decline of Jules Verne's imaginative powers. His greatest works, *A Journey to the Center of the Earth*, *A Trip from the Earth to the Moon*, *Tour of the Moon*, *Twenty Thousand Leagues Under the Sea*, *The Mysterious Island*, *Round the World in Eighty Days*, and *Michael Strogoff*, were behind him. Nothing as imaginative or dramatic would appear in the future though he wrote incessantly up to the time of his death. Even his publisher realized that he was experiencing difficulty in obtaining new ideas and encouraged him to write a number of nonfiction books of a geographical nature. Everywhere in Europe and America writers were borrowing from Verne. Now, sometimes, he borrowed in return. In the final reckoning he gave far more than he took.

Biographers, aware of Verne's declining powers after 1878, have referred to *Robur the Conqueror; or, Clipper of the Clouds*, published in 1886, as the last major flaring of that author's great talent. In it he prophesied a heavier-than-air ship held aloft by a number of moving vanes—a gigantic helicopter. The powerful characterization of Robur invested the novel with drama and purpose and, in a dozen or more later books by other writers, illustrations can be found that copy Verne's helicopter, *The Albatross*.

It in no way detracts from the quality of his book nor does it substantially take anything away from a man who has fame to spare to point out that the idea of the multivaned helicopter was taken by Verne from Luis Senarens. The boy finally answered him and a spasmodic correspondence sprang up. Before the date of *Robur the Conqueror*, Lu Senarens had written no less than three Frank Reade, Jr., stories centered around sky-borne ships carried aloft by the helicopter principle. So popular were these stories in *Boys of New York*, where they first appeared, that all three of them were reprinted in *Wide Awake Library* in 1884 and 1885 and the *reprints* were issued before Verne's work!

The three short novels were *Frank Reade, Jr., and His Air-Ship*, *Frank Reade, Jr., in the Clouds*, and *Franke Reade, Jr., With His Air-Ship in Africa*. These may very well have been the earliest works of fiction built around the theory of the helicopter and almost certainly the first to propose that an air vessel be driven by electric engines powered by storage batteries.

It was no coincidence that Jules Verne's *Albatross* in *Robur the Conqueror* was lifted by the helicopter principle, powered by an electric engine from storage batteries and accumulators of advanced design. As if to trademark the derivation of his ideas, Verne had for comic relief a Negro servant, Frycollin, a cowardly counterpart of Pomp, the Negro aide who accompanied Frank Reade, Jr., on all his adventures.

Verne also exploited ideas first set forth by Edgar Allan Poe, Alexandre Dumas, Johann Rudolf Wyss, and H. G. Wells, and his biographers have acknowledged those debts, but no credit has ever been extended for his borrowing from Luis Senarens and the Frank Reade series.

If Lu Senarens felt anything, it was a sense of pride that so great an author would consider any of his ideas usable. Writing two, and sometimes three, novels a week, constantly reaching for new ideas himself, he was sympathetic to the plight of the prolific author. He took payment by incorporating a facsimile of Verne's *Albatross* into one of the longest serials he ever wrote for *Boys of New York—Frank Reade, Jr., and His Queen Clipper of the Clouds*. Here, every detail of Senarens' Queen Clipper of the Clouds imitates Verne, including the use of compressed paper as the material from which the ship is constructed and the use of plastics ("gelatinized fibers") for the propeller screws. Verne had copied him, so now he copied Verne. It seemed fair enough to a busy writer.

By 1890 Lu Senarens, under his pseudonym of Noname, was one of the most beloved and best-selling dime-novel writers in America, predominantly for his Frank Reade, Jr., stories. As fast as serialization was completed in *Boys of New York* they were reprinted as five-cent novels in the *Wide Awake Library*.

Beadle and Adams, the first of the dime-novel companies, did relatively few invention stories, but Street & Smith, another big publisher in the field, decided to get in on a good thing. They had a five-cent boys' serial paper called *Good News*, and in that paper they ran a Tom Edison, Jr., story written by a staff member disguised as Philip Reade to identify with the Frank Reade, Jr., type. Eight of these stories were written and published as complete novels in *The Nugget Library* during 1891 and 1892 dealing with heavier-than-air craft, various types of submersibles, and steam- and electric-propelled land vehicles. Some of the novels are interesting because of the author's faith in the future of aluminum as a structural metal, but the most unusual thing about the novels is the stylistic fact that they all are written in the second person.

Several more of the Tom Edison, Jr., stories appeared in another Street & Smith periodical, *New York Five Cent Library*, started in 1892. At the same time an entirely new invention series concerning Electric Bob alternated in the same Library, featuring the inevitable new invention, always of electrical design (including an electric pistol), and a Negro aide for comic relief.

So much a fixture had the invention story become on the dime-novel scene that a specialist in comic adventure for *Wide Awake Library*, Peter Pad, had published in the November 15, 1889 number a take-off on all such stories titled *Bulger Boom, the Inventor*. In quick succession, Bulger Boom invented an airship, an insecticide, a super horse liniment, a remarkable fertilizer, a mechanical chicken plucker, a hand-cranked multiple-boy spanker, a rodent killer, a catamaran, an incubator for chicks, and a spring-driven carriage, all of which bring him increasing grief, instead of the fame that is the lot of Frank Reade, Jr. Finally, broken in body if not in spirit, Bulger Boom spends his declining years looking for the secret of perpetual motion.

It is ironic that this story, intended only as a parody, was to inspire a school of humorous science fiction writing built around the slapstick of misguided scientific experiments, with the unspoken message that man's meddling in the unknown will eventually bring him to grief. The most famous of these were The Hawkins series by well-known humorist Edgar Franklin, which began in *The Argosy* in May 1903 and ran through dozens of stories; the Prof. Jonkens stories by the beloved creator of Uncle Wiggily, H. R. Garis, which began in *The Argosy* for August 1905 and established his first reputation; *The Scientific Adventures of Mr. Fosdick* by Jacques Morgan, which started in the October 1912 issue of *Modern Electric*, the world's first radio magazine; and the more advanced *Dr. Hackensaw's Secrets* by Clement Fézandié, which created a chuckling following in *Science and Invention* beginning in May 1921.

Spurred by the threat of encroachment on his audience from the Tom Edison, Jr., series, Frank Tousey prevailed on Lu Senarens to sit up still later at night and add to his heavy schedule a new series of invention stories for a companion to *Boys of New York* called *Young Men of America*, which he also published. Hero of this series was Jack Wright, and starting in 1892 more than fifty novels with such titles as *Jack Wright, the Boy Inventor; or, Hunting for a Sunken Treasure, Jack Wright and His Electric Locomotive; or, The Lost Mine of Death Valley*, and *Jack Wright and His Electric Flyer; or, Racing in the Clouds for a Boy's Life* began thrilling youngsters across the nation with an effectiveness second only to that of Frank Reade, Jr.

Such great circulation builders were the Frank Reade, Jr.,

and Jack Wright stories that Tousey boldly gambled on a weekly, to be titled *Frank Reade Library* and to be devoted *entirely* to "invention" stories. The first issue, dated September 24, 1892, featured *Frank Reade, Jr., and His New Steam Man; or, The Young Inventor's Trip to the Far West* by "Noname." Technically, the *Frank Reade Library* was the first regular periodical completely devoted to science fiction and the debate has never ceased as to whether or not those novels qualify as magazines or as a series of paper-bound books.

Regardless of the definition, collectors would prefer to forget their existence, for their rarity has been compounded by the disintegration of the cheap newsprint used in their publication and the fact that they are sought after by devotees of early dime novels and aeronautica as well as science fiction enthusiasts.

The compendium of inventions and adventures involving Frank Reade and Frank Reade, Jr., in the 191 issues of the *Frank Reade Library* constitutes a truly remarkable cache of Americana. Lu Senarens' stories can be divided into five major categories of prophecy: robots, air craft, submersibles, armored vehicles, and powered land and sea vessels. In each of these groupings there are literally dozens of variations of the inventions. The robots are powered by both steam and electricity, are used as means of drawing vehicles, and can perform no voluntary act. They are machines for motive power in the shape of a man, horse, or steer. Nevertheless, they constitute the single greatest mass of robot literature ever written by one man. It is quite probable as well that Lu Senarens wrote more about the possibility of air flight, projecting regular winged planes and dirigibles as well as helicopters, than all the rest of American writers up to his time combined. The variety and ingenuity of his air concepts represent adequate material for a major thesis in itself. This multiplicity of aircraft is matched by the range of imagination he shows in the construction of submarines of diverse types. Still further, his armored tanks and cars ingeniously outdo considerably those that were used in World War I or II, though the endless metal track apparently never entered his mind. With similar thoroughness he powered by steam or electricity every type of vehicle from tricycle to trackless freight car, making them completely believable to the readers of his period.

He usually did not venture beyond the earth's atmosphere, but a notable exception is one story, *Lost in a Comet's Tail*, discussed in the preceding chapter.

The *Frank Reade Library* continued as a weekly through to its February 5, 1897 number when it became a semi-monthly, finally closing down in August 1898, almost six years from the time of its inception. During the period of its publication it reprinted *all* the Frank Reade stories prior to 1892. The value of the set is greatly enhanced by the remarkable line drawings of the artist, a personal friend of Senarens, whose name was never signed to his illustrations nor was it ever recalled by Senarens' children. The drawings frequently fill in specific details of the inventions where Senarens' text is couched in vague generalities. It is almost inconceivable that a book on the early history of aeronautics, for example, could go to press without reproducing several of them.

Strangely enough, the demise of the *Frank Reade Library* and, at about the same time its sturdy companion *Boys Star Library*, which featured in every other issue the adventures of Jack Wright, was not brought about by reader satiation. On the contrary, their popularity helped raise to a new frenzy the anti-dime-novel fever that had been running for decades. Western, detective, and sea stories with their necessary violence, criminality, and piracy were bad enough, but stories of aircraft, submarines, robots, and tanks seemed to some segments of the population to be drawn from the dark pits of madness. Everybody knew such things were impossible and the destructive influence of such subject matter upon the minds of the younger generation was projected as beyond calculation. The scientific stories of Frank Reade and Jack Wright became the subject of impassioned sermons against

dime novels from the pulpits across the nation. Dealers' boy-
cotts were enforced and were extended to other Tousey publications. The press of America helped feed fuel to these fires
of ignorance. Faced with publishing disaster, Frank Tousey
capitulated and discontinued publication of the *Frank Reade
Library* and the *Boys Star Library*.

Ironically, in 1897, even as these campaigns were at their
height, Simon Lake announced that he had tested the first
practical submarine, but even this seemed to have no effect
on the determined campaign to "clean up" dime novels. Yet
all through those years the man responsible for the fabulous
popularity of the juvenile science fiction story and the nation-
wide crusade which was to push Frank Tousey, one of the
great pioneers of the dime novel, down a gentle slope to ruin,
remained, under the cloak of "Noname," as anonymous to
those who condemned his works as he was to his readers.

Luis P. Senarens was born in Brooklyn, New York, April
24, 1865, the son of a Cuban father and an American mother
of French-German extraction, who raised him in the Dutch
Reformed Church. His father, a tobacco merchant whose
family were well off as growers of sugar and mahogany in
Cuba, died when he was only four years old.

Senarens financed his own college education with the
money from his writing, for he earned an average of $150 a
week from the time he was fourteen years of age, in years
when $10 a week was considered a liberal salary for a man
with a family. He studied at St. John's College of Arts and
Sciences in Brooklyn, finally obtaining a law degree. But he
never practiced, protesting fear that his skill might be employed inadvertently to convict an innocent man.

All his work before 1900 was written in very neat Palmer
method longhand; deadline pressure was so great that he
never revised his work but rushed first drafts through to the
printer. In a bit more than thirty years, he wrote some forty
million words and fifteen hundred individual stories under
twenty-seven pseudonyms. Among the pen names that have
definitely been established are Capt. Howard, W. J. Earle,

Ned Sparling, Kit Clyde, Frank Doughty, Cecil Burleigh; highly probable are Alan Drayper and Gaston Garne. Senarens also was responsible for many of the Buffalo Bill and Old King Brady series.

Senarens spoke five languages fluently: Spanish, Italian, French, German, and English. Early balding added dignity to his six-foot frame, which looked almost spare despite his 190 pounds. He made one trip to Cuba to visit his relatives and contracted yellow fever. At a time when fatality rates were almost 100 per cent, he was one of the few to recover from that disease.

His wife was scarcely five feet tall, of English-Irish parentage; he met her in Brooklyn and married her in 1895 when he was 30. Though proud of his achievements, she sometimes behaved like a spoiled child, and Senarens' two children, Sinclair V. Senarens of Amityville, New York, and Mrs. Elizabeth Gunderson of Fairlawn, New Jersey, recalled that he always treated their mother as though she were the youngest of the three.

Nevertheless, they did have one accomplishment in common—music. Luis P. Senarens was one of the highest paid church baritones of his time and his wife was one of the highest paid female singers.

An easygoing, likable personality, he was immensely popular with his Brooklyn neighbors, who looked up to him despite the fact that he was a dime-novel writer and unfailingly asked for advice on their problems; usually he had the answer. Their faith in his knowledge was buttressed by a fine library of 2,500 books, mostly scientific references, which he maintained for research purposes, to save precious time needed to meet his tremendous writing quotas. He set up a separate room as a study, where he frequently wrote twelve to fourteen hours at a stretch. The year of his marriage he was made editor in chief of Frank Tousey's publications, but still he managed to turn out one or two short novels a week in addition to his other duties.

His daughter Elizabeth was the only member of the family

he tolerated in his study while he wrote and she made herself useful by getting books from the shelves so that he might look up references. She still clearly remembers his telling her, in 1901, while checking the moon's distance from the earth for *Three Boys from the Moon*, a novel he was writing for *Happy Days*: "You'll live to see the day when they'll invent *all* the things I write about."

Feeling that hostile opinion had died down and in a desperate effort to bolster his worsening economic situation, Frank Tousey decided to revive the Frank Reade series in a weekly publication to be called *Frank Reade Weekly Magazine*. The first number was dated October 31, 1902; the series ran reprints of the earlier series for ninety-six numbers until August 26, 1904. The covers were beautifully done in full color and their imaginative depiction of future invention makes them much-sought-after collectors' items. At the same time *Pluck and Luck* began to republish the Jack Wright series with comparably outstanding cover art. Frank Tousey did not live to see the first issue of the *Frank Reade Weekly Magazine*, for he died on September 7, 1902.

Tousey's son, Sinclair, took over the company, but the era of the dime novel was drawing to a close. Pulp magazines like *Argosy, Blue Book, All Story, Short Stories, Cavalier, Popular,* and *Top Notch* were replacing them, and Sinclair Tousey found himself beating a dead horse. Luis Senarens had made a great deal of money from the Tousey organization besides inheriting a substantial amount from his grandparents. He began systematically to loan Sinclair Tousey money to keep the firm afloat. One estimate puts the cumulative amount of his loans above $100,000. All hope of its return was lost when Sinclair Tousey apparently committed suicide on July 29, 1915.

Meanwhile motion pictures were coming to the fore and, still holding his costly position as editor for Frank Tousey Publications, Lu Senarens began writing movie scenarios in 1911, selling sixty in as speedy a manner as he sold dime novels. He edited one of the earlier film fan magazines, *Moving Picture Stories*, a weekly which ran for almost ten years, featuring six stories of prominent films each issue, plus a variety of other motion picture material. During this period, the youthful Norma Talmadge, yet to make her mark on the silver screen but aware that Senarens might have connections to help her, was a perennial family visitor.

Throughout the years, Lu Senarens had received letters from admirers of Frank Reade from all over the world. Some of these were inspired by reprints in British publications, but most of them proved the ability of the dime novel to penetrate the most remote corners of the earth. The Jack Wright stories were still being reprinted in *Pluck and Luck* and would continue right through to 1920. But in England there was a brief revival of interest in Frank Reade, Jr., and Jack Wright as the Aldine Publishing Co. brought into being in 1912 *The Invention Library* which ran thirty-two weekly issues devoted entirely to the adventures of Frank Reade. Simultaneously, Aldine changed the policy in its old *The Cheerful Adventure Library* series with No. 823, May 9, 1912, so that it would run nothing but Jack Wright adventures weekly. Both these publications sold at a halfpenny and contained sixteen pages.

Sixteen more issues of *The Invention Library*, with full-color covers, appeared in England in 1913, priced "extravagantly" at one penny with double the number of pages, but by that time it was obvious that so many of the once mind-stimulating predictions of aircraft, submarines, and motor-driven vehicles were accomplished facts that the youngsters could be pardoned for wondering what all the excitement was about.

Taking the place of Frank Reade in America was Victor Appleton's Tom Swift series, which, in hard covers, was to sell many millions of copies. While many authors wrote under the house name of Victor Appleton, the first thirty in the Tom Swift series were the work of H. R. Garis. More imaginative were the Roy Rockwood *Great Marvel* stories which took their readers to the moon, Mars, and Venus, and such series as Dave Dashaway, the Speedwell Boys, the Motor Boys, and the Radio Boys. Quite literally, Lu Senarens created a whole phase of boys' fiction.

The speed with which Senarens wrote precluded the possibility of literary merit in his novels beyond the minimum needed to carry his readers along. That he had the ability to do better is attested by the fact that he was still selling motion picture scenarios until three years before his death in 1939. His daughter claims that he sold at least two stories to *The Saturday Evening Post* during his writing career, but both appear to be irretrievably lost in the anonymity of his countless pen names.

Yet his memory has been kept alive by the sentiment of boys grown old who will always cherish the excitement and awe his imagination inspired in them in the wondrous years of their youth. A typical apostle was Frank Reade fan Frank T. Fries of Orrville, Ohio, who began a dime-novel fan magazine titled *Frank Reade Weekly* which began publication in October 1928 and continued for eighty-two issues under various titles until 1935. As a side venture Fries reprinted condensed versions of six Frank Reade opuses. Another admirer, George Sahr of Kenosha, Wisconsin, in July 1931 reissued in handsome format *Frank Reade, Jr.'s White Cruiser of the Clouds; or, The Search for the Dog-Faced Men* and announced five other titles. The Dime Novel Club, headed by Charles Bragin of Brooklyn, New York, which specializes in publishing exact replicas of the old boys' literature, has included nine Frank Reade and Jack Wright stories among its selections in recent years.

Lu Senarens, plagued by a gall-bladder ailment, retired from editorial work in 1923 but continued his scenario writing. A heart condition which first became apparent in 1929 made him a semi-invalid for the last ten years of his life. Despite these troubles, he always managed to provide adequately for his family, though when he died there was no estate of any size.

At the end of his life, Luis Philip Senarens frequently found himself referred to as "The American Jules Verne." He entertained no pretensions and made no claims. Certainly, when Jules Verne's sequel to *Robur the Conqueror*, titled *The Master of the World*, appeared in 1904 Senarens must have found himself disenchanted; for the third time Verne outrageously lifted one of his ideas, this time the flying submarine which had first appeared on the cover of *Boys Star Library* in 1896, eight years before Verne's story, illustrating a scene from Noname's novel *Over the South Pole; or, Jack Wright's Search for a Lost Explorer With His Flying Boat.*

8

THE WONDERS OF
H. G. WELLS

The question most often asked about science fiction is: "But is it literature?" To this, the science fiction world has one powerful and overriding answer, and that answer is expressed in the name H. G. Wells.

Wells has produced novels and short stories of great literary distinction which are indisputably works of science fiction. It was for the imaginative quality of his works of science fiction that H. G. Wells gained fame. Those are the works which make his name known throughout the world, despite the fact that most of them were written more than fifty years ago.

When H. G. Wells was born in Bromley, Kent, England, in 1866, the French master of science fiction, Jules Verne, was already an outstanding world-wide success, with his *voyages extraordinaires.* Verne had written and scored with *Five Weeks in a Balloon, A Journey to the Center of the Earth,* and *A Trip from the Earth to the Moon.*

Thirty years later, in 1895, when H. G. Wells burst on the literary horizon with *The Time Machine,* to remain a brilliant fixed star in the firmament of masters of the scientific fantasy, Jules Verne was still alive and still writing. That very year Verne had published *Propeller Island,* a satiric "utopia" of a navigable island, whose inhabitants enjoyed the luxury of moving sidewalks.

Beyond the point in his career when he could invent really powerful imaginative concepts, and flanked by dozens of imitators and acolytes, Verne still reigned supreme in his field, though such titans of fantasy and science fiction in their own right as H. Rider Haggard and A. Conan Doyle were already displaying the potentiality to supplant Verne. Except for personality preferences and timing they might have earlier smothered Wells's bid for fame in the realm of scientific fantasy.

Haggard created a sensation with *King Solomon's Mines,* published in 1885, and followed it in 1887 with his now classic novel of immortality, *She.* In the years that followed Haggard poured out a profusion of literary successes, but his interests caused his fantasies to take a different turn. A lawyer by profession and, when he took the pains, an author capable of biblical, almost poetic, prose, Haggard merely toyed at the fringes of science fiction, preferring the color and drama of ancient Egypt, the wilds of Africa and South America, and the unprovable realm of mysticism.

As a writer of tales based on geography, Haggard was quite the match for Verne. Had he written more science fiction, his superb characterization, his classic sense of drama, and his fine imagination would have made him Verne's successor. Instead, he preferred to pioneer and explore a peculiar literary nook of his own based on the pageantry of the past, lost races and civilizations, reincarnation—all leavened with an occasional sobering dash of science. Haggard's niche in imaginative literature is secure—but not as a major writer of science fiction.

At the time Wells's *Time Machine* appeared, A. Conan Doyle had already assured his literary immortality with the creation of Sherlock Holmes. He ventured also to write historical novels but he displayed a predilection for the supernatural that is astonishing considering the fact that Sherlock Holmes was basically a scientific detective. Doyle also wrote science fiction, but in this early period it took the form of short stories which occupied a very minor place in his writing. Had A. Conan Doyle written his Professor Challenger novels before 1895, he might have succeeded to Jules Verne's seat among the science fiction immortals. As it was, he wrote too little science fiction at first and then much too late wrcte his famous science fiction novels, *The Lost World* and *The Poison Belt*, in the years 1912 and 1913 respectively. By that time, he could not hope to gain serious attention for them, since they would be matched against the brilliant works produced by H. G. Wells in the realm of science fiction.

Throughout his long literary career, H. G. Wells stoutly denied any suggestion that he was influenced in any way by Jules Verne. Wells once wrote:

> There's a quality in the worst of my so-called "pseudo-scientific" (imbecile adjective) stuff which differentiates it from Jules Verne, e.g., just as Swift is differentiated from Fantasia —isn't there? There is something other than either story writing or artistic merit which has emerged through the series of my books. Something one might regard as a new system of ideas—"thought."

He stormed at the characterization of himself as the "English Jules Verne" and repeated to the end of his days that if there was any strong influence reflected in his work it was that of Jonathan Swift, the satirist of *Gulliver's Travels*.

In all truth, Wells could not afford to permit the idea to circulate that he was in any way an imitator of Jules Verne.

The shadow of Verne's success, particularly in his early days, threatened to obscure his own, merely because they both wrote science fiction.

For his part, Verne recognized the fact that Wells seriously challenged the one great distinction he possessed, that of being a fictional prophet and seer.

In commenting upon Wells's work Verne said, in an interview published in *T. P.s Weekly* in England, for October 9, 1903:

> I do not see the possibility of comparison between his work and mine. We do not proceed in the same manner. It occurs to me that his stories do not repose on a very scientific basis. No, there is no rapport between his work and mine. I make use of physics. He invents. I go to the moon in a cannon-ball discharged from a cannon. Here there is no invention. He goes to Mars in an air-ship, which he constructs of a metal which does away with the law of gravitation. *Ca, c'est très joli*, but show me this metal. Let him produce it.

The truth of the matter is that neither of them was on very firm ground. Proof that Verne exerted some influence on Wells is quite apparent in the text of *The First Men in the Moon*, where the inventor of the moon spaceship, Cavor, is asked how it will be possible to get in and out of the vessel and gives a description of an airlock, after which the questioner comments: "Like Jules Verne's apparatus in *A Trip to the Moon?*"

Wells, on the other hand did use a gun in firing his Martians across space in *The War of the Worlds*. In Chapter 7 of Book II of that novel, where English survivors of the Martian invasion are trying to muster hope for their situation, we read:

> "After the tenth shot they fired no more—at least, until the first cylinder came."
> "How do you know?" said the artilleryman. I explained. He thought. "Something wrong with the gun," he said. "But what if there is? They'll get it right again."

The impression that Verne attempted to convey, that Wells's material was not true science fiction because it did not minutely stick to the rules of scientific accuracy, is an unfair one. Verne's scientific knowledge was obtained from his personal observations and wide reading; by occupation he was a lawyer. Wells, on the contrary, had a fine scientific education under the instruction of one of the greatest scientists of his day, T. H. Huxley. In a good many respects his knowledge of science was superior to that of Verne's.

To top it off, Wells was more than a writer; he was an artist, using words to paint a picture and, when the spirit moved him, brilliantly poetic in his evocations of the strange, the unknown, and the unusual. As an innovator of plot themes for science fiction, he ranks supreme, and the years since his passing have secured that distinction for him beyond any dispute.

However, he refused to limit the scope of his storytelling or of his imagination because of scientific technicalities. Verne, who would not permit his characters to land on the moon because he could not contrive any known scientific method of having them take off again from that satellite or send their messages back to earth, regarded Wells's antigravity metal in *The First Men in the Moon* as placing that novel outside the pale of respectable science fiction. Yet it enabled Wells to land his characters on the moon and return them to earth, and to give the reader some of the finest descriptions of other-worldly environment that have ever appeared in a novel of space travel.

Verne had good reason to stay within bounds. His formula had earned him the plaudits of the masses around the world. It is little wonder that in his later years he came near to throttling his talent with restrictions on his imagination for fear he would kill the goose that laid the golden egg.

Verne would never have considered a device as questionable as a time machine. Wells not only considered it; he was obsessed by it. The idea originated in *The Chronic Argonauts*, published in 1888 in the April, May, and June issues of *The Science Schools Journal.* Wells afterward condemned this early attempt as an "experiment in the pseudo-teutonic, Nathaniel Hawthorne style," and in later years bought up and destroyed all copies of the early version he could find, thus making it a rare collector's item.

Another component of *The Time Machine.* titled *The Rediscovery of the Unique,* appeared in the July 1891 issue of *The Fortnightly Review.* Wells subsequently said he did not think that any copies survived, but he forgot that some copies had been sent to America.

A third try, *The Universe Rigid,* was set up in type for *The Fortnightly Review* but was never printed.

In 1894, a series of articles, containing sections from *The Time Machine,* appeared in *The National Observer.*

The near-final version of *The Time Machine* was to be published as a serial in *The New Review* during the years 1894–1895. This version, extremely hard to find, contains at least one episode which was not published in the book, a section referring to descendants of man, built somewhat like kangaroos, and giant centipedes that preyed upon them.

The first American edition of *The Time Machine* is distinguished by the fact that the author was referred to, both on the title page and in the page headings throughout the book, as H. S. Wells.

This chronology of *The Time Machine* is important because that story has generally come to be regarded as H. G. Wells's greatest work, already a classic of world literature. This story is undoubtedly and primarily a work of science fiction.

While the concept of the time *machine,* which Wells was the first in the history of literature to use, though other authors had traveled in time by other means, is highly unlikely, Wells nevertheless obtains in his readers a "willing suspension of disbelief" through the use of actual scientific theory.

This short novel, really an extended tale, which carries its hero first to the year 802,701 and then by hops past the year

30,000,000, when the sun has grown cold and man extinct, is not used as a vehicle for presenting utopian concepts, since the civilizations described are decadent. It is not a warning story, since the period in which it is laid is long past the peak of man's future Golden Age. Nor is the slightest attempt made at satire.

Projection of the sciences of physics, biology, astronomy, and chemistry are integral to the narration of the story. Though there is depth of thought and concept, the story always comes first and is a fascinating chronicle, beautifully, superbly written. Most important, the events that occur could not possibly have been related in any literary genre other than science fiction.

A special point is made of this because it is the habit of the public and some literary critics upon reading really outstanding works of science fiction, such as *Brave New World* by Aldous Huxley or 1984 by George Orwell, to say in effect: "That isn't really a work of science fiction; basically it's an allegory." Even more prevalent is the phrase: "Well, that isn't science fiction. It's *good!*" Through the use of this weird logic, whenever a work of science fiction is truly outstanding it ceases to be science fiction. Thus denuded of its masterpieces, the field is then usually challenged to prove its worth.

Wells, the master writer and prophet of the field, has become the margin of respectability for science fiction as a literary craft.

World events have vindicated the subject matter of science fiction for Wells and the hundreds of other writers who also used future invention, atomic power, and space travel as basic ingredients of their fiction. Today, the rise and fall of nations and the very survival of mankind depends on how well the world understands those very topics that were previously discussed almost exclusively by writers of science fiction. Science fiction thereby reveals itself as being something significantly more than simply a literature of escape. To deny that fact is to deny that the hydrogen bomb exists or that the dawn of space travel has arrived.

Proper credit has never been granted to H. G. Wells for his major role in the development of the British short story. Probably the only British writer at the turn of the century who surpassed H. G. Wells as a writer of short stories was Rudyard Kipling, and as a writer of short science fiction stories Wells has never been surpassed.

Undoubtedly Wells's greatest short story is *The Country of the Blind.* Though intended as an allegory it can be appreciated on the merits of the story alone, and either way it emerges as a profound and stirring work. The story takes place in a valley whose original settlers were attacked by a rare malady which gradually blinded the entire population. The valley is completely cut off from civilization by natural upheavals, and the people, though blind, have adjusted to their environment, their other senses becoming more acute. The blindness is hereditary and after a while the concept of sight becomes meaningless. A man from the outside world stumbles into this valley and instead of being able to seize control because he alone can see he finds himself regarded as an abnormal, not-quite-sane, "unformed" person. He falls in love with a blind girl who wants him to have his eyes put out so that he will be "normal" and fit into the social structure. In the end he escapes from the valley.

The Country of the Blind originally appeared in the April 1904 issue of *Strand Magazine.* Thirty-five years later, in 1939, Wells rewrote the ending, adding three thousand words, and this version was published in a limited edition of 280 copies by the Golden Cockerel Press of London. It also was included in a collection titled *The College Survey of English Literature,* edited by B. J. Whiting and published in 1942.

In the revised version, the hero vainly attempts to save the village from a rockslide he sees is about to start. The villagers do not believe him. He escapes from the valley with his blind sweetheart and they are later married. The girl rebuffs attempts on the part of the doctors to restore her sight, because she is "afraid" to see.

While the new version is as well written as the old, the

allegory becomes so labored that it destroys the impact of the original story. It should be noted that anthologists have generally ignored the revision.

In most of his short stories, Wells strove for a single departure from the norm, with all other elements kept in the focus of the familiar. His stories were characterized by the originality of their central themes and the wide range of ideas. Today, most of the ideas that Wells presented have been rehashed dozens of times. At the time he wrote them, they were either completely original or the first really competent presentation of the concept.

Among the short stories with ideas that have become part of the fabric of modern science fiction are *Empire of Ants*, in which the ants threaten to conquer the world; *Flowering of the Strange Orchid*, which deals with man-eating ter tacled plants; *The New Accelerator*, concerning a drug which can speed up the motions of men dozens of times; *The Remarkable Case of Davidson's Eyes*, about a man who could see through walls; *Aepyornis Island*, in which the ancient eggs of extinct creatures hatch; *The Star*, in which a wandering body from space almost collides with the earth; *The Crystal Egg*, which is really an interplanetary television receiver; and *The Grisly Folk*, a tale of prehistoric people. There are quite literally dozens of others. His mind seemed a bottomless well of diverse and new—for his time—scientific ideas. One would be hard put to name another writer of science fiction who possessed his versatility.

The success of *The Time Machine* and the originality of this continuous stream of short science fiction stories built a tremendous demand for Wells's work. Jules Verne had created an audience for popular science fiction, and H. G. Wells not only captured that audience but gave it works of literary quality as well. H. G. Wells not only made it pay, but gave it literary standing.

The very popularity of his short scientific fantasies emboldened Wells to work them in longer lengths. *The Island of Dr. Moreau*, an extraordinarily well-done story reversing an incident in Homer's *Odyssey*, where Circe, through the use of a vapor, changes Ulysses' men into swine, finds modern science, through surgery and glandular injections, turning animals into human beings. Essentially this is a scientific horror story and one of such impact that at first publishers rejected it. When it was finally published, outraged voices were raised against its theme. Yet time has softened the outcry and the stature of the story is secured by the consummate skill with which it is related.

The Invisible Man, published in 1897, was an instant success and is undoubtedly the finest work ever done in fiction on the subject of invisibility. When made into a motion picture in the United States, it had the bizarre effect of making a renowned star of a man whose face was not seen until the last sequence of the picture—Claude Rains.

The War of the Worlds, which appeared in book form in 1898, scored an immediate and deserved hit. Wells was by this time a world-renowned figure. The great imagination and literary artistry he displayed in tale after tale were as much a wonder as his subject matter. Hard as it is to believe, *The War of the Worlds* appears to have been the first science fiction story written about the invasion of the earth by creatures from another planet bent on conquest. The theme has been treated so many hundreds of times since that Wells's originality is lost sight of.

While *The War of the Worlds* was running as a serial novel in America's *Cosmopolitan Magazine* during the latter part of 1897, the distinguished United States astronomer and popular science writer Garrett P. Serviss wrote a sequel to the story, titled *Edison's Conquest of Mars*, which ran serially in the newspaper *The New York Journal*, starting January 12, 1898. It related how Thomas Alva Edison and a group of other scientists built a fleet of spaceships armed with disintegrator rays and traveled to Mars to punish the Martians for their abortive invasion of the earth. This is a striking example of the impact *The War of the Worlds* had on first publication and how popular H. G. Wells had become.

The effectiveness with which Orson Welles retold the story, in a different setting, in 1938 during a radio broadcast that scared the wits out of a nation underscores the vitality of the work. Though it has dated to the point where we know that modern science and weaponry would have made short work of Wells's Martians and their robots, the novel continues to be reprinted, read, and even brought up to date for motion pictures.

With such a string of true classics of science fiction behind him, Wells is to be excused if he stumbled with book publication of *When the Sleeper Wakes* in 1899. That novel, despite extensive revision, was, as Wells so aptly put it, "one of the most ambitious and least satisfactory of my books." A tale of a man who falls into a state of suspended animation and awakes in the future, to find a world in which power is vested in the hands of a few men, devolves into a somewhat tedious muddle of sophomoric socialism.

The publication of *The First Men in the Moon* in 1901 did much to take the bad taste of *When the Sleeper Wakes* out of the mouth of the reading public. This was the first of Wells's books to be filmed. It was produced by J. V. L. Leigh for the Gaumont Film Company in 1919, a rather unimaginative and tasteless transference of the story to celluloid.

The mature Wells chafed at being typed as a scientific romancer. While he boasted of the pains he took to make his tales scientifically plausible, and claimed for them merit beyond that of entertainment, he felt barred from recognition as a contributor to mainstream literature. To Arnold Bennett he wrote, "I am doomed to write 'scientific' romances and short stories for you creatures of the mob, and my novels must be my private dissipation."

Finally the mainstream novels poured forth: the brilliant *Tono-Bungay*; the popular *History of Mr. Polly*; *Kipps, Ann Veronica, The New Machiavelli*, and many others. Most of them were timely hits. They blasted at the prejudices and inhibitions of the period. They rocked the people out of their warped ideas of righteousness and replaced smugness and complacency with indignation and doubt.

Interspersed among the Wells novels were nonfiction works on the future of mankind and various aspects of socialism. He was becoming more and more convinced that he had a message to impart to the world. Though the scientific fantasies continued to come—*The Food of the Gods* in 1904, *In the Days of the Comet* in 1906, and the truly prophetic *The War in the Air* in 1908, which clearly foresaw the dramatic change the airplane would make in future warfare—and though a number of marvelous collections of short stories and a few out-and-out fantasies such as *The Wonderful Visit* and *The Sea Lady* appeared with them, it became apparent that the tenor of Wells's thought was changing.

Clearly evident in *The War in the Air* was Wells's tendency to halt his story to deliver a sermon, although he should have had ample outlet for his ideas in such nonfiction works as *Anticipations*, *The Discovery of the Future*, and *New Worlds for Old*.

Already impatience had overcome him. Whether in a scientific fantasy, such as his master-prophecy, *The World Set Free*, published in 1914, wherein he predicted the atomic bomb and world destruction, or his "realistic" novel, *The World of William Clissold*, appearing in 1926, he could no longer be bothered with the story. He had to stop and deliver sermons, interminable sermons and often boring sermons.

He never quite realized that fiction was not the way to get his educational material across to the masses. *The Outline of History*, the first of a trilogy in which he tried to impart a factual picture of what the world and mankind were like and how business and science fitted into the scheme of things, sold millions of copies; he may have made more money from this one book than he made from the combined sales of all his other books. The other two volumes, *The Science of Life*, in collaboration with Julian Huxley and his son G. P. Wells, and *The Work, Wealth and Happiness of*

Mankind, by their only slightly less enthusiastic reception should have proved to him that sugar-coating was extraneous if he really had something to say.

One by one his once famous mainstream novels dated and dropped out of print until only *Tono-Bungay* and *The History of Mr. Polly* any longer received serious consideration in literary circles.

Yet, ironically, the scientific fantasies of his youth, the scientific romances which he felt had so constrained him, refused to die. Wells often denied that he was destined to be read by posterity. Though he referred to himself as "only a journalist," it would have been less than human on his part not to have hoped that his "mature" novels would have made a lasting mark.

Wells was completely aware of the development of science fiction in recent years. Twenty-six of his novels, novelettes, and short stories were reprinted in *Amazing Stories* between 1926 and 1930, and one in *Science Wonder Stories.* There were also reprints of his tales in *Weird Tales* and *Ghost Stories* and he must have received copies of these publications.

Then there is the letter received from him by Festus Pragnell, British science fiction author of *The Green Men of Graypec,* which was first published serially in Gernsback's *Wonder Stories,* and then reprinted in book form in England under the title of *The Green Man of Kilsona.* A leading character in that story was named H. GeeWells and evoked the comment: "Dear Mr. Pragnell, I wanted something to read last night and I found your book on a table in my study. I think it's a very good story indeed of the fantastic-scientific type, and I was much amused and pleased to find myself figuring in it." Wells signed his name "H. GeeWells."

Perhaps it was instances like the latter that prompted Wells to turn halfheartedly toward the scientific fantasies of his youth during the late 1930s. Perhaps it was the obvious longevity of his work in this vein. Perhaps it was an attempt to regain some of the optimism lost because of old age, ill-health, and the way the world was going. But from his pen (and Wells wrote all his first drafts in longhand) came *The Shape of Things to Come, The Croquet Player, Star Begotten,* and *The Camford Visitation.* It was no use. Uniformly they were marred by preachments.

One thing these later science fiction stories did have in common with the old was the fact that the center of interest was generally the unusual phenomenon or world catastrophe rather than any individual. Though a master of the art of making people come alive on the printed page, Wells failed to produce a single character comparable to Jules Verne's Captain Nemo.

Despite this, except for his most badly dated works (paradoxically also his most prophetic, *The War in the Air* and *The World Set Free*), nearly all of Wells's novels and short stories of science fiction and fantasy are still in print and continue to be read. It is not the ideas that keep them alive, nor their pointed warnings to civilization, nor their sensationalism, but the word-mastery of a literary genius, who took the elements of the scientific "boys' tales" and "thrillers" and created permanent and enduring literature.

9

THE WORLD, THE DEVIL,
AND M. P. SHIEL

Matthew Phipps Shiel, the tenth child and only son of a
Methodist preacher, was born on Montserrat in the West
Indies, July 21, 1865. Shiel speaks at some length and with
affection of his Irish father in biographical reminiscences,
but for some reason he never makes a direct reference to his
mother.

Shiel claimed that his father did not preach for money and
that his real source of income came from ships he owned.
The reason for the use of "claimed" is that proven exaggera-
tions and fabrications in many of Shiel's statements were
uncovered by his friend and biographer, the British poet,
author, and anthologist John Gawsworth. Shiel's assertion
that in a puckish mood his father once had him anointed
king of an island in the West Indies by the Reverend Dr.
Semper of Antigua appears to have some basis in fact. This

event was said to have occurred July 21, 1880, when Shiel was fifteen years old. The island was called Redonda, a five- or nine-square-mile chunk of rock, depending on who was interviewing Shiel, which was eventually annexed by the British government. His father, he reported, maintained a running angry fight with the government for fifteen years as to ownership—but to no avail.

Young Shiel had a private tutor on the islands and then was dispatched to London, where he obtained his degree at King's College. Languages fascinated him and he acquired some facility in a number of them, including Greek, Latin, Italian, French, Polish, and Spanish. This aptitude at one time caused him to be accepted as an interpreter to the International Congress of Hygiene and Demography.

More important, his extensive knowledge of languages formed the foundation of a tremendous vocabulary, and translating the idioms of the many languages he knew into English produced an unorthodox and pyrotechnic style that made him the despair of purists and the envy of his fellow authors.

This style was first brought to the attention of the literati when Shiel tired of teaching mathematics after a year of it and, turning to medicine, then found he had no stomach for the knife. He produced three detective stories which were published as a book in both England and the United States in 1895 under the title *Prince Zaleski*. Strongly smitten at the age of seventeen by Edgar Allan Poe and conscious of the acclaim won by A. Conan Doyle for his Baker Street adventures, Shiel produced what might best be called "Sherlock Holmes in the House of Usher."

Prince Zaleski, a mysterious Russian, solved difficult crimes by brilliant deduction. M. P. Shiel personally assumed the role of his "Dr. Watson," but instead of London's metropolitan Baker Street there was a Gothic castle furnished with partially unwrapped mummies. The stories are primarily of historical interest, actually being no more than pastiches falling into the same category as Maurice LeBlanc's Lupin or

August Derleth's Solar Pons tales, take-offs on the Holmes stories. Nevertheless, this book caused renowned novelist Arnold Bennett to comment later: "I read, and was excited by, *Prince Zaleski* when it first appeared."

Shiel's next book was a rather ordinary romance, *The Rajah's Sapphire*, published in 1896, and followed within months by *Shapes in the Fire*, a collection of short stories. The latter is much sought after by Shiel collectors as the first hard-cover collection of a number of his most bizarre tales of horror, including *Xelucha*, *Tulsah*, and *Vaila*, the last later rewritten under the title of *The House of Sounds*. The style of all of them is berserk Poe with all genius spent.

Omitted from the collection was one of Shiel's better short stories, *Huguenin's Wife*, which appeared in *Pall Mall Magazine* for 1895. In this story, Huguenin rescues a young woman from a Greek mob which is out to kill her for setting up a temple to Apollo in the modern world. The woman attaches herself to Huguenin with great fervor and he marries her. She is an inspired artist, but one of her too realistic paintings, of a great catlike creature, covered with wings and feathers instead of fur, disgusts him so that he strikes her. She dies from the blow but her last words are: "You may yet see it in the flesh."

When the house catches fire and Huguenin, in a mental ferment, opens his wife's tomb, he releases a living replica of her painting which tears his throat out.

It is very likely that *Huguenin's Wife* could have served as the inspiration of H. P. Lovecraft's tale, *Pickman's Model*, in which a famous artist's monster paintings prove to have been posed by creatures living in tunnels beneath Boston.

In May 1871 *Blackwood's Magazine* in England published anonymously a novelette called *The Battle of Dorking*, which has since been attributed to George Chesney. This story realistically projects a future war where Great Britain, the supreme nation of the earth, is crushingly defeated and then humbled by its conquerors. The speculation deservedly created a sensation with its prophetic analysis of the factors which would bring about the rise of Communism and the future loss of Britain's colonies. There were a half-dozen or more sequels by as many authors, the most famous of them being *What Happened after the Battle of Dorking*, and even such personal accounts as *Mrs. Brown on the Battle of Dorking*.

This sparked a vogue for future war novels which reached its zenith when George Griffith added imaginative inventions to the projected clash of nations in his best-seller, *The Angel of the Revolution*, and its sequel, *Olga Romanoff*, published in 1893 and 1894 respectively.

A popular author of the period, Louis Tracy, had cashed in on this cycle with *The Final War* issued in 1896. As a friend and collaborator, he prevailed upon Shiel to follow the trend, with the result that Shiel's *The Empress of the Earth* was serialized in England in *Short Stories* magazine from February 5 to June 18, 1898, and the same year was published as a book titled *The Yellow Danger*.

The thought that England might be conquered by the yellow men of Asia was Shiel's contribution to the literature of future wars. In later years, Shiel's publishers made the claim that the phrase "the yellow danger" was coined by him.

The book suited the mood of the times and went into three editions in Britain and one in America. Through the lips of his Chinese strategist, Dr. Yen How, M. P. Shiel expresses his view of the inherent superiority of the white man over the yellow when he tells his compatriots: "Poh! Your Navy! Who built it for you? It was they. Your Navy is like a razor in the hands of an ape which has seen its master use it. The brute may or may not cut its own throat with it."

Yen How urges that the yellow races strike before the white man's progress has made the dream of yellow supremacy a forlorn hope. Uniting China and Japan, Yen How, through political manipulations in Asia (where the leading European nations were involved at the turn of the century), starts a frightful war on the continent. In chapter after chapter, Shiel spares no detail in describing the battle movements of every naval unit of the Great Powers of that period, even to the extent of drawing sketches of the battle formations, which are included in the book.

When Europe has almost exhausted itself in war, the yellow horde pours out of Asia, conquering everything up to the British Channel.

A series of torpedoes aimed at the massed Chinese and Japanese fleet by the British starts a chain reaction of explosions which destroys the invaders' fighting units, turning the tide. Barges with twenty million Chinese are towed north into a maelstrom and sucked to the bottom of the sea. One hundred and fifty Chinamen are injected with cholera and released on the Continent. The plague wipes out one hundred and fifty million. England thus becomes ruler of the world, since the only remaining power, the United States, cannot remain a single free island in a world otherwise ruled by England. The quality and importance of this work are on a par with the plot outline, but the book reached a wide audience.

Following this heartening success, Shiel's next science fiction novel, which appeared in 1901, was again a future war tale, but with a difference. Frequently referred to as the second best of Shiel's novels, *The Lord of the Sea* reaches an intensity of anti-Semitism that provokes comparison with Hitler's *Mein Kampf,* for which it could have served as an inspiration.

This is the background: The Jews, after being systematically expelled from every nation in Europe for buying up half the land and holding mortgages on the rest (literally), flood into England, where they begin the process anew. One third of all members of Parliament are Jews. After initial prosperity, the poor British farmers, who must pay rent to the Jews, bend under the heavy yoke.

The prime Jewish villain, Frankl, is pictured as lewdly grasping for Irish girls with "phylacteried left arm." He also routinely forecloses mortgages as a prelude to Sabbath rites.

Frankl, described by one of Shiel's characters as a "dirty-livered Jew," is interrupted at his prayers by the hero, Richard Hogarth, who whips him with a riding crop.

Tired from his exertions and bleeding from a stab wound in the shoulder inflicted by a servant attempting to save his master from the beating, Hogarth, whose physical description amazingly parallels that of Shiel, returns home to receive the staggering news from his Irish father that he was actually born of Jewish parents; therefore he should take pride in his people: "*They* are the people who've got the money." Semiconscious from loss of blood, Hogarth fails to absorb the full impact of the confession.

Framed by Frankl for the "murder" of a servant who actually committed suicide, Hogarth is sent to prison. He escapes, finds a meteorite on Frankl's property that is almost solid diamond, and with the money from its sale secretly constructs a number of huge floating forts, strategically placed to command the seas. He exacts tribute from every ship that passes and becomes not only the "Lord of the Sea," but the highest official of England.

In this capacity he has Parliament pass a law to the effect that "No Jew might own or work land, or teach in any Cheder or school, or be entered at any Public School or University, or sign any stamped document, or carry on certain trades, or vote, or officiate at any public service, and so on: parentage, not religion, constituting a 'Jew.'"

In a fit of generosity, the Jews are reimbursed for their lands, and Palestine, then almost a wasteland, inhabited by 300,000 nomads, is given to them to settle upon if they so desire. Scarcely have the Jews left England when the British government, through stealth, accomplishes what it had been unable to do by force and succeeds in scuttling most of Hogarth's forts.

His power gone, Hogarth has confirmed to him and in turn makes public that he is a Jew. He is banished to Palestine where he is revealed to be a new incarnation of Jesus who, for the next sixty years, rules his people. During that period,

Shiel says, his followers took the commandment "Thou shalt not steal" to heart, and "therefore, Israel with some little pain attained to this."

Only in his prediction that Palestine would flourish under the Jews does Shiel's novel show any merit, either in prophecy, prose, or decency. It need scarcely be emphasized that the only difference between his method and the Nazis' rests in the fact that he would have permitted the Jews to emigrate with their lives.

The same year as *The Lord of the Sea*, Shiel's most applauded novel, *The Purple Cloud*, was serialized in *The Royal Magazine*, London, January to June, 1901, in six installments, and in September of that year appeared in hard covers. This is justifiably the most highly regarded of Shiel's works and the one that eventually brought him literary recognition as well as, in his old age, a pension for "his services to literature" from the British government.

In delivering Shiel's funeral oration before an audience of thirteen on February 24, 1947, Edward Shanks, himself noted for an end-of-the-world story, *People of the Ruins*, which was admittedly inspired by Shiel's epic, said:

> In speaking of Shiel it is difficult not to give the impression that he was a 'one-book' man. To some extent at any rate, that he must always be. There is a parallel case worth mentioning. Herman Melville will always be first and foremost the author of *Moby Dick*. For as many generations ahead as one can see, critics and readers will continue to pay, at any rate, lip service to that one book. But among the readers thus influenced, some will always seek in other books the qualities, however attenuated, which made that one great.
>
> So it will be with Shiel.

The Purple Cloud shows strong influence of Mary Wollstonecraft Shelley's *The Last Man* in its seemingly interminable yet individually potent episodes describing a world from which virtually all human life has departed. When the book was written, the North Pole had not been reached. A bequest by Charles P. Stickney of Chicago (a character who also appears in *The Lord of the Sea*) offering $175,000,000 to the first man to reach the Pole inspires the organization of an arctic exploration team. A physician named Adam Jeffson succeeds, with the aid of his lady friend, in doing away with a member of the party so that he may be substituted. After many hardships, the objective is reached and the area is found to be littered with diamonds from meteorites attracted by the Pole's magnetism. Killing most of his party, Jeffson, in passages reminiscent of *The Captain of the "Polestar"* by A. Conan Doyle, makes his way overland to the sea to find that those left aboard the ship are dead. On reaching civilization, he discovers that the entire earth is a vast graveyard. The cause, a purple gas issuing from fissures, has killed everyone.

On this device, H. G. Wells commented, "No one can dispute that some great emanation of vapour from the interior of the earth, such as Mr. Shiel has made a brilliant use of in his *Purple Cloud*, is consistent with every demonstrated fact in the world."

Jeffson's twenty-year, detailed search through the ruins of the world, since it is presented in synoptic diary form with frequent self-conscious flarings of rhetoric, is scarcely easy reading. Nor is the description particularly pleasant, of Jeffson's shift toward madness that causes him to burn city after city. Neither is his unreasonable brutality when he finally discovers, alive in Constantinople, a girl who was so young when the catastrophe occurred that she doesn't even know how to speak.

The reaction on finishing the novel is similar to that experienced on completing Franz Kafka's grim *Metamorphosis*: It was worth reading, but you would hate to do it again!

Primarily as a result of this novel, Shiel has received high praise from such literary greats as Arthur Machen, Jules Claretie, Hugh Walpole, J. B. Priestley, and Charles Williams. Shiel, though weak at plotting, was a writer's writer stylistically. His mad literary rhythms, seemingly improvised, like a jazz artist's at a jam session, were a bubbling fountain at which new techniques of phrasing could be drunk. While the artistry was rarely sustained, it had flashes of splendor. For 1901, a passage like "Pour, pour, came the rain, raining as it can in this place, not long, but a torrent while it lasts, dripping in thick liquidity like a profuse sweat through the wood . . ." anticipated the method of innovators like Thomas Wolfe at a much later date.

Again Shiel turned to the theme of future war for *The Yellow Wave*, published in 1905. This is really a love story projected against the background of a war between Russia and Japan which threatens to involve the other nations of the world, which have at last learned the ways of peace. Never one to coddle his lead characters, Shiel sacrifices the two lovers at the end to bring peace between the combatants.

In *The Last Miracle*, published in 1906, fiction is once more used to project one of Shiel's fanatical hatreds, one as violent as that against the Jews. Though he was the son of a minister, Shiel knew no bounds in his almost paranoid vilification of organized religion. He felt that the only true religion was science and that science was the only thing that uplifted a man, whereas to the great faiths he attributed most, if not all, of the blame for man's problems and ignorance.

In this novel, a scientist, through undisclosed means, causes the disappearance of people, and their various crucifixions appear as "visions" in churches throughout the world. The novel terminates so abruptly as to be virtually unfinished. Its purpose seems to be a vast orgy of antireligious diatribe, rather than the telling of a story. For the solution of men's problems, Shiel offers, in notes to the book, some deep-breathing exercises which resulted in unfavorable, but deserved, comparison with Bernarr Macfadden, who, even then, was promoting "physical culture" to commercial success.

Shiel's *style* in storytelling was so spectacular that many tend to think all his books are fantasies. Collectors read and collect his books for the bizarreness of his method, regardless of their literary classification. Therefore, while other books written during the same period as those outlined, such as *Contraband of War, Cold Steel, The Man-Stealers, The Weird o' It, Unto the Third Generation, The Evil That Men Do, The Lost Viol, The White Wedding,* and *This Knot of Life,* might interest the Shiel devotee, they are neither science fiction nor fantasy.

A borderline case is *The Isle of Lies* (1909), in which a youth is trained to virtual infallibility of memory and clear thinking, but fails in an attempt for political control of the globe because of his weakness for women.

One of the books listed, *This Knot of Life* (1909) is of special importance, inasmuch as it strengthens the certainty of Shiel's tendency to a Nazi-like anti-Semitism. In many of his books appears the superman, forerunner of the super race. Shiel has a new term for such men. He calls them "Overmen," and in *This Knot of Life* admits to having derived the term from the German "*Ubermensch.*" His villain here is a fiendish Jew named Sam Abrahams. Some student might, as an exercise, try to find a single Shiel book in which there is not a direct or implied slur at the Jews, usually accompanied by another at religion. *The Dragon,* issued in 1913 and later reprinted as *The Yellow Peril* in 1929, is no exception—in it he classifies a group of English traitors as "pure Jews, only, with their bad heredity, lacking the brains of Jews."

As might be inferred from the title under which it was reprinted, *The Yellow Peril* is almost a paraphrase of *The Yellow Danger.* Again, a diabolical Chinese ("the only man who can outwit a Jew in business is a Chinaman—don't forget") sets the European nations at one another's throats so they are weakened for the poised Oriental invasion. The Chinese again come galloping across Asia and Europe, like a movie retake. Shiel heartily approves of this, because it will destroy Christianity and religion. "Good!" he says. "Now, the scientist denies that apes, Negroes, bishops, bouzis, dervishes, are religious."

In the nick of time, when England is about to be invaded,

the Overman ("*Ubermensch*") comes up with a ray that blinds all the invaders. The Overman issues the following dictum, the epitome of Shiel's lifelong philosophy:

> That Great Britain be considered my private property by right of Conquest.
> That taxes (except "death-duties") be abolished; and "customs."
> That citizens be liable to daily drill, including running and breathing.

At the age of seventy, Shiel claimed he was still running six miles a day for reasons of health.

> That Research and Education be the nation's main activities.
> That education, transport, power, medicine, and *publishing* be taken over by the government.
> That Doctors be "consecrated"; and be Bachelors of Science; and be taught in "Consecration" ... it "To the pure, all things are pure."
> That Clergymen now leave off uttering in public, for money, whatever comes to seem childish to average people.

With this book, Shiel ended a period of eighteen years of writing and did not resume again for ten years. The only other book worthy of serious attention in this era is the short story collection *The Pale Ape*, issued in 1911, which contains some of Shiel's better short stories, including *Huguenin's Wife* as well as a unique detective character, Cummings King Monk, who is adept at ventriloquism in addition to his deductive accomplishments.

The purchase of *The Purple Cloud* in 1927 as possible material for a motion picture probably motivated Shiel's revival of interest in the writing of science fiction. Though the book was considered as the basis of a dozen screen plays, it remained sidetracked, though not forgotten by Sol C. Siegel, who bought an option on the novel in 1957 after he became vice-president of Metro-Goldwyn-Mayer.

The movie appeared in 1959 as *The World, the Flesh and*

the Devil, starring Harry Belafonte, Inger Stevens, and Mel Ferrer. It was a milestone in cinema ingenuity since all the outside scenes were shot in an "empty" New York City. It was taboo-shattering as far as race relations were concerned, since the "last" man on earth is a Negro, and the last woman white. When a surviving white man floats in from the sea, he forces a grim duel to the death with the Negro for possession of the girl. The senseless fight is stopped when the girl steps in, indicating her preference for the Negro.

Shiel ventured into science fiction again in 1928, this time with *2073 A.D.*, a short story, which, despite its minor length, was serialized in *The Daily Herald*, a London newspaper, on March 12, 13, 14, and 15, 1928. Later, retitled *The Future Day*, it was included in a collection, *The Invisible Voices*. An undistinguished piece of work, it deals with a future in which all cities are suspended in the air and men ride about in "air boats." A girl, wishing to test the bravery of her poet suitor, pretends that the power has failed in her "air boat" and that they will fall to earth. He comes through with flying colors and she agrees to marry him.

Though he was well into his sixties and living alone after his second wife left him in 1929 (his first wife had died after only five years of marriage), a great deal of energy and venom still remained in Shiel when he wrote *This Above All*, a fable of immortality, published in 1933. Based on the idea of the eternal woman, possibly inspired by Karel Čapek's *The Makropoulos Secret*, Shiel's volume centers around a Jewess who has come down through the ages as an imperishable thirteen-year-old, and her efforts to get Lazarus (who is still alive after being touched by the hand of Christ centuries earlier) to marry her. In the meanwhile, so as not to get rusty while waiting, she has married a whole string of mortal men whom she discards as they age. The plot is constantly being interrupted by her blasts against Christianity and religion, her advocacy of science and research as well as long fasts, and her slow and silent eating (preferably honey and nuts).

It soon develops that Jesus is still alive and that Jesus, Lazarus, and the "young" girl are all members of a special race of long-lived human beings. Here, Shiel attempts to alter the theological picture of Jesus. While he concedes that the man was basically good and kind, he warns that he was also a Jew and, if alive, might favor his own people. He also retranslates from the original Greek and reinterprets New Testament passages, to the effect that Jesus may have occasionally imbibed too much wine and that he was really not against divorce. The reader is faced with a decision: Does Shiel hate the Jews because they created Christianity, or does he hate Christianity because it was created by Jews?

If the book has any worth-while message, it lies in the preachment that age/immortality does not mean wisdom. Shiel, himself, seems an excellent case in point.

Probably Shiel's single best short story is *The Place of Pain*, to be found in the collection *The Invisible Voices*. It deals with a Negro preacher in British Columbia, once highly respected in the community, who falls from grace and declines into drunkenness after apparently making an unusual discovery in the wilderness. This discovery he eventually confides to a white man who has been kind to him, when he feels he is dying from tuberculosis. It seems that he had by accident found that a rock placed in a mass of froth at the bottom of a waterfall would convert the water into a pool that acted as the convex lens of a telescope. Through this lens, he has seen, or so he implies, nightmarish and monstrous sights on the moon. He dies just as he wades out to place the stone in the correct spot to form a lens for the white man to look through.

The story is magnificently handled and Shiel exercises unaccustomed restraint in its telling. Though the Negro does not duplicate his discovery for the reader or actually describe what he saw on the moon, one is led to believe that he is telling the truth. If there is any flaw, it is that Shiel cannot excise his racial prejudice: "He had called them frankly a

pack of apes, a band of black and babbling babies; said that
he could pity them from his heart, they were so benighted,
so lost in darkness; that what they knew in their wooly nuts
was just nothing."

Shiel's last important work of fiction was *The Young Men
Are Coming*, and it is at once one of his most imaginative
and one of his most damning novels. A sort of super flying
saucer lands in England and fantastic flaming-haired creatures
whisk away an aging Dr. Warwick. They travel three times the
speed of light to the first moon of Jupiter. There, the un-
hatched egg of one of the space creatures engages Dr. Warwick in a prolonged discussion on philosophy, science, sociology, and religion. Dr. Warwick is given a draught of immortality and a parting message from the space creatures:

> Farewell. I bear you this message from the Egg's Mother;
> that she sets a detector to resonance with your rays: so, if in
> an emergency worthy of her notice you, having on your
> psychophone, send out your soul in worship to her, she still
> journeying in this eastern region of worlds, your wish will
> reach her.

Returned to earth and immortal, Dr. Warwick organizes
the "young men" into a group of virtual storm troopers to
defeat the "old men" who are planning a "fascistic" movement. The political goal of the "young men" is to overthrow
religion and substitute science (reason) in its place.

A revolutionary war ensues. To win over the people, Dr.
Warwick tells them he will perform a *scientific* "miracle"
and challenges religion to duplicate, top, or stop him. He
sends a message out to the space creatures to create a universal storm, thereby illustrating the power of science over
religion. They respond with a globular hurricane which sinks
land masses, drowns or kills millions, and inadvertently destroys the air fleet of the "old men" who have the "young
men" just about licked in a fair fight.

As far as bloodshed is concerned, Shiel scoffs at the notion that "the next war will wreck civilization." Wars are merely "inconveniences," he avers, concluding, *"Cursed* are the meek! For they shall *not* inherit the earth."

If one were to assume the role of apologist for M. P. Shiel, what could be said for him? It could be said that while he made no impact on mainstream literature, he did make a minor, if flawed, contribution to science fiction. It might be said that faults aside, his work displayed unquestioned erudition and scholarship, and that there were honest flashes of power and brilliance in his writing.

It would have to be admitted that, in the psychiatrist's vernacular, the man had a "problem." Its manifestations were obvious, but its cause can only be speculated upon. Descriptively, Richard Hogarth in *The Lord of the Sea* comes very close to being a replica of Shiel down to the three moles on the cheek and the Irish father. Somewhere along the line did Shiel learn something about his ancestry that he could not reconcile with his early religious training? Is there a link between this information and a mother of whom he never speaks? Was it really the ubiquitous Jewish villain, Dinka, speaking in *The Young Men Are Coming,* "If I am a bit of a Hebrew inside, isn't my coat as Christian as they make 'em?"—or is it Shiel?

It is indeed ironical that a man who was an anti-Semite, anti-Christian, anti-Negro, anti-Oriental, an ardent believer in Aryan superiority, and a war lover is to be posthumously ennobled as an apostle of peace and racial tolerance every time *The World, the Flesh and the Devil* is shown, as it will be for many years to come.

10
ARTHUR CONAN DOYLE:
A STUDY IN SCIENCE FICTION

Professor George Edward Challenger, a fictional character created by Arthur Conan Doyle, has frequently been referred to as "The Sherlock Holmes of Science Fiction." To literary critics and researchers alike, he presents unshakable evidence that outstanding characterization is possible within the fabric of the true science fiction story. Professor Challenger appeared first in *The Lost World*, a novel serialized by *Strand* in England in 1912, and continued to figure prominently in Doyle's literary output until the publication of *The Maracot Deep*, a collection of stories issued in 1929.

"Challenger was one of his favorite characters and in private conversations he often alluded to him," recorded the Reverend John Lamond, D.D., in *Arthur Conan Doyle, A Memoir*, published by John Murray, London, in 1931. Lamond pointed to the Challenger science fiction series as an "indication of what he might have produced if other interests had not occupied him."

The other interests were, at first, Sherlock Holmes and, later, spiritualism. The time Doyle spent on Sherlock Holmes added immeasurably to the development of the detective story and the reading pleasure of the world, but the inordinate demands on his time made by his obsession with spiritualism prevented him from devoting more effort to science fiction, which his correspondence indicated he wanted to do.

In the course of his long career as a storyteller Doyle chose themes in a variety of fields. By the creation of Sherlock Holmes he became the greatest single writer of detective stories of all time. He loved the historical novel, and *The White Company, Micah Clarke,* and *The Refugees* are creditable and popular accomplishments in that genre. Because of Doyle's early training as a physician, medical science plays an important role in a large number of his stories. His intense preoccupation with spiritualism resulted in many ghost stories and weird tales, of which *The Bully of Brocas Court,* published in 1921, is frequently mentioned as his best.

His output included straightforward tales of adventure which showed a particular fondness for the sea and for Africa. Doyle also wrote *The British Campaign in France and Flanders,* a history of World War I in six volumes, as well as several collections of poetry. Toward the end of his life there were volumes of nonfiction on spiritualism and allied subjects, the publication of a few being subsidized by Doyle himself.

Though his best science fiction was written long after the fame of Sherlock Holmes had made his name a household word throughout the world, for a brief time in his early years science fiction competed with the historical novel, the detective story, the adventure thriller, and the weird tale as the vehicle which Doyle hoped to ride to substantial literary recognition.

Arthur Conan Doyle was born in Edinburgh, Scotland,

May 22, 1859, the son of Charles Doyle, an architect and artist, and Mary Foley Doyle, both Irish Catholics. He received his medical degree from Edinburgh University in 1881, but two years previously had already earned his first check of three guineas for a short story, *The Mystery of Sasassa Valley*, published in *Chambers' Journal* for October 1879. That tale was a horror story concerning a legendary demon with glowing eyes who happily turned out to be two giant diamonds embedded in rock salt.

A. Conan Doyle hung out his shingle in Elm Grove, Southsea, England, a town near Portsmouth, in September 1882, and waited for patients. Few came. He was not then a success as a doctor, nor was his later effort to establish himself as an eye specialist to bear any fruit.

At the best, as a medical practitioner, he scarcely eked out an existence. Part of his trouble lay in complete lack of support from his family and relatives when they discovered that he espoused no religion. Setting up medical practice as a religious conformist or a "Catholic" doctor would have helped him in the England of 1882, but his disenchantment with theology, arising from the belief "that the evils of religion, a dozen religions slaughtering each other, have all come from accepting things that can't be proved," would not permit him to do so in good conscience.

In the England of that day, a graduate of a medical school could not legitimately claim the title of "doctor" until he had spent a number of years in practice and qualified further through a special thesis and examination. A. Conan Doyle obtained his doctorate in medicine in 1885 and a month later married Louise Hawkins, an attractive girl whom he had long admired.

Since his medical income was inadequate, he redoubled his efforts to write in his spare time. As a student, Doyle had enjoyed reading Poe's works aloud to his parents. It was in Poe's detective stories involving C. Auguste Dupin—*The Murders in the Rue Morgue, The Mystery of Marie Roget,* and *The Purloined Letter*—that Doyle received his inspiration for

Sherlock Holmes. Poe's Dupin solved his criminal cases through the use of scientific deduction. Sherlock Holmes did the same.

Dupin was an engaging character who had a friend who roomed with him and who told the story, a role performed by Dr. John Watson for Sherlock Holmes. Dupin always had the French prefect of police dropping in on him for help when a particularly knotty criminal problem arose. Holmes paralleled this by condescendingly aiding Scotland Yard's Inspector Lestrade and others.

The first Sherlock Holmes story, A *Study in Scarlet*, appeared in *Beeton's Christmas Annual* for 1887. In it Sherlock Holmes refers to C. Auguste Dupin as "a very inferior fellow." Years later, Doyle poetically apologized for Holmes's ingratitude:

> To put down to me my creation's crude vanity?
> He, the created, would scoff and would sneer,
> Where I, the creator, would bow and revere.
> So please grip this fact with your cerebral tentacle:
> The doll and its maker are never identical.

The influence of Poe was later to be found in Doyle's science fiction.

Strangely enough, the first Sherlock Holmes story created no great stir: it was published in 1888 as a separate entity—with six illustrations by the author's father, Charles Doyle—by Ward, Lock & Co., London, the publishers of *Beeton's Christmas Annual*.

Micah Clarke, a historical novel, appeared in 1888, but resulted in no unusual success. Adventure stories and stories with a background of medical research continued to come from Doyle's pen, but the first important science fiction story was a short novel published in 1891, *The Doings of Raffles Haw*. The subject matter was derived from Poe's *Von Kempelen and His Discovery* and dealt with the experiences of a man who discovers a method of converting baser metals into gold.

This story remains today one of the finest ever written on the theme. Usually, in such tales, the method by which the transmutation process is accomplished serves merely as a backdrop for the story. Doyle, possibly because of his excellent scientific education, convincingly describes the laboratory, machinery, methods, and theory by which such transmutation is made possible.

That Doyle's plots and character types were not to any marked degree original has been pointed out many times by discerning critics. Ordinarily an imitator would have to play second fiddle to the man he copies, but Doyle was never an imitator in a commonplace way. *The Doings of Raffles Haw* reveals, as do the Sherlock Holmes and other stories, an almost uncanny ability to make characters come alive from the printed page.

The intrigues surrounding the manufacture of gold are completely convincing and as the invention brings widespread unhappiness the story builds in power right up to its tragic finale. In the end the inventor destroys himself, his secret, and his laboratory, after reconverting the tons of gold already created into a worthless metal.

The Sign of the Four, the second of the Sherlock Holmes stories, appeared in *Lippincott's Magazine* for February 1890, and was received with even less enthusiasm than the first. Doyle was now convinced that his bid for recognition must be made with the historical novel, so he began research for *The White Company*.

Doyle loved the historical books best of all his works. In all probability he would have confined himself to historical writing exclusively if he could have been assured of success in that field.

The Doings of Raffles Haw enjoyed some success, and it is interesting to speculate whether he would have alternated his historical novels with more science fiction if the third of the Sherlock Holmes series, *A Scandal in Bohemia*, published in the popular *Strand* for July 1891, had not finally sparked reader interest and caught on. Almost overnight Doyle was famous and the *Strand* was literally begging for more of his work.

Doyle wrote more Sherlock Holmes stories but kept setting the price higher and higher, not because he was greedy for money, but because he resented the fact that the labor involved allowed him less time for his "more important" work. The *Strand* met each new demand and gradually Doyle grew to dislike his most illustrious character and his indebtedness to him.

The Captain of the "Polestar" and Other Tales was published by Longmans, Green and Co. in 1894. The title story was obviously inspired by Edgar Allan Poe's *The Narrative of Arthur Gordon Pym* and by plot elements and atmospheric touches in Jules Verne's *Captain Hatteras* and *The Desert of Ice.*

In this story, the captain of a sailing ship imagines he sees the floating image of a woman in the arctic whiteness. He narrowly escapes death several times as he pursues the spectral figure, which is visible to him alone. Finally he deserts his ship in the vicinity of a giant ice floe, and when his shipmates find him several days later, frozen and with a strange smile on his face, one of them relates how the many little crystals and feathers of snow which had drifted onto him had been whirled about in a mysterious way by the wind. "To my eyes it seemed but a snowdrift, but many of my companions averred that it started up in the shape of a woman, stooped over the corpse and kissed it, and then hurried away across the floe."

The same volume contains the frequently reprinted *Great Keinplatz Experiment*, in which a professor and his student, through the use of hypnosis, exchange bodies. A number of years earlier, in 1882, F. Anstey (T. A. Guthrie), the literary godfather of Thorne Smith and John Collier, had caused a minor sensation with *Vice Versa*, in which, through the use of an ancient talisman, father and son switch bodies. The derivation is almost incontrovertible, although the actual style of the story is markedly reminiscent of Nathaniel Hawthorne.

Nevertheless, *The Captain of the "Polestar"* is an extraordinarily well-written story and *The Great Keinplatz Experiment* is amusing.

The Captain of the "Polestar" was dedicated to Major-General A. W. Drayson, an outstanding late Victorian astronomer and mathematician. What made the dedication particularly significant was the fact that General Drayson introduced Doyle to spiritualism, which was to have a most profound influence on his thinking toward the end of his life.

That year Methuen published *Round the Red Lamp,* another collection of short stories, which included *The Los Amigos Fiasco,* a tale with more obvious originality and grounded more strongly in science than the previously mentioned short stories. When this story was written, experiments were being made in the employment of the electric chair for capital punishment in the United States. The locale is a western American city called Los Amigos, noted for its tremendous electrical generating plants. The peace officers of Los Amigos capture a train robber, and decide that in executing him they will utilize the full power of their generators. Disregarding the warning of a local electrical experimenter, Peter Stulpnagel, they proceed. As the tremendous current surges through the condemned man, he bounds forward from his chair shouting, "Great Scott!" His hair turns white. His eyes brighten, but he does not die.

They try another power surge, but it merely lends the unfortunate man's cheeks a healthy glow. Giving up on the electricity they string him up, but after dangling for hours he still lives.

The United States marshal, exasperated, empties a six-shooter into the desperado, but only evokes the complaint that they have ruined a perfectly good suit.

Peter Stulpnagel advances the explanation that, since electricity is life, while small shocks will kill, great voltage has merely made a superman out of the victim, and even if they put him in jail, he probably will outlast the prison. That is how the affair came to be known as the *Los Amigos Fiasco.*

In short, up until 1894, Doyle had increasingly begun to experiment with tales that roughly were recognizable as science fiction, but he was to drop this tack for another eighteen years, conceding by default to the young H. G. Wells, who was to become pre-eminent as a writer of scientific romances during the same period.

The reasons were obvious. Sherlock Holmes had by now achieved a fabulous world-renown, although Doyle tried to kill him off in 1893. The public began to buy Doyle's historical work, *The White Company*, *The Refugees*, and *Micah Clarke*, in great quantities, despite the less-than-enthusiastic reviews of the critics. The year 1894 also saw the creation of another Doyle character which the public took to their hearts, Brigadier Gerard. With all these successes contributing to his prominence at the same time, Doyle could well afford to let the science fiction slide.

Each year after 1894, his fame progressed with giant steps. Medical practice he abandoned as an encumbrance. He volunteered nd participated in the Boer War. He almost refused a knighthood, because there was some question about whether it was being offered to him for the creation of Sherlock Holmes or because of his objective work, *The War in South Africa: Its Cause and Conduct*, which, translated into many languages, refuted most of the atrocity charges brought against the British.

For ten years he abandoned the writing of Holmes stories, resuming only to disprove the charges brought against him that he had lost his skill in detective fiction. But no one challenged him to write science fiction. So when *The Terror of Blue John Gap*, a short science fiction story, appeared in *The Strand Magazine* for September 1910, it was little more than a happenstance. But it signified that in science fiction, as in other fields, he had matured as a writer.

This little-known story shares with *The Horror of the Heights* the distinction of being Doyle's finest short science fiction. It deals with a bearlike creature, as large as an elephant, which is a nightly marauder in northwest Derbyshire.

The creature is stalked to its lair by Dr. James Hardcastle, but outwits and overcomes him. Dr. Hardcastle is fortunate to escape with his life. The writing is excellent and the theory as to the creature's origin postulates the existence of giant caverns inside the earth, where bizarre conditions have given rise to plants and animals that ought never to see the light of day.

While the theoretical concept stems from Verne's *A Journey to the Center of the Earth*, we begin to find Doyle adding a new dimension to an old idea, and plotting and writing in a manner distinctly his own.

There seemed to be no special reason why Doyle should have returned to the serious writing of science fiction, as he did in 1912. If it had happened in 1909 it might have been attributed to his presiding at the centenary dinner at the Metropole of the birth of Edgar Allan Poe, in which he paid homage to the memory of a man whose inspiration had profoundly influenced every aspect of his early work. Perhaps it was the example of H. G. Wells, a friend and correspondent, who had established his reputation in the world of the scientific romance. Whatever the reason, he wrote to Greenhough Smith, editor of *The Strand*, regarding *The Lost World*:

> I think it will make the very best serial (bar special S. Holmes values) that I have ever done, especially when it has its trimming of faked photos, maps, and plans. *My ambition is to do for the boys' book what Sherlock Holmes did for the detective tale. I don't suppose I could bring off two such coups. And yet I hope it may.*

A goal had been set. A. Conan Doyle was determined to build for himself a reputation in science fiction as great as the one that caused him to be canonized by detective story lovers. When *The Lost World* appeared it seemed that it was almost within his ability to accomplish that feat. Though the basic idea, like that of *The Terror of Blue John Gap*, was unabashedly inspired by Verne's *A Journey to the Center of the Earth*, the superior elements of characterization, humor, and pace that Doyle added to the idea set it distinctly apart.

The main character, George Edward Challenger, if not the finest drawn character in all science fiction, is at least on a par with Verne's Captain Nemo, Burroughs' John Carter, and Stanley G. Weinbaum's alien entities. The dumpy, barrel-chested, black-bearded, bad-tempered, intolerant, egotistical, driving, but truly brilliant Professor Challenger, despite his faults, or possibly because of them, bubbles into believability from the black type of the printed page.

We enjoy reading about him, even when his exploits and accomplishments fail to involve fantastic events. As we get to know him better we find that he is a man of sincerity, possessing true loyalty for his friends and acquaintances, a redeeming sense of humor, and a wealth of tender affection toward his tiny, fragile wife. The people who surround him —E. D. Malone, the young, athletic Irish reporter; Lord John Roxton, the adventurer; and Professor Summerlee—are all cut from fine literary cloth.

Professor Challenger attempts to persuade the leading scientific society of England that he has evidence to support his claim of the existence of prehistoric monsters on a South American plateau. In answer to ridicule, he offers to prove it if the society will send an observer with him on an expedition. Professor Summerlee is assigned. Together with Malone and Roxton they locate the plateau and also the fabulous and truly terrifying beasts from out of earth's past, long presumed extinct. After a series of adventures which involve saving a race of virtually modern natives from primeval, apelike dawn men, they return to England.

The ending is unforgettable. They have lost most of their evidence in making their escape back to civilization. As Challenger tells what he has seen and Professor Summerlee confirms it, they find themselves confronted with derisive laughter. The audience demands as proof nothing less than one of the antediluvian beasts in the flesh. Sardonically, Professor Challenger orders a cage brought onto the platform. The door is opened. He makes coaxing little noises and abruptly there is pandemonium as an immense, leathery-winged, red-eyed, saw-beaked pterodactyl sails out into the auditorium in blundering, fear-inspired flight. It squeezes through an open window and later is seen perched on the roof of Queen's Hall for two hours. Soldiers bolt their posts in wild terror when they glimpse the demon shape flying across the face of the moon. It is last sighted by a ship in mid-ocean as it wings its lonely way toward South America. Professor Challenger has won his point!

Superb characterization, coupled with fine humor and good science, lifted *The Lost World* above the level of the average adventure story. As a result, the novel was an instant success and new editions began to multiply. The following year, 1913, *The Poison Belt*, "being an account of another amazing adventure of Professor Challenger," began in *The Strand* for April.

This novel has always been overshadowed by the fame of *The Lost World*, but it is outstanding in its own right. For this story, Doyle borrowed again from Edgar Allan Poe, enlarging on the idea presented in *The Conversation of Eiros and Charmion*: the atmosphere of the earth is "poisoned" by a change resulting from conditions in outer space. In this novel, Challenger, foreseeing catastrophe, gathers his wife and the three companions of his previous adventure in an airtight room in his home. There, sustained by containers of oxygen, they watch the entire world come to a catastrophic stop. The penetrating British humor stands up even across the gulf of the years. As they prepare for the hour of doom, Challenger turns to his manservant, and says, quite calmly, "I'm expecting the end of the world today, Austin."

"Yes, sir," the servant replies. "What time, sir?"

Doyle strikes a telling blow at the theory of the survival of the fittest when he permits the only person in all London apparently still alive to be an asthmatic old woman, who thought she was having an attack when the character of the atmosphere began to change and fed herself oxygen out of a container she kept at her bedside for emergencies.

The philosophical description of the world's extermination provided by Doyle is worth repeating. Speaking through Challenger's lips he says:

> You will conceive a bunch of grapes which are covered by some infinitesimal but noxious bacillus. The gardener passes it through a disinfecting medium. It may be that he desires his grapes to be cleaner. It may be that he needs space to breed some fresh bacillus less noxious than the last. He dips it into the poison and they are gone. Our gardener is, in my opinion, about to dip the solar system, and the human bacillus, the little mortal vibrio which twisted and wiggled upon the outer rind of the earth, will in an instant be sterilized and out of existence.

The Lost World and *The Poison Belt* provided evidence that Doyle had it in him to be one of the greatest science fiction writers of all time. Certainly it is known that he loved Professor Challenger above all of his literary creations. It is reported that he used to assume Challenger disguises solely to startle his friends. He regarded Challenger as the science fiction version of Sherlock Holmes, unraveling scientific mysteries with the same skill his detective fiction counterpart used to solve crimes against society.

The Horror of the Heights, published in *Everybody's Magazine* for November 1913 and following *The Poison Belt*, may be the source from which flying saucer enthusiasts have derived the imaginative concept that alien and incredible life forms dwell in the upper atmosphere of the earth. The concept, for the year 1913, was a novel one and Doyle's handling of the theme was skillful indeed.

His ability as a very logical type of prognosticator was dramatically demonstrated when in *Danger!*, a novelette published in *Strand* for February 1914, he detailed in fictional form how Britain could be brought to her knees by submarines. The story recommended tunnels under the Channel and also made mention of airplanes with engine silencers as valuable war weapons. *Danger!* caused quite a stir and some people later accused Doyle of giving Germany the formula for submarine warfare.

The fantastic masterpieces of H. G. Wells were getting fewer and farther between. A great romancer of the scientific tale had arisen in America: Edgar Rice Burroughs, whose Tarzan was to challenge Sherlock Holmes for world-wide popularity. Years later, Burroughs' famous novel, *The Land That Time Forgot*, owing a debt to *The Lost World* in the development of its unique evolutionary theory, was to reveal that Doyle could lend as well as borrow. But now, this was the man Doyle had to surpass to emerge as top man in the field.

Then a strange thing happened. A. Conan Doyle, who had been an agnostic since his youth, found religion. But it was not the religion of the orthodox. Years earlier his first wife had died and he had married Jane Leckie, a woman whom he loved very dearly. Friends and relatives of Doyle's were killed during World War I, but the hardest blow was when his wife's brother, Malcolm Leckie, joined the list. He believed that he had received at a séance a very personal message from Leckie, an emotional experience which caused him to write: "It is absolute lunacy, or it is a revolution in religious thought —a revolution which gives us an immense consolation when those who are dear to us pass behind the veil."

The writing of science fiction was now forgotten. Sherlock Holmes became only an infrequent, irksome task. Doyle threw himself wholeheartedly into the cause of spiritualism. Books with titles like *The New Revelation, The Vital Message, Wanderings of a Spiritualist* poured from his pen. When no one would publish them, he paid the cost himself. He traveled widely, preaching the new religion and devoting his energies to defending its adherents. In a ten-year period he spent well over a million dollars for the cause. This took such curious turns as *The Coming of the Fairies*, published by George H. Doran in 1922, in which, in photos and text, Doyle lent his name to championing the physical existence of the "little people."

It is questionable if Doyle would have returned to science

fiction again had it not been for Hollywood. *The Lost World*, made into a motion picture and distributed in 1925, starred such prominent screen personalities as Wallace Beery, Lewis Stone, and Bessie Love. The prehistoric monsters, recreated for the screen, were masterfully done, and the public took the film to their hearts.

The year the film was released Doyle fans were electrified to learn that *The Strand* would feature a new Professor Challenger novel, the longest one yet, *The Land of the Mist*. They might have been justifiably uneasy had they known that the pre-publication title of the novel had been *The Psychic Adventures of Edward Malone*.

As it was, dismay was widespread when reading revealed that Challenger, now somewhat older and a widower, receives a message from his departed wife from the spirit world (much in the same manner as Doyle was contacted by Malcolm Leckie) and is converted to spiritualism. The characterization is as splendid as ever and the novel has some poignant moments, even though the body of the story is episodic and tarnished by preachments.

The appearance of *The Maracot Deep* as a four-part novel, beginning in the October 8, 1927, issue of *The Saturday Evening Post*, indicated a renewal of Doyle's interest in the writing of science fiction. A new scientific hero, Professor Maracot, was created and Atlantis rediscovered. There are elements of good storytelling, but the scientific premise of the tale again is marred by the introduction of spiritualism.

However, it may quite possibly have inspired Stanton A. Coblentz to write *The Sunken World*, which appeared in *Amazing Stories Quarterly*, Summer 1928. One scene in the novel, a battle of wills between Maracot and Baalseepa, lord of the dark, is duplicated in *Below the Infra Red*, by George Paul Bauer, which appeared in the December 1927 issue of *Amazing Stories*.

Two other Professor Challenger stories were to follow and these were collected into a book with *The Maracot Deep* in 1929, less than a year before Doyle's death. The shorter one,

The Disintegration Machine, deals with a man who invents a device for dissolving solids into atoms and threatens to sell it to a foreign power. Professor Challenger disposes of the problem by dissolving the inventor with his own machine. The story is as weak as it sounds.

The other, a novelette, *When the World Screamed*, is something else again. In it, Professor Challenger drills a deep tunnel into the bowels of the earth and causes all the live volcanoes on the planet to erupt simultaneously and an earth-shaking scream of pain to issue forth when a giant drill pierces a soft, membranous substance eight miles beneath the surface, thereby proving that our planet is one gigantic living creature covered by a hardened crust.

Though the tale barely escapes being facetious, the strong originality and adroit handling of its concept make it the best of the later Challenger stories. It seemed to indicate that Doyle was recapturing his old ability as a master craftsman in the genre.

Doyle had written no Sherlock Holmes stories since the appearance of *The Case-Book of Sherlock Holmes* in 1927. His last important contributions to science fiction date from that year. Twice before he had been on the verge of establishing himself as a master of prophetic fiction: first in 1894, when he was forgivably detoured by the unexpectedly overwhelming reception of Sherlock Holmes, then again in 1915, before family tragedies diverted him to spiritualism. His last creative achievements in the field were destined to be stopped by his death, which occurred on July 7, 1930.

Most of the world would never know that Doyle carried with him to the beyond two fascinating secrets. First, he had been Sherlock Holmes in real life, actually solving famous crimes by the methods Watson described in the "Sacred Writings." Second, Professor Challenger was merely an uninhibited version of himself. As far as he was concerned, it was a good joke to let everyone go on believing that it had all been just fiction.

11

TO BARSOOM AND BACK WITH
EDGAR RICE BURROUGHS

"*Tarzan, Lord of the Jungle,* is the great romance of the present day, surpassing in its popular appeal even the *She* and *King Solomon's Mines* of Rider Haggard's yesterday and the *Twenty Thousand Leagues Under the Sea* of Jules Verne's days before that," wrote editors Edwin Balmer and Donald Kennicott in the November 1927 issue of *Blue Book Magazine.*

"The touch of the great romances of tradition . . . is in *Tarzan,*" they continued. ". . . The reader feels himself also partly the writer. He himself joins in the story-telling and calls upon his own imagination to share in the delightful business of creating romance. And that's just about the best fun there is."

Edgar Rice Burroughs, principally as a result of his creation

of the by now almost mythical character Tarzan, far out-
stripped Jules Verne, H. Rider Haggard, and H. G. Wells in
catching public favor. Some of the Tarzan novels qualify
rather obviously as science fiction—*Tarzan and the Ant Men*
and *Tarzan at the Earth's Core* to name two—but the spirit
of science fiction underlies the entire series.

It is not necessary to rely upon borderline elements in the
Tarzan series to establish Burroughs' reputation in the science
fiction world. The first novel Burroughs ever wrote was an
interplanetary tale—*Dejah Thoris, Princess of Mars*. It was
literally a transcription on paper of daydreams engaged in by
the author to divorce himself from the cold failures of his
everyday life. When he coupled to this daydreaming his born
gift of storytelling, these same fantasies were to act to make
more bearable the problems of others.

Thomas Newell Metcalf, editor of *All-Story*, bought that
first novel, which he retitled *Under the Moons of Mars* and
ran as a six-part serial, beginning in the February 1912 number of his monthly. For the only time in his life, Burroughs
used a pen name. *Under the Moons of Mars* bore the by-line
"Norman Bean," a typesetter's corruption of "Normal Bean,"
with which Burroughs had intended to imply that though
the story was mad the author was not.

So we see that Edgar Rice Burroughs' earliest dreams were
centered on a world forty million miles beyond ours, Mars,
whose red disk at the turn of the century had become a
favorite topic of astronomical discussion. The impetus for this
interest was provided by Professor Percival Lowell's famous
book, *Mars As an Abode of Life*. In that book, Lowell advanced the hypothesis that Mars was probably a much older
world than ours, and that at one period in the past it may
have supported a high order of civilization. That the so-called
canals were actually artificial waterways created by highly
intelligent creatures, was, of course, his major premise.

Burroughs' Martian novels, for eleven of them followed
that first one, are framed against the background of a planet

in decadence, where the great civilization of the past has given way to hundreds of diverse cultures, the product of a variety of semihuman tribal groupings, who carry on a sense-less, violent, and never-ending struggle against one another as a way of life. It is a world where savagery and science live side by side and where the strength of a man's swordarm counts for as much as the achievements of science in the struggle for survival and power.

It might seem a bizarre world, if it did not bear a satiric resemblance to the one we live in. The endless contest of strength and cunning in Burroughs' Mars is no more point-less and illogical than the military history of mankind, or adventures of Ulysses. In fact, Burroughs' science fiction is a direct descendant of the travel tale typified by the *Odyssey*. It is the traditional romance brought up to date with the addition of a few modern scientific trimmings.

This variety of science fiction has become known as "scien-tific romance." In such stories, colorful adventure of the classical kind is seasoned with just enough science to lend wonder and enchantment to the background and locale. Edgar Rice Burroughs was to become the acknowledged mas-ter of the scientific romance, and the rousing enthusiasm that greeted his first novel was to usher in the golden era of escape science fiction. Indeed, the scientific romance was to domi-nate science fiction until the appearance in 1926 of the first magazine devoted specifically to science fiction and to remain a factor for ten years beyond that date.

The arrival of Edgar Rice Burroughs on the scene eclipsed the rising star of George Allan England. England's novel, *The Elixir of Hate*, published in *The Cavalier* in 1911, was already regarded as a classic. The theme, a man gradually growing younger until he becomes a child, was given master-ful treatment by the author.

Almost concurrently with the appearance of Burroughs' first Mars novel, *Cavalier* ran George Allan England's master-piece, *Darkness and Dawn*, as a four-part serial, beginning in the January 1912 number.

This was truly a memorable work, presenting a grim picture of a man and a woman who awaken after a period of suspended animation to find the entire world in ruins. Apparently only degenerate half-human creatures survive. Though tarnished in spots by plush rhetoric verging on the rococo, the documentary style and graphic spots of realism make reading *Darkness and Dawn* a fascinating experience, even though the plot, development, and even the fragments of political idealism that creep in are all clearly derived from H. G. Wells's *The Time Machine.*

Together with its two sequels, *Beyond the Great Oblivion* and *The Afterglow*, this novel was published under the title of *Darkness and Dawn* by Small, Maynard and Co., Boston, in 1914. The trilogy, which is today one of the most desirable of all science fiction collector's items, proved popular enough to warrant a number of editions.

George Allan England went on to write other popular novels for *All-Story Cavalier Weekly*, including the highly imaginative *The Empire in the Air* and *The Fatal Gift*. But though *The Flying Legion*, *The Golden Blight*, and *The Air Trust* were soon to follow in hard covers, he never attained more than a fraction of the universal popularity of Edgar Rice Burroughs.

There were a number of reasons for this. First, Burroughs *completely* divorced the reader from association with reality, and carried him off to a never-never world of his own creating. Second, Burroughs was a natural storyteller. His style never jarred. It flowed along, quickly and smoothly, catching the reader up in the spell of the story. Rarely was the reader called upon to think. Whatever "messages" appeared in the story were essential to the narrative, there was no sermonizing, no separation of theme, no clearly didactic pointing out of lessons to be learned.

Burroughs had an unsurpassed sense of pace, and his ability to keep several situations moving simultaneously, coupled with his mastery of the flashback technique, established him as an authentic literary craftsman.

And by far most important, Burroughs could make characters come full-bodily alive from the page, and achieve a maximum of reader identification. This was impressively evident in his initial Mars novel, where first-person narration offered easy identification with John Carter, enabling the reader to share closely with him wondrously thrilling and romantic adventures. Particularly vivid is the memorable scene in the Mars air-manufacturing plant, the fate of the entire planet resting upon the telepathic ability of John Carter to open the doors and permit a Martian to crawl in and restart the stalled air machinery.

This talent for apt characterization was to provide a firm foundation for Burroughs' fame. He would have been a successful author if he had written the Mars stories alone. But the creation of the character Tarzan in *Tarzan of the Apes*, his second published novel, which appeared in the October 1912 issue of *All-Story*, elevated him to literary greatness and world renown.

According to Alva Johnson, in his article *Tarzan, or How to Become a Great Writer*, published in the July 29, 1939 issue of *The Saturday Evening Post*, Rudyard Kipling was a great fan of the Tarzan stories, believing that they were inspired by his own *Jungle Tales*.

If the influence of any writer can be strongly discerned in the theme and style of *Tarzan of the Apes*, it would seem to be that of Kipling. But Burroughs stoutly and vigorously denied this. He has been quoted as saying: "I started my thoughts on the legend of Romulus and Remus who had been suckled by a wolf and founded Rome, but in the jungle I had my little Lord Greystoke suckled by an ape."

Characterization in Burroughs' novels was not confined to the lead character. Read a Tarzan story and the very lions, leopards, elephants, apes, and monkeys come to life as distinct personalities in their own right. The effect is heightened by giving the jungle creatures names and identifying their peculiarities. There was the female ape who mothered Tarzan, Kala, and her mate, Tublat. They even had family quarrels over raising Tarzan. Numa was the lion and Sabor the lioness, Histah the great snake, and Tantor the elephant. Through the magic of Burroughs' pen, all come into being as three-dimensional fictional people.

Of the literature mankind has ever produced from its imagination, only Sherlock Holmes is nearly as well known as Tarzan. And *Tarzan of the Apes* is a great and fabulous adventure epic. The development of the story is inspired. The young English couple who are cast away on the shores of the Dark Continent . . . the child who is born to them in a primitive cabin . . . their deaths . . . the female ape, Kala, who finds and raises the child with all the patience and love of a human mother . . . the self-education of the ape-boy Tarzan as he grows to manhood . . . his encounters with human beings . . . his love for the American girl Jane Porter and, finally, his act of self-sacrifice when he steps aside to let William Cecil Clayton, a British nobleman, marry her, add up to one of the world's great romances, which ends with his rival for the girl asking:

> "If it's any of my business, how the devil did you ever get into the bally jungle?"
> "I was born there," said Tarzan, quietly. "My mother was an Ape, and of course she couldn't tell me much about it. I never knew who my father was."

This was no corn, no Pollyanna-ish cliché. The hero does not get the girl. The novel ends on a realistic and powerful back-to-earth note. As a concession to readers, Tarzan does get Jane at the end of the sequel, *The Return of Tarzan*, but the artistry of the first story remains unimpaired.

With *All-Story* readers of *Under the Moons of Mars* frantic about whether the atmosphere plant on Mars had been put back into operation in time to save the planet, Burroughs wrote a sequel, *Gods of Mars*. It was signed with his own name this time and ran for five monthly installments, beginning in the January 1913 issue of the magazine.

After learning that Mars had been saved, the readers sat

back to revel in an even more enthralling series of adventures which culminated in a cliff-hanger of movie-serial intensity. The book ends with Dejah Thoris, queen of Helium, most beautiful woman of the planet Mars and beloved wife of John Carter, trapped in a revolving chamber with two other women, Thuvia and Phaidor.

The chamber, which revolves deep in the earth and permits entrance for only one day in a Martian year—almost twice as long as our terrestrial year—moves out of sight as Phaidor, who has developed a jealous passion for Carter, dagger in hand, lunges at Dejah Thoris. Thuvia bravely attempts to slip between them. As the chapter, and the book, ends, the chamber closes and John Carter will not know for an entire Martian year whether his beloved has died under the knife of her murderous assassin.

Burroughs' first Mars novel, published in 1912, brought him less than a third of a cent per word, or $400. His second Mars novel, published a year later and shortly after *Tarzan of the Apes*, brought many times that sum. Before the appearance of his first hard-cover book, *Tarzan of the Apes*, published by A. C. McClurg in 1914, he was earning twenty thousand a year from magazine sales alone.

Tarzan of the Apes proved a runaway best-seller, accounting for almost a million book sales under the McClurg imprint and many others when it went into A. L. Burt and Grosset & Dunlap lower-priced reprints. These rewards came to Burroughs after he had attempted a score of jobs and businesses and considered himself a complete failure.

Edgar Rice Burroughs was born in Chicago, September 1, 1875. His father, a manufacturer of electric batteries, sent him to a number of private schools. He flunked entrance exams for West Point and gave up hope of a military career. At the age of twenty-five he married Emma Centennia Hulbert and went to work in his father's battery plant at fifteen dollars a week. In the next ten years he tried a succession of jobs and enterprises, including clerk, cowboy, railroad policeman, gold miner, and shop-owner. He failed likewise at a series of selling jobs but he is said to have ghost-written a book, shortly before he made his first fiction sale, on how to be a success in business.

The fact that he did not make his mark until the age of thirty-five has been pointed to by Burroughs as proof of his ineptness in business matters. The facts do not bear him out. It is doubtful if any writer in the history of literature earned more money than Burroughs. Before his death, he admitted to having assembled an estate worth over ten million.

The adroitness with which he merchandised his products, successfully obtaining magazine, book, reprint, newspaper syndicate, radio, cartoon, and motion-picture sales for the greater part of them, in addition to the new Tarzan movies released annually, indicated business ability of the highest order. While he never undersold himself he never priced himself out of the market either. He was an easy man to do business with, agreeing without pressure to changes deemed necessary to adapt his work to various media.

An editor could revise a Burroughs story for magazine publication and never hear a word of complaint from the author. However, the hard-cover edition would always contain Burroughs' original version. A comparison of hard cover with magazine versions of his stories reveals few instances where the editor was right in tinkering with the proven formula of a superlative storyteller who, in the final analysis, knew better what the public wanted than any other writer—or editor—of the first half of the twentieth century.

With the publication of *Tarzan the Invincible* in 1931, he formed his own publishing company, Edgar Rice Burroughs, Inc., situated in Tarzana, California, a town named after his most famous character. Though it was begun during a period of bitter national economic depression, the venture proved well starred. Burroughs was to demonstrate that he was a better businessman than his previous publishers when, in 1949, he reissued ten of the Tarzan series to which he owned book rights, plus the entire Mars and Venus series, as one dollar reprints.

Other publishers, following the fashion of literary thought prevalent at the period, claimed that the mood of the times had left such works behind. As orders poured into Tarzana, Burroughs, almost with a humble note of astonishment, told a reporter for *Writer's Digest*, "The books are selling better than ever."

The Gods of Mars was followed in 1913 by *The Cave Girl*, a Jack Londonish novel in which a skinny, overprotected Bostonian is stranded on a Pacific Island where a primitive cave culture still exists. Casting off the veneer of civilization, he rebuilds himself into a Tarzan-like character, survives, and wins for his mate a beautiful cave girl. *A Man Without a Soul*, which was first published in *All-Story* in 1913 and later appeared in trade book form as *The Monster Men* (1929), deals with the creation of synthetic humans through the use of tissue-culture. It is unquestionably one of the pioneer stories of its type and Burroughs later used the theme in *The Synthetic Men of Mars*, first published in *Argosy*, January 7 to February 1, 1939, in four weekly installments.

The skillfully executed *The Eternal Lover*, a tale of a prehistoric man who falls into a state of suspended animation and wakes to find himself on Tarzan's estate in Africa, was Burroughs' first offering for 1914, and was followed a month later by *At the Earth's Core*, the novel which began the Pellucidar series. This exciting story, first published in *All-Story Weekly*, April 4 to April 25, in four weekly installments, postulated that the center of the earth was hollow, and its interior another world—heated and lighted by the molten core of the earth which hung suspended like a sun at its center. It was an ideal setting for marvelous adventure and Burroughs was eventually to write six sequels: *Pellucidar* (*All-Story Cavalier Weekly*, May-June 1915), *Tanar of Pellucidar* (*Blue Book*, March-April 1929), *Tarzan at the Earth's Core*, *Back to the Stone Age*, *The Land of Terror*, and *The Return to Pellucidar*. *The Land of Terror* has appeared only in book form and is one of the rarest of all Burroughs novels. *The Return to Pellucidar* appeared as three complete short stories in *Amazing Stories*, the title story February 1942, *Men of the Bronze Age* March 1942, and *Tiger Girl* April 1942. It has not appeared as a book.

The magazine publishers could not gainsay the monumental popularity of Burroughs' work. Until the advent of Burroughs, the influence of Jules Verne and H. G. Wells was primary in the development of the field. In England, George Griffith, taking a more adventurous tack, but still predominantly guided by Verne's logical method, had turned out interplanetaries like *A Honeymoon in Space*; future war stories such as *The Angel of the Revolution, Olga Romanoff,* and *The Stolen Submarine*; a prediction of weather control in *The Great Weather Syndicate*; future air stories like *The Outlaws of the Air,* and a score of other science fiction and fantasy volumes. His popularity was limited primarily to Britain, but there it was extremely great, his better books going into a number of editions.

In addition to George Allan England, America had the popular astronomer, Garrett P. Serviss, writing with a note of scrupulous scientific accuracy his sequel to Wells's *War of the Worlds*, titled *Edison's Conquest of Mars*; his famous interplanetary *The Columbus of Space*; the swashbuckling saga *The Sky Pirates*, and, most praised of all, *The Second Deluge*, probably the greatest science fiction novel yet written based on the biblical story of the Great Flood.

Both of these men took the scientific progress of the present and convincingly extrapolated from it, trying to keep from straying too far from what was theoretically possible. Their tales took place in the world as we know it and, given certain postulates, might conceivably occur. Burroughs diverged sharply from their method. He divorced the reader completely from problems. His background, while made acceptable by his own brand of artistry was no more real than L. Frank Baum's Land of Oz. His aim was to provide pleasure through complete escape, and he succeeded.

Charles B. Stilson was one of the first to follow Burroughs' lead, offering his trilogy, which began in the December 18,

1915 issue of *All-Story Weekly* with *Polaris—of the Snows*, and continued with *Minos of Sardanes* and *Polaris and the Goddess Glorian*. The never-never land of Stilson was a volcanic valley in the antarctic, and his hero Polaris is a Tarzan in his own right. It must be pointed out that the mark of George Allan England is also to be found in the style and treatment of Stilson, as well as in many of the other scientific romanticists.

Austin Hall, a writer capable of writing science fiction in the tradition of Verne or scientific romance à la Burroughs, was the next to follow, thrilling his *All-Story* magazine readers with *The Rebel Soul, Almost Immortal*, and, in collaboration with Homer Eon Flint, *The Blind Spot*.

J. U. Giesy, who had been writing scientific detective stories, science fiction pranks, and other oddments, turned to the scientific romance in 1918 with *Palos of the Dog Star Pack* and went on to the popular sequels, *Mouthpiece of Zitu* and *Jason, Son of Jason*.

From that period on there was a veritable flood of strong talent attempting to cut cloth to the pattern. Most of the authors are so famous that little elaboration is required here. The great A. Merritt belongs to the group as does atom-explorer Ray Cummings, Victor Rousseau, Ralph Milne Farley, Otis Adelbert Kline (who most closely imitated Burroughs), Francis Stevens, and, to a limited extent, Murray Leinster and Garrett Smith. Innumerable others also made more or less regular excursions into the realm of the scientific romance, contributing their bit to an era of memorable scientific enchantments.

The critics, judging Edgar Rice Burroughs by absolute literary standards, have never been kind. They have pointed out that his plots are repetitious and his prose often hasty, with an overwhelming emphasis on action and violence and a seemingly pointless procession of incidents rather than a completely co-ordinated whole. Most sternly they condemn the lack of significance for our times in the themes forming the essential framework of his efforts.

Burroughs never denied the charges and with almost a note of apology explained that it was his purpose to write for those who desired entertainment and escape, that he expected his works to be judged by that standard. He noted that his books were clean without being prudish and while he did not know if they had potentialities for good, he was sure that no one had been harmed by them. The near-farce of 1962, when a western school board banned and then reinstated the Tarzan books on the ground that Tarzan and Jane were never legally married might have amused Burroughs, though precision requires noting that he carefully had married them.

The truth is somewhat removed from either the viewpoint of the critics or Burroughs' claims. As to literary worth, it seems likely that *Tarzan of the Apes*, at least, will be printed and read long after many books "with pointed messages for our times" have been forgotten.

As food for thought: Burroughs did try to convey a message of social import on many significant subjects. *The Mucker*, published in *All-Story* in 1914, deals with the influence of environment on character. Billy Byrne was Burroughs' Studs Lonigan, raised on the rough West Side of Chicago. "There was scarce a bartender who Billy did not know by his first name . . . he knew the patrolman and plainclothesmen equally as well, but not so pleasantly."

For at least half its length *The Mucker* is a revelation of the power Burroughs was capable of commanding when dealing with grim realism instead of escape. *The Girl from Hollywood*, originally published in *Munsey's Magazine* from June to November, 1922, is a straight-from-the-shoulder exposé of drug addiction in the film capital; *The Oakdale Affair*, which first appeared in *Blue Book* for March 1918, forcefully dramatizes the author's disgust at mob violence and lynching; *The Girl from Farris's* (*All-Story Weekly*, September 23 to October 14, 1916) has as its central theme prostitution; *The Efficiency Expert*, from *Argosy-All Story*, October 8 to 29, 1921, is a prototype of the novel of behind-the-scenes-doings in big business, along lines of the much-later *Executive Suite*;

and *The Outlaw of Torn* (*New Story*, January to May 1914) is as carefully researched a historical novel of the age of chivalry as you are likely to read anywhere.

All of which proves that Burroughs was far from being a writer without social conscience. It was simply that he discovered that other authors could play that role with greater impact than he. To refuse to recognize that fact and waste the great talent he possessed for entertaining millions would have been pointless.

Absolute literary standards apart, judged by their own standards, two Burroughs novels are most frequently nominated by science fiction devotees as established classics. Those two are *The Moon Maid*, a trilogy collected into a single book in 1926, and *The Land That Time Forgot*, another trilogy which appeared as a single volume in 1924.

The means of interplanetary travel in the early novels of Mars were so ill-defined as to border on the mystical, but in *The Moon Maid* the Mars of John Carter supplies earth by radio with the plans for constructing a spaceship which functions on reaction principles. Led by a renegade earthman, the people of the moon invade and devastate the earth. Primitive earth societies evolve in the wilderness and, eventually, the descendants of the Americans drive the moon men from the North American continent. Though some of the science is dated today, the scenes depicting the reconstruction of civilization are superbly conceived.

The Land That Time Forgot tells of the discovery of a giant island in the South Pacific where prehistoric creatures still survive. There are also seven species of human beings, in various stages of evolutionary development. In a single lifetime, each of these creatures evolves from a point a little higher than the ape to humanity, comparable to modern man. This concept is highly original, and most other elements of the book are as well thought out and effectively developed.

Burroughs' early Martian stories all went into hard cover. *Under the Moons of Mars* became *A Princess of Mars*, to be followed by *The Gods of Mars*, *The Warlord of Mars*, *The*

Chessmen of Mars, and *Thuvia, Maid of Mars.* All were rollicking, swashbuckling scientific romances in the grand tradition. None displayed too careful a regard for scientific accuracy until the appearance of *The Master Mind of Mars.* This novel was first published complete in *Amazing Stories Annual,* 1927.

The title and the author's name were featured on the cover in larger letters than the magazine's own title. *Amazing Stories Annual* was intended to test the feasibility of publishing a companion to *Amazing Stories* and a big name was needed to help put it over. Gernsback had previously reprinted *The Land That Time Forgot* in *Amazing Stories* and claimed that all he did to obtain *The Master Mind of Mars* was to write Burroughs asking him for a novel with some good scientific thought behind it.

Except for the opening scene, where the story's hero, Ulysses Paxton, is *wished* to Mars, the inventions and machinations of Ras Thavas, Martian scientific genius, are meticulously described. The novel also contains surprising philosophical passages. It is difficult to believe that Burroughs wrote this novel specially for Gernsback, yet it is even harder to conceive of *Argosy—All-Story* or *Blue Book* rejecting it merely because it was more thoughtful than the others. Certainly not *Blue Book,* which during this very period thought nothing of giving *six* covers, one for each installment, for a serialization of an Edgar Rice Burroughs novel—which occurred not once but several times. It was in *Blue Book* that the majority of Burroughs' novels were printed in their first magazine appearance. What is probably close to the truth is that Burroughs, a good businessman and skillful professional, would not decline a good offer from anyone and would write to order for a guaranteed sale.

The writing of the Venus novels with Carson Napier as that watery world's heroic counterpart of John Carter came about through a literary rivalry. Otis Adelbert Kline, who had written for early issues of *Weird Tales* and *Amazing Stories,* had watched Burroughs' rise with undisguised admiration. He attempted to get on the bandwagon with a facile imitation of Burroughs' style and method in *The Planet of Peril*, a novel serialized in 1929 by *Argosy*, with Venus as its locale. Readers' raves resulted in a sequel, *The Prince of Peril*, which appeared in 1930.

Impressed by their popularity, A. C. McClurg & Co., Chicago, put the novels into hard covers immediately following magazine publication. Grosset & Dunlap issued low-priced editions soon afterward. Both of these companies had been Burroughs' traditional publishers, but he had gone to the newly formed Metropolitan Books, Inc., New York, in 1929, with *Tarzan and the Lost Empire*. Their action may have been a result of this move, or possibly, Burroughs, piqued by the scheduling of a competitive kind of novel, had withdrawn his books in retaliation.

This did not end the matter. A simulation of Tarzan by Kline appeared as *Tam, Son of the Tiger* in *Weird Tales* in 1931. So substantial was Kline's popularity at the time that the rumor prevailed that *Tam, Son of the Tiger* saved *Weird Tales*, which had gone bimonthly, from extinction and restored it to monthly publication. Adding insult to injury, Kline ran still *another* carbon copy of Tarzan, *Jan of the Jungle*, in *Argosy* the same year.

Stung into action, Burroughs launched a counter-invasion, setting his *Pirates of Venus*, his next novel, in Kline's territory, The Evening Star. It arrived at the editorial offices of *Argosy* just as they were evaluating a new Kline novel, *Buccaneers of Venus*. Caught on the horns of a dilemma, the editors of *Argosy* decided in favor of the more famous name, Edgar Rice Burroughs, especially since his Venus story, in thrills, action, and characterization, was at the top of his form.

Filled with righteous indignation, Kline, now forced to peddle his jilted Venus novel to *Weird Tales* at a lower rate, came back with a haymaker, turning out a novel of the Red Planet, *The Swordsman of Mars*, which was *Argosy's* lead-off serial of the year. Burroughs thundered back with *Lost on*

Venus, a sequel to *Pirates of Venus,* which was the equal of his first, and Kline then countered with another Mars story, *The Outlaws of Mars.*

From an entertainment standpoint there seemed little to choose between them, but from the aspect of economics, Kline was unable to get further book publication for his Venus and Mars stories, while Burroughs, who had formed his own publishing company, was parlaying every blow of the feud into profits. As far as sales were concerned, Burroughs was still the bigger draw.

The contest continued through 1935, when Kline's popularity began to fade. He was an imitator, and though he was an outstanding one, his success did not rest on solid ground. Burroughs nevertheless continued to grind out Venus stories even after Kline turned his attention away from writing to steering the destinies of other authors as head of The Otis Adelbert Kline Literary Agency.

However, relieved of the pressure of competition, the quality of Burroughs' Venus stories, after the first two, suffered seriously, and they are not among his better works. They consisted of *Carson on Venus* (*Argosy,* 1938), *Slaves of the Fish Men, Goddess of Fire, The Living Dead,* and *War on Venus,* all in *Fantastic Adventures,* the first three in 1941, the last in 1942 (collected as *Escape on Venus,* 1946). *The Wizard of Venus* appeared posthumously in 1964.

Of great interest is the serialization of *Tarzan and the Lion Man* in *Liberty Magazine,* beginning with the November 11, 1933 number. *Liberty,* then one of the three leading weekly slicks, along with *The Saturday Evening Post* and *Collier's,* solicited this story from Burroughs. The style is slick-magazine throughout. The novel is loaded with dialogue, often good dialogue. The sentences are direct and modern and crisp. The book version does not differ from the magazine's— a good bet that it was Burroughs' original.

Considering the fabulous popularity of Tarzan, why did Burroughs bother to write anything else? Of the fifty-nine books published during his lifetime, twenty-four featured Tarzan. Burroughs has been quoted as claiming thirty-five million sales for all of his hard-cover books in North America alone. Of this number, he credited only fifteen million sales to Tarzan. The thirty-five other books accounted for another twenty million sales, an average of better than half a million copies per title. While we know a few to have been "lemons," we can see where his science fiction tales of Mars, Venus, and Pellucidar must have enjoyed greater popularity and profit than is generally believed.

During World War II, though in his sixties, Burroughs served as a war correspondent; the strain resulted in several heart attacks. Ill almost to the point of becoming a semi-invalid, he knew that he did not have long to live. In the foreword to *Llana of Gathol*, probably the best written of all the Martian books—it was published just before his death in March 1950—John Carter, the character who first brought his creator success, reappears to Burroughs. Here is the episode in the author's own words:

> ". . . I never expected to see you again."
>
> "No, I never expected to return."
>
> "Why have you? It must be something important."
>
> "Nothing of Cosmic Importance," he said, smiling, "but important to me, nevertheless. You see, I wanted to see you."
>
> "I appreciate that," I said.
>
> "You see, you are the last of my earthly kind whom I know personally. Every once in a while I feel an urge to see you and visit with you, and at long intervals I am able to satisfy that urge—as now. After you are dead, and it will not be long now, I shall have no Earthly ties—no reason to return to the scenes of my former life."
>
> "There are my children," I reminded him. "They are your blood kin."
>
> "Yes," he said, "I know; but they might be afraid of me. After all, I might be considered something of a ghost by Earth men."
>
> "Not by my children," I assured him. "They know you quite as well as I. After I am gone, see them occasionally."
>
> He nodded. "Perhaps I shall," he half promised.

12
THE MARVELOUS
A. MERRITT

The weekly adventure fiction magazine *Argosy*, fifty-eight years old in 1938, conducted a poll of its readers to determine the most popular story it had ever published. That story was to be reprinted. *Argosy*, then the most prominent adventure story magazine in the history of the western world, at one time had achieved a greater circulation than any other magazine in America, regardless of type.

The votes pouring in honored a fabulous group of storytellers: Edgar Rice Burroughs, creator of *Tarzan*; Albert Payson Terhune, gifted writer of dog stories; Frank L. Packard, renowned for *The Miracle Man* and his Jimmy Dale series; John Buchan, whose *Thirty-Nine Steps* is a cloak-and-dagger showpiece; James Branch Cabell, author of perhaps the most widely discussed novel of the twenties, *Jurgen*; Howard R. Garis, beloved chronicler of the children's animal favorite,

Uncle Wiggily; Johnston McCulley, whose flashing tales of *Zorro* still thrill on TV; Erle Stanley Gardner, father of Perry Mason and perennially best-selling detective novelist; Gaston Leroux, universally known through the motion-picture versions of *Phantom of the Opera*; Max Brand, one of the truly great writers on the Old West; and Ludwig Lewisohn, whose fiction will probably endure as long as any of our time, to name only a few of the many outstanding authors who made it possible for *Argosy*, in 1938, to "point with pride" to a record of more than seven hundred hard-cover books reprinted from its pages.

The winner was *The Ship of Ishtar* by A. Merritt and the reprinting of that story in six weekly installments began with the October 29 issue of *Argosy*. The ranks of adventure writers, the legions of pulp magazine followers, and, more particularly, the editorial vote-counters were astounded. But to Albert J. Gibney, associate publisher of The Frank A. Munsey Company this evidence of popularity confirmed and justified a top-level *Argosy* decision made many years before.

"We paid A. Merritt the highest word-rate given anyone in the history of the magazine," he revealed in a fascinatingly candid appraisal. "This only proves he was worth it!"

A. Merritt loved writing. It is doubtful if he wrote a single line of fiction with monetary considerations in mind. For twenty-five years he had been right-hand man to Morrill Goddard, editor of *The American Weekly*, a magazine supplement distributed with the Hearst newspapers, its weekly circulation five million copies. Morrill Goddard earned $240,-000 a year in that capacity.

It seems reasonable to suppose that as second man in the organization Merritt also received rather exceptional remuneration. That such was the case was evidenced by a second home in Indian Rock Key, Pinellas County, Florida; a seventy-five-acre experimental farm in Bradenton, Florida, where he raised avocados, mangoes, and litchi, and an experimental farm near Clearwater, where he planted the first olive groves in Florida. He also maintained a hothouse of rare poisonous plants. In 1937 Morrill Goddard died and Merritt became the editor of *The American Weekly*.

Recognition similar to *Argosy's* had been given Merritt by science fiction readers a few years earlier. *Wonder Stories*, under Hugo Gernsback, conducted a survey of its readers to determine the favorite science fiction of their entire reading experience. *The Moon Pool* by A. Merritt headed the list, even though the story had been published in magazine form almost a decade previously and no Merritt stores had ever appeared in *Wonder Stories*.

The first notice science fiction readers had of A. Merritt was his six-thousand-word short story *Through the Dragon Glass*, which appeared in the November 24, 1917 issue of *All-Story*. Merritt's initial effort might have attracted little attention if the cover of that issue had not illustrated a new four-part interplanetary novel, *The Cosmic Courtship*, by Julian Hawthorne, son of Nathaniel Hawthorne.

Lured by the promise of Hawthorne's cosmic romance, science fiction readers found themselves considerably more enthralled by Merritt's brief fantasy of Herndon, who raided the Imperial Palace of Peking during the Boxer rebellion and came away with a green stone on which were carved twelve dragons with emerald eyes.

Herndon passes through this stone into another world, where seven artificial moons revolve perpetually around a mist-shrouded valley walled with fire. There he meets the maiden Santhu and is attacked by a winged beast, whose master hunts him as a quarry in a cruel and ingenious game. Badly clawed, he escapes from the Dragon Glass, to pass through a second time with an elephant gun. He never returns.

The next tale from Merritt's typewriter was bona fide science fiction. The January 5, 1918 issue of *All-Story* carried *The People of the Pit*. This story of an Alaskan explorer who discovers a stairway leading down into a volcanic crater, at the bottom of which exists a strange city inhabited by ten-tacled, transparent, snail-like monstrosities who float in the air and exert a powerful psychological influence upon him, is a polished masterpiece. It is sometimes condescending to state that a work is worthy of Edgar Allan Poe, but had Poe written *The People of the Pit* it would today be held up as one of the brightest jewels in the diadem of masterpieces which crown his genius.

Fame was not to come to Merritt the hard way. He would not have to build a tremendous literary pyramid to show above his contemporaries. One more novelette, *The Moon Pool*, published in *All-Story* for June 22, 1919, and letters by the hundreds began to pour across the desk of Robert H. Davis, the Munsey editor who had discovered Merritt.

The master touch in the highly individualistic prose so conspicuously evident in *The People of the Pit* was repeated in *The Moon Pool*. The concept of a pool of force created by the vibrational pattern of seven different lights, the transfer mechanism from the earth's surface to some strange realm below, and "The Shining One," an alien entity of radiant matter which acted as a guide between worlds, fired the imagination, arousing a clamor for a sequel which could not be ignored.

Bob Davis, who had felt that fifty dollars a story had been generous pay for Merritt's shorter work, dangled forty times that sum if he would write a full-length sequel.

With the publication of only two short stories and a novelette, Merritt had become the "hottest" writer in science fiction. Merritt represented the furthest extreme that the scientific romance—ushered into phenomenal popularity when Edgar Rice Burroughs' *Under the Moons of Mars* delighted the *All-Story* readership of 1912—was to go. Much of Merritt was then, and would continue to be, sheer fantasy. His stories, which because of their scientific aspects—never obtrusively introduced—qualified as science fiction, were, in mood and spirit, fantasy. Like Burroughs, Merritt's intent was solely to entertain.

Son of Quaker parents, Abraham Merritt was born January 20, 1884, in Beverley, New Jersey, a small community near Philadelphia. Merritt, in his youth, had a predilection for the law. He attended lectures at the University of Pennsylvania but was mostly self-educated. Family finances compelled him to abandon law, and at the age of nineteen he obtained a reporting job with the *Philadelphia Inquirer*. That first job was the turning point of his life.

As a cub reporter he was eyewitness to an event—the nature of which he assiduously kept secret—which was to have serious political implications. To avoid repercussions and to prevent young Abe Merritt from "spilling the beans," he was prevailed upon by parties unknown to leave the country, all of his expenses paid.

The following year, spent in Mexico and Central America, made a deep and permanently lasting impression on Merritt. As a youth he had been profoundly influenced by the physician-novelist S. Weir Mitchell, who had encouraged free inquiry into folklore and odd phenomena. Reading Dr. Charles Euchariste de Médicis Sajous, renowned for his pioneer studies into the functions of the ductless glands, taught him a respect for science and the scientific method. Both of these intellectual fevers he fed at the "sacred well" of Chichén Itzá; he explored the Mayan city of Tulum, hunted treasure in Yucatán, and underwent rites by which he became the blood-brother of an Indian tribe in Miraflores.

When the heat lifted, he returned to the *Philadelphia Inquirer* and eventually became night city editor. Veteran companion journalists James J. O'Neill and Colonel George Kennedy remembered him as a "superlative" newspaperman whose flair for vividly covering executions, murders, suicides, hangings, and at least one lynching, was unsurpassed.

Never able to harden himself, Merritt drank himself into restfulness after events of violence. This wholesale contact with the more gruesome and soul-sickening aspects of life was later compensated for by escape into fantasy.

His work as Philadelphia correspondent for Morrill Goddard, editor of *The Sunday Supplement* of the Hearst newspapers, resulted in an offer which brought him to New York in 1912 and a lifetime career on the publication which was to evolve into *The American Weekly*.

Always a six-day-a-week job during Goddard's reign, life on *The American Weekly*, while well paid, permitted a young writer little time for side ventures. Yet, encouraged by the reception of his first stories, Merritt plunged into the writing of his first novel, a sequel to *The Moon Pool* entitled *The Conquest of the Moon Pool*. The reaction that followed the last of the six weekly installments, which had begun in the February 15, 1919 *All-Story*, verged on hysteria.

Speaking of his personal feelings, Edmond Hamilton, veteran science fiction author, echoed the fascination of thousands when he said: "I had a newspaper route about that time and when Merritt's long-awaited sequel to *The Moon Pool* came out, I carried papers one night each week with the *All-Story Magazine* held three inches before my eyes, avoiding automobiles and street-cars by the grace of God, and heaving every paper on the wrong porch."

From the vantage point of the somewhat more sophisticated modern reader, *The Conquest of the Moon Pool* reveals glaring flaws. In contrast to *The Moon Pool* there are sequences that show obvious signs of haste. The movement of events follows the standard pattern of thrillers of an earlier period. The characters of the Moon Pool stories are stereotypes: Larry O'Keefe, the Irishman; Olaf, the Scandinavian; Von Hertzdorf, the treacherous German (who, in a later edition and in different political climate, is converted to Marakinoff, the Russian devil); Lakla, the handmaiden (personification of good), and Yolara, dark priestess of evil.

Along with them are such stock chillers as frog men, dwarf men, and dead-alive men, and the love scenes make no concession to a world climbing out of Victorian prudery.

Yet the novel holds magic for its readers. It is an honest story. It evokes more than a hint of the strangest mysteries, and the imagination of the author never falters in his brilliant preoccupation with the unearthly, the terrifying, and the bizarre. It also promises rich, colorful, heroic action and it keeps that promise. The age-old struggle between good and evil, with the cleavage sharply differentiated, forms the basis of the plot. In this contest, the reader is thrilled by flights of imaginative fantasy equal to the best of H. Rider Haggard.

Greatest victory of all, Merritt transcended the coldness and dehumanization that frequently accompany pure fantasy. His word pictures shape a mood.

Humanity shines from this work. For every stock character there is a brilliantly original one of his own creating. The Shining One, a robot of pure force with fantastic powers, becomes believable as its intelligence acquires humanlike drives of personal pride and desire for achievement and power. The Silent Ones, ageless, godlike men from an ancient civilization which created The Shining One—now aloof and inscrutable—call upon ancient science to thwart the ambitions of this strange thinking force and its dreadful omniscience. When they have destroyed their creation: "No flames now in their ebon eyes—for the flickering fires were quenched in great tears, streaming down the marble white faces."

Basic patterns for other Merritt novels were established in *The Moon Pool*. Later stories would always be built on the conflict of light against darkness. There would always be a beautiful priestess of evil, and the villains would be memorably, brilliantly characterized. Forms which are generally symbols of repulsion—the frog men in *The Moon Pool*, the spider men and the snake women in *The Snake Mother*, Ricori, the gangster in *Burn Witch Burn!*—are converted by literary sorcery into sympathetic and admirable characters.

One of the most impressive aspects of Merritt's success was the period in which it was achieved. Within the space of not much more than a year, the era of the scientific romance, which had begun with Burroughs, had blossomed to its fullest flower. Competing with Merritt for the public's attention, often in the same publications, were a glittering assemblage of fantasy classics by masters of the art. J. U. Giesy had broken new ground only eight months previously with the first of his occult-interplanetary trilogy, *Palos of the Dog Star Pack*. Praise for Victor Rousseau's surgical fantasy, *Draft of Eternity*, still echoes in the readers' departments of magazines. *Citadel of Fear* was the work of Francis Stevens, a woman whose stories displayed such beauty of style and narrative skill that for years it was thought that Merritt had written them under a pen name. *Who Wants a Green Bottle?*, a brilliant effort by the greatly underrated Tod Robbins, had appeared less than three months before *Conquest of the Moon Pool*, on December 31, 1918.

A young man who—forty years later—would earn the title of "The Dean of Science Fiction Writers," Murray Leinster, had an early story, *The Runaway Skyscraper*, in that year's *Argosy*. Max Brand was also making memorable contributions to fantasy with *Devil Ritter*, *John Ovington Returns* and the grisly *That Receding Brow*, which ran in the very same issue, February 15, 1919, as the first installment of *The Conquest of the Moon Pool* in *All-Story Weekly*.

While Merritt's novel was still being serialized, Ray Cummings' *The Girl in the Golden Atom* appeared and clamor arose for a sequel, only slightly less intense than that which had greeted Merritt's *Moon Pool*. *The Planeteer*, *The Lord of Death*, and *The Queen of Life*, the three interplanetary epics that established Homer Eon Flint's reputation, were soon to follow.

Scarcely was Merritt's novel concluded than Austin Hall's imaginative triumph, *Into the Infinite*, was begun. Before the year's end the popular scientific romancer, George Allan England, was to thrill a wide audience with a new novel, *The Flying Legion*.

Blue Book had, a short time previously, published what many believe to be Edgar Rice Burroughs' best story, *The People That Time Forgot*, second in the trilogy *The Land That Time Forgot*. In the same magazine, a brilliant Englishman William Hope Hodgson, increased his reader following with *The Terrible Derelict*. *Argosy* had Garrett Smith with

After a Million Years. On every side, competing for attention were such renowned storytellers as Sax Rohmer, Edison Marshall, Philip M. Fisher, Charles B. Stilson, and Loring Brent.

That Merritt was singled out and accorded unique prestige amidst such a galaxy of fantasy and science fiction favorites reveals how completely he captivated the imagination of the readers, and explains why no one has contested the title conferred on him—A. Merritt: Lord of Fantasy.

Using the battlefields of France as a locale, Merritt next wrote a short story entitled *Three Lines of Old French*, which appeared in the August 9, 1919 issue of *All Story*. The style was an abrupt departure from that of his just-published novel. It was restrained, almost journalistic in tone, but still had about it much of the same hauntingly imaginative quality which had characterized *The People of the Pit* and *The Moon Pool*.

It deals with a surgeon in France who decides to conduct a psychological experiment on a soldier almost paralyzed with battle fatigue and half-hypnotized by strain. The medical man presses a piece of paper in the soldier's hand with a line from a French ballad,

And there she waits to greet him when all his days are done.

Then he passes a sprig of flowers before the man's eyes.

The soldier's subconscious mind accepts these symbols and he is plunged into a fantasy world in which he is carried into the past, to the garden of beautiful Lucie de Tocquelain. He falls in love with her, but rejoicing in the knowledge that there is another life he wills to return so that he can tell his comrades that death is an illusion. Before he leaves, the French lass scribbles three lines on a piece of paper and thrusts it into his pocket.

Emerging from his trance, the soldier is crushed by the realization that it was all an experiment—until he finds the crumpled slip of paper and reads the girl's brief and moving message.

> Nor grieve, dear heart, nor fear the
>   seeming—
> Here is waking after dreaming.
>   She who loves you,
>   Lucie

As a work of art, there is no question that *Three Lines of Old French* would not be out of place in an anthology of outstanding American short stories, even though some of it shows the influence of Robert W. Chambers' *The Demoiselle D'Ys*. A stranger tribute was to be Merritt's reward, however, one similar to that experienced by Arthur Machen when his short story *The Bowmen* appeared in the *London Evening News* for September 29, 1914. Letters began to pour in, particularly from England, praising Merritt and thanking him. Bereaved parents, grasping for a spark of reason in the tragic loss of a loved one in battle had taken hope from Merritt's intimation of a life after death.

The Moon Pool and *The Conquest of the Moon Pool* were combined under the title of the original novelette and issued in hard covers by Putnam in 1919. The book sold well and Liveright later took over the reprint rights. *The Moon Pool* has been constantly in print for forty-one years, selling steadily through prosperity, war, and depression, despite three magazine reprintings and two soft-cover editions in the hundreds of thousands of copies. Never a hard-cover bestseller, it has nevertheless become an established classic of fantasy.

The most controversial work of Merritt's has always been *The Metal Monster*, published as an eight-part serial in *Argosy—All-Story*, beginning with the August 7, 1920 issue. Merritt said of the story: "I have never been satisfied with it. It has some of the best writing in it that I ever did and some of the worst. It has always been a problem child."

The novel is in a sense a sequel to *The Conquest of the Moon Pool*, since one of the lead characters, the narrator Dr. Walter T. Goodwin, appears again, and references are made to incidents in the *Moon Pool* stories. Sensitive to the slightest criticism, Merritt lost confidence in this work when reader reaction proved mixed.

He had let out all the stops on *The Metal Monster*. That it is overwritten, Merritt himself was the first to acknowledge, but far from being a failure it is probably his most successful novel. It begins with this opening passage:

> In this great crucible of life we call the world—in the vaster one we call the universe—the mysteries lie close packed, uncountable as grains of sand on ocean's shores. They thread gigantic the star-flung spaces; they creep, atomic, beneath the microscope's peering eye. They walk beside us, unseen and unheard, calling out to us, asking why we are deaf to their crying, blind to their wonder.

The novel thus immediately strikes a serious philosophical and, later, intellectual note which interpenetrates the action.

Ray Bradbury in his short story, *Forever and the Earth*, tries to imagine how Thomas Wolfe would have described space and other worlds had he put his mind to it or had the opportunity to visit them. Wolfe could hardly have improved on the inspired cosmic passages in which Merritt visualizes a world of metal intelligences hurtling through interstellar space, seeding uncounted worlds with offspring—one of them our earth!

The Metal Monster is the best unified of all Merritt's early novels and the passages delineating the alien concept of sentient, intelligent, metallic life succeed in transmitting a mood of near-belief. A triumph for so difficult a theme.

Three years passed before Merritt completed another work, *The Face in the Abyss*, a 35,000-word short novel. Restraint was evident throughout the narrative, a restraint enlivened by a masterful technique and a bell-like clarity. There were invisible flying snakes, dinosaurs, spider-men, and, most striking of all, a superb characterization of the Snake Mother —part woman, part serpent. The last survivor of an ancient race, she was custodian of secrets and wisdom far in advance of human achievement. All this Merritt projected against the inspired backdrop of a tremendous carven image of an evil face, from which flowed tears of molten gold.

Readers who had reservations as to Merritt's entertainment value, and who had found *The Metal Monster* too much for them, were completely won over by the spell of this new fantasy. With so much hinted at, and so very much left unsaid, *The Face in the Abyss*, which appeared in the September 8, 1923, issue of *Argosy—All-Story*, obviously required a sequel. But Merritt was no longer compelled or disposed to drive himself night and day to turn out inspired follow-ups for fickle audiences. His revenge was incomparable.

He made them wait six years for the sequel! He could hardly have been pressed for time, because two other novels appeared in the interim, but he had apparently ma-le up his mind to write only what he wanted, when he wanted.

Some months after the appearance of *The Face in the Abyss*, Bob Davis received a novelette from Merritt entitled *The Ship of Ishtar*. He returned it to the author, saying it was a shame to cramp so wondrous an idea by confining it to novelette length. Why not expand the basic concept to full novel length?

Merritt tried, but chafed under the task.

He wrote some of the last chapters first as independent episodes, then gradually filled in the gaps between. The novel shows it. The early portion, where the two ends of an ancient ship are separated by a wall of force, is quite clearly a different sort of tale from the central section, which hinges on action adventure, or the final portion, which is composed of a series of superbly wrought literary exercises. Yet consummate craftsmanship is evident in every line and the singing rhythm of the prose carries one along with intense fascination to the very end, despite inadequacies of plot and narrative construction.

This story is not science fiction, even by courtesy. It is sheer fantasy, but a truly remarkable fantasy with at least one chapter—"The King of Two Deaths"—closer to genius than to talent.

The Ship of Ishtar began in *Argosy—All-Story* for November 8, 1924, and ran for six weekly installments. The applause that followed was sincere, as *Argosy's* poll fourteen years later confirmed. But now something new was happening in the science fiction world. Even as the period of the scientific romance blossomed and reached its height, another concept of science fiction was being revived. It challenged the romance written solely for entertainment's sake, and demanded that science fiction incorporate the plausible logic of Edgar Allan Poe and the prophetic vision of Jules Verne to become an expression of man's thirst for knowledge and progress. It was headed by Hugo Gernsback, who, as far back as 1911, in his popular scientific magazine, *Modern Electrics,* had written *Ralph 124C41+,* a true miracle of plausible prophecy.

As his *Modern Electrics* metamorphosed into *Electrical Experimenter* and finally into *Science and Invention,* Gernsback continued to promote science fiction of this type. Shortly after *The Ship of Ishtar* appeared, *Argosy—All-Story* was forced to take cognizance of the new trend by introducing Ralph Milne Farley, with a great hullabaloo about his scientific qualifications and the technical accuracy of his *The Radio Man.*

The immediate success of the first science fiction magazine, *Amazing Stories,* introduced in 1926 by Gernsback with the accent on more science, was the handwriting on the wall for the scientific romance. As high priest of the old order, A. Merritt stood to lose most.

Then a remarkable thing happened. With the entire honor roll of the past to choose from in the field of reprints, with the necessity of selecting stories that most closely typified his ideas imperative, Hugo Gernsback made a startling exception. That exception was A. Merritt. He elected to reprint every science fiction story Merritt had written up to that time —the book version of *The Moon Pool, The Face in the Abyss, The People of the Pit* (twice, once in the monthly and once in *Amazing Stories Annual,* which saw but one issue). Most astonishing of all, he had Merritt revise *The Metal Monster* and ran it as *The Metal Emperor* in *Science and Invention* in eleven monthly installments, from October 1927 through August 1928.

The reading public's response was electric. It was as if Merritt had been discovered for the first time. Readers referred to him as a "genius." Manuscripts from new writers clearly showed his influence and such later well-known names as Jack Williamson and P. Schuyler Miller openly acknowledged their literary debt to him.

The old order would die, and with it most of the "Elder Gods." But Merritt would reign on.

To conquer the specialized new world of the science fiction magazines Merritt had fired a fusillade; the realm of weird-fantasy he toppled with a single shot.

It happened this way. A novelette whose theme symbolized the ages of struggle between man and the forest, *The Woman of the Wood*, was submitted by Merritt to *Argosy—All-Story*. In one of his rare errors of judgment, Bob Davis rejected it as being "plotless." On condition that not a single word be altered, A. Merritt offered it to *Weird Tales*, where it was published in the August 1926 number. Years later, Farnsworth Wright admitted that this hauntingly atmospheric tale of the birch forest which assumed human shape to save itself from destruction was the most popular novelette which *Weird Tales* had ever published. Merritt asserted it was the only story he was completely satisfied with upon completion.

Bent on campaigns of literary imperialism, Merritt next invaded the mystery field with *Seven Footprints to Satan*, a five-part novel beginning in *Argosy—All-Story* for July 2, 1927. Loyal science fiction and fantasy fans were disappointed, but mystery fans were delighted. Built around the sinister figure of a man who calls himself Satan, the novel deals with the activities of a cult formed to play a deadly game where the stakes are fortune or death. With its dozens of unique melodramatic devices and a full retinue of stock ones, the novel was a set-up for Hollywood, and First National had it in movie houses even before the appearance of the Boni & Liveright hard-cover edition in February 1928. Within a month the book had gone through three printings and into a low-priced Grosset & Dunlap reprint, illustrated with stills from the motion picture.

This was heady brew for A. Merritt. Only one year earlier, Putnam had been unable to sell a pitifully small edition of a thousand copies of *The Ship of Ishtar* in book form and the sheets for the last three hundred copies were finally purchased by Munsey, and were bound and distributed to readers of *Argosy—All-Story Magazine*.

For the next three years Merritt rested on his laurels, toying with a new novel he had been picking up and putting down without completing since 1923—*The Fox Woman*. Unable to develop the plot properly he put it aside with only about 15,000 words completed—he never did finish it, but when it was published in 1946 it contained a section written by Hannes Bok titled *The Blue Pagoda* which completed the story—and started work on a sequel to *The Face in the Abyss*.

Seven years had passed since that story had first appeared in *Argosy—All-Story*. With *The Snake Mother* he returned to the long-dropped theme. The title character is the best rounded, most sympathetic, most memorable he ever created, though in this novel, which ran to seven installments beginning in the October 25, 1930 *Argosy*, he fashioned a truly captivating villain—Nimer! Nimer is a disembodied intelligence—evil incarnate—who is able to take over a human body as easily as if he were merely changing to a new suit. The caliber of his strategy and his unquestionable courage, even against formidable odds, make him a figure of irresistible appeal.

A marvelous blend of action, superb characterization, philosophy, poetic prose, involving such elements as atomic powers and the strange Dream Makers (who can fabricate a hypnotic illusion like a story on a motion-picture screen) *The Snake Mother* is an imaginative triumph.

If there had ever been any doubt that Merritt was escaping from the brutalities and injustices of the world in his novels and short stories, it was dispelled by *The Dwellers in the Mirage,* which began in the January 23, 1932 number of *Argosy.* The yellow-haired Leif Langdon is unquestionably the youthful A. Merritt. Tsantawu, the Cherokee, Leif's guide, parallels the Indian who accompanied Merritt during his early sojourn in Mexico. The architecture and surroundings in the fictional land of the mirage are reminiscent of the Mayan ruins he explored.

For many Merritt readers this story is an all-time favorite. The tiny golden people, the nightmarish Kraken, the good and beautiful Evalie, Leif himself (whom all believe to be a reincarnation of Dwayanu, once lord of the hidden valley) are elements unified by the struggles of two women to gain the love of Leif. One, the dark witch woman Lur, believes him to be the reincarnation of Dwayanu, who once loved her and whom she loved in return. The other, Evalie, is the epitome of everything fine, noble, and good in women. In the magazine and book version, Lur, with her faithful white wolf, is killed trying to destroy Evalie. Then Leif takes Evalie back to the outside world.

Laying bare the human temptation and gnawing doubts that haunt all men, the author has Leif reflect:

> "Ai, Lur—Witch-woman! I see you lying there, smiling with lips grown tender—the white wolf's head upon your breast! And Dwayanu still lives within me!"

Abruptly, Merritt then made another switch. With a theme borrowed from Fitz-James O'Brien's *The Wondersmith,* he produced a tale of witchcraft which he originally called *The Dolls of Mme. Mandilip,* but which *Argosy* changed to *Burn Witch Burn!* The novel, which began in the October 22, 1932 number, bears the stamp of a skilled professional as it moves at a breathless pace to unfold the story of a sinister old woman who sends her animated mannikins from a night-shadowed doll house with their poisoned needle-swords to slay her unsuspecting victims. As they had done with *Seven Footprints to Satan*, the film producers quickly seized upon this one, casting Lionel Barrymore in the role of Mme. Mandilip in *The Devil Dolls*.

Creep, Shadow!, commencing in *Argosy* for September 8, 1934, marked the end of Merritt's most productive period. *Creep, Shadow!* is a sequel to *Burn Witch Burn!* This time Merritt dwelt in somber imaginative fashion on the near-lost powers of witchcraft surviving from 10,000 years in the past, implying shadow life and shadow creatures. Where before he was impatient to plunge into his wonder-worlds, now he proceeds deliberately, examining the problem intellectually before increasing the tempo of the action. There are some memorable scenes and fine artistic passages in the novel, but it reveals a Merritt more concerned with the method than the substance of his medium. Though he lived another nine years, Merritt never completed another story, contenting himself with revising his old ones.

Pride in his art remained, but he ceased to dream.

Always gracious toward his admirers, Merritt gave generously of his time to the science fiction fan movement. When *Argosy* begged for something from his pen, he pleaded lack of time, but he presented, as a gift to the editors of *Fantasy Magazine*, a short story, *The Drone*, to commemorate the second anniversary of that fine fan magazine in 1934.

Even in this tiny realm of amateur publication, Merritt was to establish his supremacy. Seventeen authors were asked by the editors of the same magazine to write a chapter each in a round-robin novel, *Cosmos*. Each writer was requested to continue from where another left off, but the chapters had to be complete stories in themselves. The authors were Ralph Milne Farley, David H. Keller, Arthur J. Burks, Bob Olsen, Francis Flagg, John W. Campbell, Jr., Otis Adelbert Kline, E. Hoffman Price, Abner J. Gelula, Raymond A. Palmer, J. Harvey Haggard, Edward E. Smith, P. Schuyler Miller, L. A. Eshbach, Eando Binder, Edmond Hamilton, and Merritt. A vote of the readers established that Merritt's chapter,

"The Last Poet and the Robots," describing how a scientist-poet destroys a world of robots who have rebelled and conquered man, was overwhelmingly the favorite.

Emile Schumacher, a well-known feature writer for *The American Weekly*, returned to New York on Thursday, August 29, 1943, after completing an unusual assignment given him by Merritt, who had now been full editor for some years. He had been sent to secure eyewitness material about a volcano, Paricutín, that had blasted out of a Mexican cornfield to cover seventy-five square miles of surrounding countryside with ash.

"I knew the story would appeal to A. Merritt with his tremendous fondness for the occult," Schumacher said, quite possibly to justify his linking of the mysterious volcano's eruption with the dying curse of an Aztec emperor, which he fabricated from whole cloth. He found Merritt cheerful, but looking tired and haggard and about to fly down to Florida for a rest.

"Have the library dig up a really spectacular photograph of the volcano belching smoke and fire" was the last order that Merritt gave him. "Then I'll have Lee do a portrait drawing of Moctezuma the Second, who mistook the invading Cortés for the fair god Quetzalcoatl of the Aztec legend—a mistake that subsequently proved fatal," he added contemplatively.

The next morning Merritt was dead of a heart attack, suffered at the age of fifty-nine while at Indian Rock Beach, Florida.

His work lives on. Popular Publications, Inc. brought out a periodical—*A. Merritt's Magazine*—so entitled because of his continuing popularity with readers everywhere. It appeared every other month, beginning in December 1949 and ran five issues. No other fantasy author has been so honored.

Avon Publications, publishers of pocket editions, reprinted *all* of his fiction. Edition followed edition for eighteen years. The seven novels and one short story collection sold upward of four million copies, Avon estimated in 1959. *Seven Foot-*

prints to Satan had sold one million copies alone, and *Burn Witch Burn!* 500,000.

"Expensive" paperbacks of Merritt novels were issued in 1962 by two publishers.

Liveright reports that five Merritt novels are still in print and selling steadily in hard covers, despite the pocket book editions. The five are *The Moon Pool, Dwellers in the Mirage, The Face in the Abyss, Seven Footprints to Satan,* and *Burn Witch Burn!*

Abraham Merritt could not have wished for a more appropriate memorial.

13
KAREL ČAPEK:
THE MAN WHO INVENTED ROBOTS

While the passage of the years had given science fiction an unshakable stature as prophecy, and the efforts of Edgar Allan Poe and H. G. Wells had admitted it to the canon of recognized literature, its material had not lent itself readily to theatrical adaptation. Though Mary Shelley's *Frankenstein* enjoyed more than a century of revivals as *Presumption, or the Fate of the Monster*, with script by Richard Brinsley Peake, it scarcely can be treasured as one of the masterpieces of the stage. Nor could the early Tarzan pictures, the several Verne epics, or the Méliès fantasy films be said to have contributed much to dramatic art.

Science fiction as meaningful drama came into its own under the brilliant efforts of Karel Čapek, "father of the Czechoslovakian theater." Together with his brother Josef Čapek, he produced, in the period between World War I

208

and World War II, these science fiction and fantasy plays:
R. U. R., *The Insect Story*, *The Makropoulos Secret*, *Land of
Many Names*, and *Adam the Creator*.

Today there is scarcely a collection of great modern European plays that does not include one of them. Čapek has become the most internationally renowned of all Czech playwrights.

The quality of his plays far exceeds the requirements of dramatic entertainment; the plays distinctly affected the thinking of the western world, and from one of them the word "robot" has entered the language of many nations. Interspersed among his plays were books, three of them science fiction novels which further enhanced his already glittering reputation and which profoundly changed the direction of science fiction.

Karel Čapek was born January 9, 1890, in Male Svatonvici, northern Bohemia, an area then part of Austria-Hungary. The son of a physician, he found means readily available for his education. He studied at Prague, Paris, and Berlin, finally graduating from the University of Prague in 1917.

Philosophically, he was a disciple of the Americans William James and John Dewey, exponents of pragmatism, which regards "the practical consequences and useful results of ideas as the test of their truthfulness, and which considers truth itself to be a process." Čapek's college thesis was written on the subject of pragmatism.

More immediately, Karel Čapek was influenced by the views of his talented brother Josef, born three years earlier, who was to make a reputation as a playwright, fiction writer, artist, producer, scene designer, and art critic. Their attitudes and outlook were so similar that collaborations were extraordinarily successful.

A series of short stories and sketches, some in collaboration with his brother, created Karel Čapek's first literary reputation. They showed so deft a touch in their handling that he deservedly was termed the Czech Chekov. A collection published in 1916, *Luminous Depths*, is of special impor-

tance, for it contains a short story, *L'Éventail*, which utilizes
mechanical dolls much in the manner of E. T. A. Hoffmann.
An even earlier reference to robots may be found in Čapek's
essay, *System*, which appears in in collection, *Krakonos's
Garden*, issued in 1918 but actually written between 1908
and 1911. Obviously the idea of the artificially created man
intrigued Čapek over a period of years.

In his short stories, Čapek openly acknowledges a debt to
Edgar Allan Poe, Oscar Wilde, and Charles Baudelaire. In
·method he was an experimental modernist, at the forefront
of a group of European writers attempting to write what
amounted to impressionistic prose. Readers sampling Čapek
for the first time are frequently startled by the daring, almost
sensational prose. Though his spectacular methods struck a
chord of affinity with the youthful generation, it was his
subject matter and not his style that brought him fame.

Almost without exception his short stories were off-trail,
either in theme or approach. Lovers of the detective story will
find his volume *Wayside Crosses*, published in 1917 and
later translated as *Money and Other Stories*, to be a bitter
but highly original collection of "whodunits" without solu-
tions.

The end of World War I and the creation of the new republic of Czechoslovakia marked the turning point in the
career of Karel Čapek. During the war, Karel, with his brother
Josef, managed a theater in Vinohrady, in what was later to
become Czechoslovakia. With the coming of Czechoslovak
independence on October 28, 1918, the National Theater
became the cultural center of the new nation and Karel
Čapek allied himself with it.

World renown followed unexpectedly and swiftly. The increasing trend toward mechanization, the scientific slaughter
of World War I, and the efficient mass-production methods
of the United States made a profound impression on Čapek.
A modernist in thought and action, he did not feel that the
idea of scientific progress in itself was bad. However, he was

concerned with the use to which new discoveries were being put and their effects on the lives of people around him.

Čapek conceived the idea of R. U. R. "quite suddenly in a motor car when the crowds around him seemed to look like artificial beings," claims Jessie Mothersale, a close friend. The label "robot" for the synthetic men in the play is said to have been suggested to him by his brother Josef and was derived from the Czech word *robititi* or *robata*, meaning "to work" or, in certain connotations, "a worker."

The play R. U. R. (Rossum's Universal Robots) opened in Prague, the capital of Czechoslovakia, January 26, 1921, and was a stunning success. Overnight it made Čapek Czechoslovakia's top dramatist, a distinction he was to retain for the remainder of his life. The audacious drama, though even in the narrowest sense bona fide science fiction, still proved magnificently effective theater.

In the near future, on an island whose location is not specified, a formula to produce artificial humans chemically for use as workers and servants has been adapted to mass production, and hundreds of thousands of such creatures are being made and sold annually. These chemical machines are replacing human workers everywhere; the only thing staving off worker revolt is the fact that the lowered cost of labor has dropped prices of the essentials of life to an all-time low. The robots are even increasingly being purchased for armies. The manufacturers justify their position on the grounds that eventually robots will free men from all toil and a utopia will emerge.

Unfortunately, one of the chemists alters the formula and the robots, who have hitherto been without emotions, assume the desires for freedom and domination that previously have been characteristic only of the human race.

The emotionally advanced leaders among the robots organize a revolt of their minions, which now number millions in key positions throughout the world. The rule of man is cast off and the human race is ruthlessly exterminated.

At bay on their little island, the robot manufacturers stave off robot attack, but are betrayed by the misguided Helena Glory, president of the Humanitarian League, who even burns Rossum's original formula for the creation of robots. Since the sexless robots cannot reproduce their kind without it, they might have accepted it in barter for the lives of the remaining human beings.

Remorselessly the robots destroy all but one man, whom they command to rediscover Rossum's formula. They offer him the world if he can help them rediscover the secret of the creation of life. But he is only a builder, not a scientist, and he cannot duplicate the method. Finally, he turns to them in recrimination and asks why they destroyed mankind.

"We had learnt everything and could do everything. It had to be," Radius, leader of the revolt, replies.

"We had to become masters," explains a second robot.

"Slaughter and domination are necessary if you would be human beings. Read history," says Radius.

With almost all hope gone for the continuation of any type of human life, a male and a female robot who apparently have naturally developed sex organs are discovered, and the implication is that they may become the new Adam and Eve of the world.

The fame of *R. U. R.* spread rapidly. It was soon produced in Germany, and Erica Matonek, writing for Britain's *Life and Letters Today*, in 1939 recalled, "that it was a 'smashing success in Germany, too.'" The play opened in London and New York simultaneously, October 9, 1922. The Theatre Guild production at the Garrick Theatre, New York, was the event of the season, and it ran 184 performances. Reviews were enthusiastically provocative:

> It is murderous social satire done in terms of the most hair-raising melodrama. It has as many social implications as the most handy of the Shavian comedies, and it also has so many frank appeals to the human gooseflesh as "The Bat" or any other latter-day thriller. In melodramatic suspense and in its general illusion of impending and immediate doom,

this piece from Vienna makes on the alarmed playgoer across the footlights somewhat the same impression as would an infernal machine of which the mechanism had been set and the signal given.—*New York Herald.*

Bernard Shaw did not write R.U.R. but he probably will. Possibly later on we shall have a variation of R. U. R. by Mr. Shaw and then what we accepted last night as an exceedingly enjoyable and imaginative fantasy will become a dull diatribe. For R. U. R. is Shavian but entertaining. It has force, energy and the sort of "fantasy" that Barrie has striven unsuccessfully to administer in allopathic doses.—*New York American.*

. . . Like the H. G. Wells of an earlier day, the dramatist frees his imagination and lets it soar away without restraint, and his audience is only too delighted to go along on a trip that exceeds even Jules Verne's wildest dreams. The Guild has put theatregoers in its debt this season. R. U. R. is supermelodrama—the melodrama of action plus idea, a combination that is rarely seen on our stage.—*The Evening Sun.*

There can be no question that in this piece, whether it happens to strike the fancy of the public or not, the Theatre Guild has got something that is worthwhile—but this fantastic composition, even if it is somewhat indebted to the ideas of authors as far apart as Mary Shelley, Hauptmann, and Lord Dunsany, is in form at least a veritable novelty full of brains and purpose.—*The Evening Post.*

Under the critical microscope of the most absolute standards, R. U. R. showed some scar tissue holding its components together. Yet time, the supreme judge, finds that, with the possible exceptions of Rostand's *Cyrano de Bergerac* and Molnár's *Liliom*, this is the most frequently anthologized of modern European plays in English translation.

While an acknowledged lightning bolt to world theater, R. U. R.'s effect was even greater on the development of science fiction. The theme which had resulted in a few isolated stories of the past about the creation of artificial life, such as Mary Shelley's *Frankenstein* and Ambrose Bierce's *Moxon's Master*, had been given by Čapek such thematic richness that henceforth it would constitute a phase of science fiction exceeded in popularity only by the interplanetary story. Never before, in science fiction, had artificial life been created in wholesale, factory lots. With that as hypothesis, the robot could influence the entire pattern of man's culture and through its numbers create its own culture. The plot potentialities were vast.

If the author wanted to imagine a civilization in which machines gained absolute control, it was now possible; see Miles J. Breuer's novel, *Paradise and Iron*, published in the Summer 1930 *Amazing Stories Quarterly*. On the necessity for built-in safety factors to protect humans from the fate Čapek described, see Isaac Asimov in his book, *I, Robot* (1951). For a metal man with beneficent motives, see the Eando Binder series concerning Adam Link. The possibility of an affectionate relationship between androids (science fiction terminology for humanlike robots as opposed to all-metal ones) was touchingly explored by Lester Del Rey in *Helen O'Loy*. And eventually there came the humorous tale built around robotic machines, notably Lewis Padgett's *Robots Have No Tails*, a swing to the other extreme from that of the Frankenstein-monster concept.

That *R. U. R.* was written in and first electrified audiences of Prague, the home of the Golem, synthetic monster of Hebrew legend, is no coincidence. Not only did Čapek admit to being thoroughly familiar with and influenced by Rabbi Judah Löw's mass of clay cabalistically infused with life, but he had several reminders that may have directly sparked his inspiration.

The Golem was first filmed in Germany by Paul Wegener in 1914, and a second version of the same story, in which Paul Wegener played the monster, appeared in 1920. This later film was widely circulated in Czechoslovakia and 1920 was the year in which Čapek wrote *R. U. R.*

What was the background and origin of the golem leg-ends, whose influence on the writing of *R. U. R.* specifically and on science fiction generally proved so powerful?

The mythology of the golem grew out of the plight of the Jews of eastern Europe in the sixteenth century. They were so taxed, degraded, and subject to pogroms that the status of the Negro at its worst in the South of the United States was utopian by comparison. To fight back meant ex-termination. There was no place to hide and no place to run. Therefore, the rabbinical elders built a wall of everyday law, based on the Talmud and called the *Shulchan Aruch*, which set down as firm rule every act of Jewish life, even to the extreme of what shoe to put on first when dressing.

The object was to make the Jews satisfied with their plight, no matter how mean, by forbidding the acts and possessions that were the right and pleasure of others. Even the reading of outside literature was frowned upon.

Late in the thirteenth century, a book had been compiled by a Spanish Jew named Moses de Leon, *Zohar* (Splendor), which purported to reveal the secret behind the words of the Torah (Bible). Since *Zohar* was theoretically a commentary on the Bible, even religious Jews could not be prevented from reading it. Its pages, filled with a fantastic melange of magic words and numbers, demons, angels, incantations, evil eyes, spells, and in general the paraphernalia of superstition, was seized upon as an intellectual plaything by the learned, and as a ray of hope in their drab existence by the ignorant.

The advent of the printing press and the stepped-up tempo of persecution found this book the new "bible" of a group of Jewish mystics, who gloried in its intimation that every man was part of God's being. Eventually the book itself was often referred to as the *Cabala*.

Few men could unravel the "secrets" of the *Cabala*, but the supreme master of its magic and certainly the most fre-quently quoted authority was Rabbi Judah Löw of sixteenth-century Prague. Records still exist of the manner in which he defended his faith and his people in an interrogation be-

fore three hundred church leaders. His "Gentlemen's Agreement" with the Emperor Rudolf II of Hapsburg was said to
have canceled an order for the expulsion of Jews from the
Hapsburg dominions. The legends of the life of Rabbi Löw
seem to contain circumstantial evidence that he was pro-
ficient in hypnotism.

Small wonder that not only his disciples, but most of the
people of sixteenth-century Prague, were ready to accept the
story that the brilliant man had created a Golem to save the
Jews who were then under the once-more revived accusation
of mixing the blood of a Christian in the dough for the
Passover matzos. The Golem he created was said to be able
virtually to read minds and thereby detect those who meant
harm to the Jews. The Golem was impervious to pain, could
not be killed by fire or water, and had immense physical
strength.

Golem in Hebrew means "embryo." The reference to an
embryo (Golem) appears once in the Scriptures, and is translated in English (Psalm cxxxix, line 16) as: "Thine eyes did
see my substance, yet being unperfect; and in thy book all
my members were written, *which* in continuance were fashioned when *as yet there was none of them*."

Anything in a state of incompletion is a golem and Adam
in the third stage of formation by God was called a "shape-
less mass," a golem. In Hebrew literature there is the reference: "God created Adam as a golem."

Golems were created, according to cabalistic lore, with the
aid of a combination of letters forming a *shem* (any one of
the names of God), which was written on a piece of paper
and inserted either in the mouth or forehead of the golem,
which had been prefabricated from clay, bringing it to life.
The golem was "a symbol of God's help, which always comes
in due season, although frequently in the last, most anxious
moment."

Though Rabbi Löw's Golem is the most famous, it was
by no means the first or the last such creature attributed to
the children of Israel. The first is credited to Elijah of Chelm,

in the middle of the sixteenth century. This golem is reputed to have grown to a monster resembling that created by Frankenstein. Fearing the golem might destroy the earth, Elijah finally managed to extract the *shem* from the forehead of his creation, thereby returning it to dust.

The last golem was said to have been created by David Jaffe, rabbi of Dorhiczyn, Grodno, Russia, about 1800. This golem was manufactured to cut down labor costs. It was intended to replace the gentile who came in to light the ovens of the Jews on the Sabbath. A slight error in instructions resulted in the golem burning the entire town to the ground.

The idea of the golem came to the Jews from general European tradition. In this mass of legends, the Roman poet Virgil took on many of the aspects of a magician, and was said to have described in his writing a statue which moved, spoke, and did his will. There are many other significant points of similarity between this and the golem legends. The statue of Virgil begins an orgy of destruction as a result of an incorrect order by a disciple. This happens in the golem legend from Grodno. The Virgil statue further saves an adulteress in trouble, as does Rabbi Löw's Golem. In this respect it should be noted that golems were sexless, as were Karel Čapek's robots in *R. U. R.*

Attending the opening performance of *R. U. R.* in Prague was Thomas G. Masaryk, founder and first president of Czechoslovakia. He and Čapek became the closest of friends, so close, in fact, that nearly every Friday night was spent by Čapek at Masaryk's palace.

Čapek's success with *R. U. R.* proved no accident. In 1921, in collaboration with his brother Josef, he wrote *The Insect Play*, a fantasy in which he invented a society of insects whose foibles parallel in composite those of humans. Alternatively known as *The Insect Play*, *The Insects*, *The Insect Comedy*, *The Life of the Insect*, *The World We Live In*, *And So Ad Infinitum*, and *From Insect Life*, it not only achieved international success, but was hailed by many critics as a better unified piece than *R. U. R.* The critic of the *New York Globe* wrote: "A finer thing than *R. U. R.* Finer in scope, feeling, philosophy. Better than the original production in Prague." (The critic had seen the play abroad.) His feelings were echoed throughout America as the play was taken on a triumphal tour.

The satirical lines of the script are pointed, pungent. Čapek unmercifully flails the shortcomings of humanity; at the same time, the insect characteristics, authentically transferred from J. H. Fabre's *La Vie des insectes* and *Souvenirs entomologiques*, gives the lie to the banality that the animals and insects of the field are more noble or more sensible in their actions than mankind.

Though he gives credit to a theory of Professor Elie Metchnikoff, famous Russian scientist, as the origin of the idea for his next play, *The Makropoulos Secret* (sometimes called *The Makropoulos Affair*), first produced in 1923, actually Čapek has borrowed from the legend of the Wandering Jew. This play did not enjoy the success on the boards of Čapek's previous two efforts, but its effect on the immortality theme in science fiction was at least as emphatic as that of *R. U. R.* on the development of robot stories.

In *The Makropoulos Secret*, a woman is discovered who has lived three hundred years as the result of an elixir perfected by her father. The woman seeks to regain the formula, which is no longer in her hands, so she can renew her life. Others, suspecting the value of the document, vie with her for its possession. Finally, through an appeal for understanding, she convinces her opponents that immortality becomes a frightful vacuum as too much is seen and felt and eventually nothing has value or desirability because there is no end to it. When they give her the formula, she destroys it.

To the well-read individual, even at the time of its appearance *The Makropoulos Secret* might have seemed just another repetition of an old idea. In fact, the charge was brought against Čapek that he had received his inspiration from George Bernard Shaw's *Back to Methuselah* which had appeared several years earlier. Čapek denied ever having read or seen Shaw's play, and pointed out that from what he had heard *Back to Methuselah* regarded the achievement of immortality as a prerequisite of paradise, whereas his play took the opposite view.

In correspondence, he later debated the desirability of longevity with Shaw, finally topping Shaw with: "We still have no experience in this sphere."

While in the early versions of the legend of the Wandering Jew, immortality is a curse which finds its possessor yearning for eternal peace and rest, it is also true that the desire for eternal life is ingrained in humanity. Čapek tries to show that in reproducing its species the human race does have a certain kind of immortality.

Čapek's plot device of the meeting of a lover, grown senile, with the ever-youthful Makropoulos woman, echoes in the achingly beautiful and popular lines of *Mr. Moonlight*; it is sketched poetically in Stanley G. Weinbaum's *Dawn of Flame*, where old Einar totters again into the life of Margaret of Urbs, the immortal woman who loved him in his youth; it appears again in the ironic whim of Naga, heroine of Ross Rocklynne's *The Immortal*, published in *Comet*, March 1941, who commands her lover to go away for "awhile." But how long is "awhile" to an immortal woman?

The same year as *The Makropoulos Secret*, Josef Čapek, without the aid of Karel, produced a science fiction allegory, *Land of Many Names*, which deals with a continent that suddenly rises from the bottom of the sea. This new continent is offered as the land of hope, where each may build anew and achieve his innermost desires.

Nations venture war for its control and possession. Instead of being a land of dreams, the newly risen mass becomes the land of the dead. Finally, when one of the nations has triumphed and while engineers and government officials lay plans for its exploitation, the continent sinks back into the sea.

The moral is obvious: wars are organized by the greedy

and selfish and fought by the deluded dreamers who ultimately wake to reality and disillusionment. The play enjoyed
only a modest success, possibly because the blank verse which
set out to be expressionistic resolved itself into stylized
tableau.

The year 1924 was a year of transition for Karel Čapek. He
had begun as a lyric poet, made his mark as a short story
writer, won international renown as a playwright, and now
he would become a novelist. A science fiction idea—the discovery of atomic energy—carried by a daringly experimental
narrative technique, combined with his proven artistry at
dialogue and characterization, won him success with *Krakatit*.

"And I've discovered atomic explosions," Prokop, the inventor, tells his associate Thomas. In trying to get the secret,
Thomas blows himself—and most of the countryside—up,
and Prokop loses his memory.

The point Čapek makes is that a discovery that is too big,
like atomic energy, can do more harm than good. "It is better
to invent something small and useful" is Čapek's credo.
Čapek saw clearly, in 1924, the implications of atomic energy
and the fact that it was more likely to be used for war than
for the betterment of mankind.

He scores the telling point made by L. Frank Baum, author
of *The Wizard of Oz*, who, in an earlier book entitled *The
Master Key: An Electrical Fairy Tale*, published in 1901, has
a demon give to a small boy the power of antigravity as well
as an offer of force screens, wireless communicators, and life
restorers. The demon is the slave of whoever strikes the
"master key" of electricity, but is chagrined when, after various misadventures, the boy thrusts his gifts back like an
ingrate.

"Why, oh why did not some intelligent person strike the
Master Key!" the Demon moans.

"Accidents are always liable to happen," the boy replies.
"By accident the Master Key was struck long before the
world of science was ready for it—or for you. Instead of con-

sidering it an accident and paying no attention to it you immediately appeared to me—*a mere boy*—and offered your services."

Krakatit was made into a motion picture by Artkino, Czechoslovakia in 1951.

Convinced of the possibility of atomic energy, Karel Čapek wrote a second novel on the theme, *The Absolute at Large,* in 1927. It follows the plot pattern of *R. U. R.* The inventors of the process have set up a company and sell atomic devices to anyone who will pay.

> "The division for atomic motor cars has got the roof on," the company head is informed. "The section for atomic flying-machines will begin work during the week. We are laying the foundations for the atomic locomotive works. One wing of the department for ships' engines is already in operation."
> "Wait a minute. You should start calling them atomobiles, atomoters, and atomotives, you know. How is Krolmus getting along with the atomic cannon?"

Atomic energy brings about overproduction and war. The world destroys itself and in the end the secret is lost.

Though clumsily constructed, the fault of many of Čapek's novels, *The Absolute at Large* is written with a light touch and the reader is rewarded with frequent flashes of brilliant wit and shining humanity.

One last time Karel Čapek ventured a fantasy play, again in collaboration with his brother. *Adam the Creator,* which was first produced in 1927, was not a commercial success in the theater. Yet in printed form it possesses undeniable potency, which probably accounts for its frequent appearance in anthologies.

Adam, dissatisfied with the world God has created, wipes the slate clean and begins a new process of creation. However, everything turns out wrong. Some of the outstanding men and women he creates adopt an air of pagan superiority

and revile him. Where temples of worship are set up, he finds
that he is barred; and commercialism, not piety, seems to be
the objective. When, occasionally, humans accept him as
their creator, he is reminded that his lack of foresight, not
their own actions, is responsible for the plight of the world.

When Adam, in his wrath, threatens to destroy the world
with his Cannon of Negation, it is the wretch who personi-
fies the poor and downtrodden who most determinedly acts
to prevent him. Finally, Adam realizes that he has botched
the matter of creation, and decides the only thing to do is to
give the sorry world a chance to work out its problems alone.

To follow was a gracious period during which Karel Čapek
traveled and wrote books with such titles as *Letters from
Spain, Letters from Holland, Travels in the North*; books
on dogs and cats, gardening, fairy tales, newspapers, and the
theater. These volumes are filled with a charm, wit, humanity,
and sagacity that can only be compared to Mark Twain's.

These were the good years when Čapek was one of the
illustrious literary figures of Europe, the epitome of the civilized human being. He had married the beautiful Czech
actress Olga Scheinpflugowa, and enjoyed a gracious social
life as well.

However, the seeds of his influence were coming to the
surface in European literature. As a result of the motion picture produced by her husband, Fritz Lang, for Germany's
UFA in 1926, Thea von Harbou's melodramatic but compelling novel, *Metropolis*, became a best-seller across the
Continent. A focal figure in the novel was a metal and glass
robot, fabricated in the form of a woman, who turns the
head of the son of a great industrialist. The basis of the story
is enslavement of the workers to the machine by the greedy
few.

The all-metal robot appears in the work of American-born
author Franz Harper, who made a hit by writing, and having
published (1929) in German, his post-Expressionist novel,
Plus and Minus, later translated into English. The creation
of an industry manufacturing homunculi (metal robots) for

use as servants and workers serves as the backdrop for a sprightly work of fate and romance.

As the world moved into the thirties, Čapek added two best-sellers about the president of Czechoslovakia to his list: *Masaryk on Thought and Life* and *President Masaryk Tells His Story.*

His trilogy, *Hordubal, Meteor,* and *An Ordinary Life,* won him critical acclaim as a novelist, *Hordubal* generally being regarded as his finest non-fantasy novel. *Meteor* has erroneously been listed as a science fiction novel, but though there is reference to an unspecified chemical discovery and a clairvoyant is a character in the book, it can hardly be considered science fiction.

When it seemed that Čapek's years of writing science fiction were a thing of the past, *War with the Newts,* sometimes called *The Salamander War,* appeared in Czechoslovakia in 1936. This long novel is Čapek's masterpiece of science fiction.

In the sea a strange, nonhuman race called the Newts evolves. The Newts are intelligent creatures, easily taught, with gentle, pliable natures. Gradually, man manages to exploit them for profit, but in the process the Newts learn. The day comes when they revolt and slowly begin to undermine the continents so that they sink into the sea. In the end they have all but destroyed the human race and have set up their own nations and culture.

However, the Newts develop factionalism, warring among themselves, finally exterminating their kind; man comes out of hiding to build anew. There is one puzzling note. The world capitalist tycoon in *War with the Newts,* G. H. Bondy, has the same name as the leading industrialist in *The Absolute at Large.* If the choice was deliberate, it can only mean that Čapek felt that such men were all of the same mold and it was senseless to distinguish them with different names.

Despite his blows against the evils of capitalism, Čapek was anything but a communist. In his book, *On Political Things or Zoon Politics,* published in 1932, Čapek states:

When all is said, communism is out to rule, not to rescue; its great watchword is power, not help. For it poverty, hunger, unemployment are not an unendurable pain and shame, but a welcome reserve of dark forces, a fermenting heap of fury and loathing.

In addition to his other activities, he worked daily in the editorial offices of a newspaper from 1917 to 1938. To him, a newspaperman, the ominous implications of Adolf Hitler's Germany were frightfully clear. When it became unmistakable that Czechoslovakia's existence was threatened by its warlike neighbor, his friend Eduard Beneš enlisted Čapek's aid.

On June 22, 1938, Karel Čapek addressed the Sudeten Germans over Prague Radio, reasoning for tolerance:

> If we could in one way or another collect all the good that is, after all, in each one of us sinful human creatures, I believe that on it could be built a world that would be surely far kinder than the present one.

Four months later, the robots marched. Goose-stepping, eyes empty of all but hate, they moved on Prague.

As Čapek had predicted, the robots would look like humans.

At the age of forty-eight, on Christmas Day, 1938, Karel Čapek died of pneumonia, his will crushed by the realization "that an alliance of violence and treachery was stronger than truth."

He was spared from knowing that a few years later his brother Josef would be murdered in a Nazi concentration camp. From the earliest years Čapek's work had reflected his fascination with Hebrew thought and legend. In his last hours, he must have realized that his fate and the fate of the Jews were as one.

14

HUGO GERNSBACK:
"FATHER OF SCIENCE FICTION"

On April 5, 1926, the initial issue of the world's first science fiction magazine, *Amazing Stories*, made its appearance on the newsstands of America. Its publisher, Hugo Gernsback, in an editorial in that April issue, wrote:

> "*Amazing Stories* is a *new* kind of fiction magazine! It is entirely new—entirely different—something that has never been done before in this country. Therefore, *Amazing Stories* deserves your attention and interest."

Nothing even approximating a science fiction periodical had appeared previously. *The Thrill Book*, a magazine Harold Hersey edited for Street & Smith in 1919, has erroneously been referred to as a science fiction magazine, but in fact, though Hersey seriously considered making it just that, he was reluctant to take the gamble. Instead, he ran a potpourri of adventure, off-trail, weird, and fantasy tales with only about a half-dozen science fiction yarns sprinkled through the magazine's brief sixteen-issue existence.

Writing his memoirs, *Looking Backward Into the Future,* for *Golden Atom Magazine* in 1953, Hersey said:

> It was too late to rectify an error that the brilliant Hugo Gernsback was not to commit when he launched *Amazing Stories* seven years later. Gernsback had the courage and vision to set a pattern from the very start that was to lead to success.

The pattern Hersey referred to was also clearly expounded in Gemback's first editorial, which said:

> By "scientifiction" I mean the Jules Verne, H. G. Wells, and Edgar Allan Poe type of story—a charming romance intermingled with scientific fact and prophetic vision.

There is no equivocation, no indefiniteness. Gernsback had clearly and unmistakably set forth the nature of the stories his magazine would publish. The very first issue contained stories by the two greatest nineteenth-century masters of the art—Edgar Allan Poe and Jules Verne—as well as an early H. G. Wells story.

More than that, Gernsback was determined from the first to stress literary quality:

> Many great science stories destined to be of an historical interest are still being written, and *Amazing Stories* will be the medium through which such stories will come to you. Posterity will point to them as having blazed a new trail, not only in literature and fiction, but in progress as well.

Gernsback gave his magazine a distinctive format by producing it letter-size and printing on paper so heavy that its ninety-six pages had a front-to-back thickness of more than half an inch. As managing editor, he selected Dr. T. O'Connor Sloane, a distinguished scholar seventy-five years of age, who was an inventor, science writer, and former professor, and was Thomas A. Edison's son-in-law.

Sloane's role was not to select stories, but to check on the accuracy of the science, handle the mechanics of expediting copy for text and illustrations and generally to co-ordinate the publication's functions. His title was changed to associate editor in the second issue of the magazine.

The man Gernsback leaned on most heavily for the selection of stories was C. A. Brandt. Gernsback learned of Brandt from a secondhand book dealer, who assured him that this German-born chemist was the greatest living authority in the world on science fiction. This was no exaggeration. Brandt, who among his other accomplishments was responsible for the introduction into America of calculating machines, possessed a fabulous library of the world's science fiction and fantasy.

Besides reading and passing on new stories for *Amazing Stories*, as first reader, he rendered invaluable service by suggesting reprints from his collection. He also translated some works into English for the magazine, including Curt Siodmak's *The Egg from Lake Tanganyika*, and *The Malignant Flower* by Anthos. A second "literary" editor, Wilbur C. Whitehead, a well-known auction bridge expert of the twenties whose avocation was science fiction, was added to the staff to help with the manuscripts.

Gernsback himself made the final decision on all manuscripts, wrote the editorials and the majority of the blurbs for the stories, and selected the scenes to be used for cover and interior illustrations.

For its art work, the magazine's most vital asset was the illustrations, both on the covers and inside, of Austrian-born artist Frank R. Paul, whose imagination captured the essence of science fiction in a manner never equaled before or surpassed since. Paul's ability to project the theme of the magazine to the public pictorially was an important factor in the almost instantaneous success of the publication.

Before *Amazing Stories*, there were only three important periodical sources of science fiction: the great weekly, *Argosy*; Farnsworth Wright's brilliantly edited *Weird Tales*; and

Gernsback's own popular science monthly, *Science and Invention*.

Gernsback got from *Argosy* the outstanding authors George Allan England, Austin Hall, A. Merritt, Edgar Rice Burroughs, Murray Leinster, and Ray Cummings. From *Weird Tales* he obtained H. P. Lovecraft, Otis Adelbert Kline, J. Schlossel, Francis Flagg, and Clare Winger Harris. *Science and Invention* produced Ellis Parker Butler, Clement Fézandié, Jacques Morgan, and Gernsback's own fiction.

Nor were the classics ignored. To Verne, Wells, and Poe were added the names of Fitz-James O'Brien, Garrett P. Serviss, and even such pieces of historical interest as Richard Adams Locke's *Moon Hoax*, which had hoodwinked the world almost a century earlier.

The precision of the publishing generalship with which Hugo Gernsback at one stroke established what he then termed "scientifiction" as a part of world literature directed attention to the fact that here was a man whose ability to convert imagination into reality transcended the bounds of what is generally referred to as "business acumen" and "talent." What was Gernsback's background and how did he come to conceive the idea of a science fiction magazine?

Hugo Gernsback was born August 16, 1884 in the city of Luxembourg. His father was a well-to-do wine wholesaler and his earliest education was from private tutors. Later he attended the Ecole Industrielle of Luxembourg and the Technikum in Bingen, Germany.

At the age of nine, Gernsback came across a German translation of *Mars as the Abode of Life*, by the renowned American astronomer Percival Lowell. Though he was highly imaginative, the concept that intelligent life might exist on other worlds had never occurred to young Hugo. He slept restlessly that night, and the next day, on the way to school, his mind wrestled with the idea, unable to resolve the enormity of its implications.

Straining for comprehension he *literally* developed a fever, which may have been psychosomatic in nature. He was immediately sent home, where he lapsed into delirium, raving about strange creatures, fantastic cities, and masterly engineered canals of Mars for two full days and nights while a doctor remained in almost constant attendance, unable to determine the cause of his condition.

The direction of Hugo Gernsback's future thinking was greatly conditioned by that experience. He was never to be content with the accumulated scientific knowledge of his day. Now he was to search the libraries for books that opened up imaginative vistas beyond the scientific knowledge of the period. Though he was to become an expert technician, scientist, and inventor, such pursuits could never satisfy him.

His mind took wings where his work left off. He almost memorized the works of Jules Verne and H. G. Wells, and wrote excursions of his own, which, despite their juvenility, displayed a sure facility for the use of words.

The telephone and electrical communications systems were fledgling science in Gernsback's youth, yet he taught himself their intricacies. At the age of thirteen he was already accepting contracting jobs for such installations in Europe. A memorable instance in that connection was the day the mother superior of the Carmelite convent in Luxembourg City obtained a special dispensation from Pope Leo XIII, so that young Hugo could equip that institution with call bells.

Among the projects that Hugo occupied himself with was the invention of a battery similar to the layer battery produced by Ever-Ready in the United States today. When both France and Germany refused him patents, he decided that there was no opportunity for a young inventor in Europe and, taking the accumulated savings from his electrical installation work, he packed up his battery and booked passage, first class, for the United States.

Not yet twenty, he landed in the United States in February, 1904, with two hundred dollars in his pocket and a stiff-necked determination that, no matter how tough things got, he would never, under any circumstances, request aid from his parents. He never did.

Despite the fact that Gernsback's layer battery could do

velop three times the amperage of any existing American unit, he had to abandon it as impractical when he learned that it could not be adapted to mass production. As a hand-produced product it would have had to sell at ten times the rate of competing products.

Though he did not have a marketable battery he did have technical know-how, so he sold his services as an expert technician to William Roche, a New York manufacturer who had a contract for producing dry cell batteries for the Navy. Gernsback was to have been head of research at $30 a week.

But, leaving Roche's office for the laboratory, Gernsback remembered some details of employment he had left unsettled. He turned back to the office, to find Roche gone. Waiting for the man to come back, he sat down and began to examine some sample envelopes of battery chemicals lying on the boss's desk. At that point Roche re-entered the office. Seeing the envelopes in Gernsback's hand, Roche leapt to the conclusion that Gernsback was an agent of a competitor, paid him a week's salary, and fired him after only three hours. Never again in his life was Gernsback to work as an employee for anyone.

He next went into partnership with the son of the inventor of a fur-processing device. They formed the Gee-Cee Dry Battery Company, for which Gernsback devised and built dry cell and dry storage batteries. His partner sold them to automobile manufacturers. Business in general was good, but little money came in. The reason, Gernsback soon discovered, was that his partner was intercepting the checks.

Nothing daunted, Gernsback got his money back from his partner's father and made an agreement with the largest distributor of motor car equipment supplies in New York to manufacture batteries. The business went along quite successfully until the depression of 1907 resulted in the loss of a contract with Packard, and his company, after paying its debts, had to be dissolved.

All this time, Gernsback roomed at a boardinghouse on 14th Street in New York. One of the boarders was Lewis

Coggeshall, a telegraph operator on the Erie Railroad. The two decided to form a company to import into the United States experimental and research material not then commonly available, such as X-ray tubes, Geissler tubes, and specialized scientific electrical equipment. This company, which Gernsback operated simultaneously with his less fortunate ventures, was called The Electro Importing Company.

For this side venture, which was to become the first mail-order radio house in the world, Gernsback designed the first home radio set in history. Called the Telimco Wireless, it was advertised in the January 13, 1906 issue of the *Scientific American*, at a retail price of $7.50. The amateur unit contained a transmitter as well as a receiver, since no commercial radio stations existed at the time.

The transmitter would ring a bell in another room without the use of wires. The police descended on Gernsback, accusing him of fraud, claiming that no wireless combination could be sold at his low price, but backed off frustrated when a personal demonstration proved the apparatus actually performed as advertised.

The set went into mass production and was sold in department stores, including Macy's, Gimbels, Marshall Field, and F. A. O. Schwartz. In 1957, a replica of this device was placed in the Henry Ford Museum, Dearborn, Michigan, the same year the Michigan Institute of Radio Engineers and the American Radio Relay League honored Gernsback for his pioneering work.

With characteristic showmanship, Gernsback helped promote his Telimco Wireless by building the first successfully operating walkie-talkie. Transmitter and receiver for this device were carried on a man's shoulders in downtown New York and the apparatus was described, with photographs, in the January 1909 *Modern Electrics*.

Gernsback's publishing endeavors grew out of his radio catalogue, also the first on record, which he began turning out in 1905. When his battery business failed in 1907, he used the publishing experience gained in catalogue work to launch the world's first radio magazine, which began publication in 1908. The periodical was distributed by the American News Company and was profitable from the first.

In 1909 Gernsback accomplished still another pioneering innovation by opening up the first radio store anywhere, at 69 West Broadway, New York. It was also in this year that he introduced the word *television* to the American public in an article, *Television and the Telphot*, in *Modern Electrics* describing early German experiments on photo transmission. By early 1910 he had formed, through his magazine, a society of 10,000 wireless radio amateurs and issued the *Wireless Blue Book*. Lee De Forest, inventor of the vacuum tube which made radio possible, became the first president of the Wireless Association of America with Gernsback as business manager.

It should also be noted, at the risk of overusing the word "first," that Gernsback in 1910 published the first book on radio broadcasting, *The Wireless Telephone*, in which he predicted radio networks.

All this might have seemed adequate achievement for any man, but Gernsback chafed at the limitations imposed by the state of scientific progress. His imagination extended horizontally, far beyond known boundaries. When he found himself a few pages short of material to fill the April 1911 issue of *Modern Electrics*, he sat down and dashed off the first installment of *Ralph 124C41+*, a work of science fiction.

He had no ideas beyond the first chapter, but each month at the approach of the deadline he would sit down and carry the story forward, with no concept of how it would develop or end. It ran for twelve monthly installments, concluding in the March 1912 number and the result was probably the greatest single work of prophecy ever written as fiction or fact.

The hero of the novel, which was subtitled "A Romance of the Year 2660," is Ralph—a "plus" man of that era—one of ten such extraordinarily endowed individuals in the entire world. A scientifically reared superman, Ralph is the prototype of the hundreds of similar heroes who have been featured in science fiction magazines in the last thirty years. The action

of the novel is best described by the description on the back
of the book jacket of the first hard-cover edition, published
by the Stratford Company, Boston, in 1925:

> Ralph's love for the beautiful stranger, his conquest of his
> rival, and the worsting of the great saturnine Martian, culmi-
> nating in a running fight in space with tragedy and terror
> conquered by almost unbelievable and incredible weapons
> make one of the most interesting and gripping stories ever
> told.

It is not the plot itself which is the truly remarkable thing
about *Ralph 124C41+*, though its picture of a running space
battle may have been the inspiration for many such thrillers
in the years that followed. Its distinction rests in the fantastic
number of accurate predictions disguised as fiction that have
come true in the forty-five years since the story was serialized.

The number of major and minor predictions is astonishing.
Fluorescent lighting, skywriting, automatic packaging machines, plastics, the radio directional range finder, juke boxes,
liquid fertilizer, hydroponics, tape recorders, rustproof steel,
loud speakers, night baseball, aquacades, microfilm, television, radio networks, vending machines dispensing hot and
cold foods and liquids, flying saucers, a device for teaching
while the user is asleep, solar energy for heat and power,
fabrics from glass, synthetic materials such as nylon for wear-
ing apparel, and, of course, space travel are but a few.

The most stunning forecast is Gernsback's inspired description and actual diagramming of radar:

> It has long been known that a pulsating polarized ether wave,
> if directed on a metal object, could be reflected in the same
> fashion as a light ray can be reflected from a bright surface
> or from a mirror. . . . If, therefore, a polarized wave generator
> were trained towards the open space, the waves would take a
> direction as shown in diagram, providing the parabolic wave
> reflector was used as shown. By manipulating the entire ap-
> paratus like a searchlight, waves would be sent over a large
> area. Then a small part of the waves would strike the metal

body of the flyer and these waves would be reflected back to the sending apparatus. Here they would fall on the Actino-

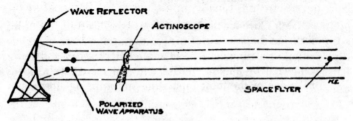

scope (see diagram), which records only the reflected waves, not the direct ones. From the Actinoscope the reflection factor is then determined. . . . From the intensity and the elapsed time of the reflected impulses, the distance between the Earth and the flyer is then accurately calculated with but little trouble. . . .

The accuracy of Gernsback's interpretation of space sickness in *Ralph 124C41 +* has already been confirmed by airforce experiments and, of dozens of other predictions yet unrealized, scarcely one seems improbable of achievement. For a popular and reliable guidebook of the future one might do worse than *Ralph 124C41 +*.

To "The Wireless Screech," a humorous department in the February 1909 *Modern Electrics*, science fiction writers owe a debt for originating matter-transmitters in science fiction. Describing "Wireless on Mars," Gernsback, writing under the nom de plume of "Our Martian Correspondent," described the sending of food by "wireless" on the red planet. This may yet prove to be one of his most inspired prophecies.

The name of Gernsback's publication was changed to *Electrical Experimenter* in 1913 and the dimensions expanded to letter-size. Gernsback, seeking a cartoonist to put across salient points in articles, in 1914 began to utilize the pen of Frank R. Paul. Then an editorial cartoonist for the *Jersey Journal*, Paul also had prior training as a mechanical and architectural draftsman. From that time on Paul's highly imaginative yet mechanically precise illustrations were to become the mark of a Gernsback technical or science fiction magazine.

The breath-taking idea of the possibility of life on Mars which had so forcibly impressed itself on the youthful Gernsback never left him. Finally, in a series titled *Baron Münchhausen's New Scientific Adventures*, which began in the May 1915 *Electrical Experimenter*, Gernsback after a brief fictional divergence in helping the Allies conquer Berlin, took Münchhausen to Mars. Here he repaid his debt to Lowell, with detailed descriptions of the life, inventions, and philosophy of the Martians, leavened with considerable humor and satire.

It is the element of wit and humor that has generally been overlooked in appraisals of Gernsback. His almost Prussian bearing, his sharp features, his habit of using a monocle when he reads restaurant menus, coupled with his serious scientific interests, have given many people a misleading impression. The truth is that Gernsback socially is a man of almost rapier-like wit, with a mischievous gleam in his eyes and with the rare ability to joke about his own misfortunes.

Writers soon came to regard Gernsback's *Electrical Experimenter* as a regular market for science fiction. His criterion for selecting stories was simple. If the story did not avoid an explanation of its unusual occurrence, and if that explanation was logical in the light of known science, he would buy it, if the literary elements made it good entertainment.

When *Electrical Experimenter* metamorphosed into *Science and Invention* in August, 1920, Gernsback frequently used two such stories in each issue, in addition to one in the companion periodical *Radio News*. At first he developed his own group of writers—among them Clement Fézandié, Charles S. Wolfe, C. M. Adams, John De Quer, George F. Stratton, and Jacques Morgan, who wrote *The Scientific Adventures of Mr. Fosdick*. Gernsback's own science fiction contributions were *Ralph 124C41+* and his quite flippant Münchhausen adventures. The reception accorded these stories was so encouraging that soon such established favorites as Ray Cummings, George Allan England, and John Martin Leahy were attracted to the new market and Gernsback decided that there might soon be a readership for a magazine devoted entirely to science fiction.

In August 1923, he published a special "Scientific Fiction Number" of *Science and Invention*. That issue contained six science fiction stories and a cover picture of a space-suited man, illustrating *The Man from the Atom* by G. Peyton Wertenbaker, a precocious 16-year old who was later to become an important authority on the Southwest.

One reason for the special issue was the backlog of science fiction stories piling up at *Science and Invention*, but it quickly persuaded *Argosy* and *Weird Tales* to alter their policies to include stories with a better grounding in science. The beginning of the end for the scientific romance which had been popularized by Edgar Rice Burroughs was brought nearer; the pattern of modern science fiction was in the process of formation.

Except for a freakish circumstance, Gernsback would have issued the first science fiction magazine in 1924. That year he sent out 25,000 circulars soliciting subscriptions for a new type of magazine, based on the stories of Verne, Wells, and Poe, to be titled *Scientifiction*. The subscription reaction was so cool that Gernsback did nothing further for another two years, at which time he placed *Amazing Stories*, fully developed, on the stands without a word of advance notice.

In the June 1926 issue of *Amazing Stories*, in an editorial titled "The Lure of Scientifiction," Gernsback took notice of the hitherto unrecognized, extremely gratifying fact that a ready-made market existed for a science fiction magazine:

> One of the great surprises since we started publishing *Amazing Stories* is the tremendous amount of mail we receive from—shall we call them "Scientifiction Fans"?—who seem to be pretty well oriented in this sort of literature. From the suggestions for reprints that are coming in these "fans" seem to have a hobby of their own of hunting up scientifiction stories, not only in English, but in many other languages.

As a result of this discovery, Gernsback started a reader's department entitled "Discussions" which actually established a forum for the organization of the science fiction fan movement, one of the most colorful aspects of science fiction today.

Taking a survey of his readers, Gernsback found that more frequent publication was desired by the overwhelming majority. To test his findings, he published in 1927 a companion to *Amazing Stories* titled *Amazing Stories Annual*. It was for this publication that he commissioned Edgar Rice Burroughs to write a new novel, *The Master Mind of Mars*, for which the author was paid $1,200. The 100,000 printing of the *Annual* was almost a sellout, despite its price of fifty cents.

Success established, Gernsback replaced the annual with *Amazing Stories Quarterly* in 1928. It ran a full-length novel as well as short stories in every issue and also sold for fifty cents. This new venture, too, showed a profit.

Amazing Stories and *Amazing Stories Quarterly* featured the work of many new authors, who wrote material to fit the needs of the magazines. Prominent among them were David H. Keller, M.D., the pioneer in what later was to become popular as "psychological" science fiction stories; Edward E. Smith, creator of the super-science tale; John W. Campbell, Jr.; Philip Francis Nowlan, whose stories of Anthony (Buck) Rogers ran in *Amazing Stories* some time before they appeared as a comic strip; Stanton A. Coblentz, poet and, in his fiction, magazine science fiction's best satirist in the tradition of Jonathan Swith; A. Hyatt Verrill, outstanding archaeologist; Fletcher Pratt, later a celebrated naval writer; Harl Vincent, Bob Olsen, Miles J. Breuer, M.D., and Jack Williamson.

The passage of the years found Gernsback's Experimenter Publishing Company grown into a veritable empire of newsstand periodicals, including in addition to *Amazing Stories* and *Amazing Stories Quarterly* such publications as *Science and Invention, Radio News, Your Body, Tid Bits* (an outgrowth of *French Humor*), *Cookoo Nuts,* and a wide variety of one-shots, comic books, radio annuals, and hard-cover books. To top it off, Hugo Gernsback for some years operated radio broadcast station WRNY in New York City.

Readers of *The New York Times* did a double take Monday, August 13, 1928, when they read: "WRNY to Start Daily Television Broadcasts." In 1928, television was still mainly a frequently used theme in science fiction. Only a few hundred crude scanning disk experimental sets capable of picking up television waves existed. The radio page of *The New York Times* for August 21, 1928 carried the program of the world's first television station. After each radio program, station WRNY televised the face of the performer. Westinghouse had occasionally transmitted motion pictures experimentally by television, but live broadcasts on a commercial basis were unknown.

Coinciding with his television broadcasting, Gernsback issued the pioneer television magazine, called simply *Television*. Its very appearance in 1928 was more fantastic than the science fiction in *Amazing Stories*.

Gernsback's fabulous success and showmanship did not go unnoticed. Bernarr Macfadden, health faddist who had climbed to fame and a publishing empire with *The New York Evening Graphic* and *Physical Culture*, a magazine featuring articles on sex, diet, nudism, and back-to-nature material, saw in Gernsback a potential competitor. True, Macfadden still frequently walked to work barefooted, trailed by a host of reporters, and did headstands on his office desk, but that was pretty tame stuff compared with television. While Macfadden's *True Story* magazine rocketed to two million circulation under the editorship of F. Orlin Tremaine, who a few years later was to head *Astounding Stories*, the weekly *Liberty*, which was bucking the well-established *Saturday Evening Post* and *Collier's*, though it sold a lot of copies, wasn't getting much advertising.

The superiority of the scientific approach in Gernsback's *Your Body*, which pointed to science as the answer to man's physical, sexual, and psychological problems, represented a threat to the blustering sensationalism of *Physical Culture*. Gernsback's offer of $10,000 to any medium who could actually contact the dead, and his use of the noted magician Dunninger to explode such fakes, threatened the existence of

Macfadden's none-to-profitable *Ghost Stories*, which appealed to the superstition and ignorance of the masses. Nor could Macfadden's *True Strange Stories*, despite its reprints of H. G. Wells and faked photos of fantastic events, hold a candle to *Amazing Stories*.

Macfadden (who lived in the same apartment house as Gernsback, at 527 Riverside Drive) now offered to buy Gernsback out, lock, stock, and barrel. Gernsback, heading what had grown to a million-dollar corporation, refused to consider the offer. The Experimenter Publishing Company and all its subsidiaries was a going and profitable concern, he asserted, and so diversified it most likely was to stay that way.

On February 20, 1929 Gernsback was awakened early in the morning by the telephone. It was a reporter from *The New York Times*. He wanted to know what was to become of radio station WRNY now that bankruptcy proceedings had been filed against the Experimenter Publishing Company. Gernsback was incredulous but the reporter insisted the story was true.

According to the law of 1929, if three or more creditors pressed the matter, a company or an individual could be forced into bankruptcy, regardless of solvency, merely because payments had been late. This was similar to the law which permitted mortgagors to foreclose when an installment was a single day late and thereby frequently gain possession of property worth more than the mortgage.

Gernsback now went to the authorities. He showed them the papers from Macfadden offering to buy him out. He claimed that all three of the creditors were also Macfadden suppliers.

The authorities, after considering the evidence, said that there was nothing they could do for Gernsback, but any attempt by Macfadden to obtain Experimenter titles would strengthen the conspiracy charges and provide grounds for an investigation. Macfadden never did bid for the titles, and the creditors, in what *The New York Times* referred to as "bankruptcy deluxe," received $1.08 for each $1.00 due them, certainly an amazing performance for a "bankrupt" company. The bankruptcy law which had brought Gernsback to grief was changed, but a week too late to do him any good.

A company called Teck Publications took over *Radio News* and *Amazing Stories*. In 1939 both of these magazines were purchased by Ziff-Davis, their publisher ever since. *Radio News*, retitled *Electronics World*, now leads the field in circulation.

Gernsback was far from licked. He sent out a series of circulars. To readers of *Science and Invention* he announced that he would publish *Everyday Mechanics*; subscribers of *Radio News* could get *Radio-Craft* and *Amazing Stories* fans found that they could look forward to *Science Wonder Stories*. Over 8,000 subscriptions poured in, so respected was the Gernsback name. If Gernsback had not possessed a cent of his own, he would have had sufficient capital to launch his new Stellar Publishing Company.

The first issue of *Science Wonder Stories* was dated June 1929. Gernsback had taken with him illustrator Frank R. Paul and most of his best new science fiction authors, including David H. Keller, Stanton A. Coblentz, Jack Williamson, Harl Vincent, Fletcher Pratt, Philip Francis Nowlan (under the pen name Frank Phillips), and Bob Olsen. Most important, he coined, in his editorial in the first *Science Wonder Stories*, the term "science fiction," which was to become the permanent name of the genre, completely eclipsing "scientifiction."

With the second issue of *Science Wonder Stories* began *The Problems of Space Flying*, translated from the German of Captain Hermann Noordung, the first factual material on an earth satellite to appear in America. Frank R. Paul depicted the space station on the cover of the magazine, painting what is probably the premiere color interpretation of such a concept.

Science Wonder Stories was soon followed by *Air Wonder Stories*, *Scientific Detective Monthly*, and *Science Wonder Quarterly*. Gernsback has received credit for publishing the first science fiction magazine in history, but the truth is that he brought into being the first seven such periodicals. While the specialized *Air Wonder Stories* and *Scientific Detective Monthly* did not last long, Gernsback kept *Science Wonder Quarterly* going for a three-year period by featuring all-interplanetary issues, taking cognizance of the fact that such stories were the most popular of all types of science fiction. Reader reaction made this fact clear, such tales as E. E. Smith's Skylark books being remembered nostalgically.

Most of Gernsback's problems during this period were caused by the fact that each month carried the nation and the Stellar Publishing Company deeper into the Depression. The passage of time found the resourceful Gernsback trying with unflagging energy to keep his new company afloat. In science fiction, his publications either combined or metamorphosed into a variety of sizes and shapes, including the first all-slick magazine of the field—*Wonder Stories*.

He was the first to lower the price to fifteen cents. He beat the drums for more science fiction movies and later attempted to organize an annual Science Fiction Day. He did form, in 1934, The Science Fiction League, patterned after his old wireless organization, one of the most constructive ideas ever promulgated by a fantasy periodical to promote the medium.

To revivify American science fiction, he introduced in translation outstanding works by German writers Otto Willi Gail, Otfrid von Hanstein, Hans Dominik, Friedrich Freksa, Bruno H. Burgel, Ludwig Anton, Max Valier, F. Golub, and Leo am Bruhl. From France he imported novels by R. H. Romans, S. S. Held, and Charles de Richter.

Finally, when all else failed, in a candid appraisal of the factors that made it impossible for him to continue to distribute *Wonder Stories* on the newsstand, he offered to send each issue to the reader in advance, with a bill for fifteen cents and a postage-prepaid return envelope, if a request form was mailed in.

Only 2,000 replies were received and, in the spring of 1936, he regretfully sold the magazine to Standard Magazines,

where it was continued under the directorship of Leo
Margulies as *Thrilling Wonder Stories*.

But this was not the last that the science fiction world was
to see of Gernsback. 1939 found him experimenting with
three issues of *Superworld Comics*, the first science fiction
comic magazine, with the principal strip drawn by Frank R.
Paul. He was too early and the magazine failed.

However, his *Radio-Craft*, which had changed with the
times to *Radio Electronics* as television came into the American home in a big way, grew into one of the leading publications of its type in the world. A daring experiment in newsstand publishing, *Sexology*, a digest-sized magazine presenting
sex in a dignified manner, paid off when the contributions
and endorsements of physicians and clergymen proved that
this delicate subject could be discussed with candor in a
magazine for newsstand distribution.

With these two successful publications well under way,
Gernsback in 1953 took one more flyer at science fiction. He
published *Science Fiction Plus*, a large-format magazine,
printed on coated stock, carrying no advertisements and
featuring five-color cover and two-color interior illustrations.
However, the mass audience necessary to support it could not
be reached and it disappeared after seven issues.

The radio-electronics industry awarded Gernsback the
magnificent silver Hugo Gernsback Trophy in 1953 for fifty
years of service to the radio electronic art. He was guest of
honor at the 1952 World Science Fiction Convention in
Chicago, and beginning with the 1953 Philadelphia meeting,
achievement awards presented at these fans' conventions were
called "Hugos."

In the first *Amazing Stories*, Gernsback's editorial contained the statement, "Edgar Allan Poe may well be called
the father of 'scientifiction.' " Today there may be argument
about this. The real "Father of Science Fiction" is Hugo
Gernsback and no one can take the title away from him.

ɔwn small chemical laboratory. "Finally astronomy dawned on me," he said, "and the lure of other worlds and inconceivable cosmic gulfs eclipsed all other interests for a long period after my twelfth birthday."

He published a small hectographed paper called *The Rhode Island Journal of Astronomy* and later wrote newspaper columns on astronomy for *The Providence Evening Journal* and the Asheville, North Carolina, *Gazette-News*.

This strong, active, and almost professional interest in the physical sciences of chemistry and astronomy, while unusual in one so young, bore no direct relation to the outré inclination his early fiction was to take. Neither did his somewhat later preference in reading matter, for the authors he championed in his early twenties stressed the romantic, scientific, or more positive aspects of science fiction.

A letter published in the March 7, 1914 issue of that early stronghold of the scientific romance, *All-Story Weekly*, sheds a revealing light on his likes and dislikes at the time.

> In the present age of vulgar taste and sordid realism it is a relief to peruse a publication such as *The All-Story*, which has ever been and still remains under the influence of the imaginative school of Poe and Verne. At the head of your list of writers Edgar Rice Burroughs undoubtedly stands. I have read very few recent novels by others wherein is displayed an equal ingenuity in plot, and verisimilitude in treatment. His only fault seems to be a tendency toward scientific inaccuracy and slight inconsistencies. I hardly need mention the author of *A Columbus of Space* further than to say I have read every published work of Garrett P. Serviss, own most of them, and await his future writings with eagerness.

When *All-Story Magazine* combined with another great adventure periodical which featured science fiction, H. P. Lovecraft wrote again enthusiastically:

> The greatest benefit derived from the amalgamation undoubtedly will be the return to *All-Story* of George Allan England, who, to my mind, ranks with Edgar Rice Burroughs and Albert Payson Terhune as one of the three supreme

literary artists of the house of Munsey. Mr. England's *Darkness and Dawn* trilogy is on a par with the *Tarzan* stories, and fortunate indeed is that magazine which can secure as contributors the authors of both.

That letter appeared in the readers' columns of the August 15, 1914 issue of *All-Story Cavalier* when Lovecraft was twenty-four years of age, hardly the juvenile fancies of a precocious child but the considered opinions of an adult critic.

Lovecraft did a variety of writing for the two leading amateur-press publications of the time—*The United Amateur* and *The National Amateur*—but the earliest work of his that can be considered of professional caliber was written in 1917. Here is evidence that Lovecraft was ready at that early date to follow a natural inclination into science fiction, if we properly evaluate his short story *Dagon*, which did not see publication until the November 1919 issue of *The Vagrant*.

The story is beyond question a work of science fiction. A packet is sunk by a German submarine during World War I, and one of its crew is set adrift in a lifeboat. His craft becomes mired in the mud of a new island which rises mysteriously from the floor of the sea. On this island he discovers an ancient monolith upon which are chiseled the forms of gigantic, froglike men, engaged in various marine endeavors. When a tremendous manlike scaled thing rises above the waters, a nearly insane fear inspires the castaway with the strength to launch his craft and escape from the island. The story ends as the protagonist realizes that the monstrous creature, which resembles the fish-god Dagon of the ancient Philistines, has searched him out in San Francisco.

Lovecraft claimed that he received inspiration for his Cthulhu mythos from his reading of Lord Dunsany in 1919. Careful reading of *Dagon* strongly suggests that the famous mythology was already in formation and the only thing Dunsany taught Lovecraft was not to attach legendary names to his horrors but to invent new ones.

The literary love affair that grew for several years after

Lovecraft encountered Dunsany's work effectively sidetracked him from moving directly into science fiction. What
entranced Lovecraft was the "crystalline singing prose" of
Lord Dunsany. Form eclipsed subject matter in his mind and
led him to other stylists of the supernatural such as Arthur
Machen, Algernon Blackwood, Lafcadio Hearn, and other
greats and near-greats of the literature of darkness.

After Dunsany, Lovecraft took turns imitating the others
but first impressions remained strongest and the clear, harp-
like chords of the Irish lord echoed periodically throughout
Lovecraft's entire lifetime of writing. Most beautifully and
true does it sound in *The Silver Key*, *The Strange High
House in the Mist*, *The Quest of Iranon*, and *Celephais*.

While Lovecraft was saturating himself with the essence
of Dunsany, he did not completely abandon the writing of
science fiction.

Beyond the Wall of Sleep, the title story of one of his collections later published by Arkham House, was written originally in 1919. It deals with an intern who electronically receives the mental impulses of an intelligence from a distant
star system. The later flaring of a nova near Algol, the Demon
Star, as predicted by the alien from far outer space, confirms
the authenticity of the contact.

The following year Lovecraft wrote *From Beyond*, in which
a machine utilizing the ultraviolet principle makes it possible, with disastrous results, to see creatures normally invisible to human sight.

Both these stories, despite stretches of excellent writing,
are minor excursions. But the same cannot be said of *The
Temple*, written the same year and published in *Weird Tales*
for September 1925. This tale, in writing and plotting, is a
science fiction masterpiece.

A German submarine in World War I is trapped on the
ocean's floor and only one of its crewmen, a Prussian officer,
remains alive. He discovers he is near the ruins of an undersea city which may be the legendary Atlantis. Lovecraft
brilliantly delineates the slow disintegration of the German's

military poise as his supplies of power, food, and water slowly give out. The desperately trapped Prussian explores parts of the ruins in a diving suit. Then, with lights burned out and air almost exhausted, he leaves the submarine a final time to investigate what he thinks is a glowing radiance in a temple-like structure in the distance.

The Temple has not received the attention it deserves as one of Lovecraft's most successful and forthright presentations.

The first professional opportunity Lovecraft obtained was with an evanescent periodical of the early twenties titled *Home Brew*. In 1921 and 1922 he wrote for the editor and publisher, E. D. Houtain, a strange series of six short stories built around the scientific attempts of Herbert West, a brilliant young medical student, to bring the dead back to life. The intent was to horrify through use of the time-worn theme of restoring the dead, but the explanations for the experiments were not in any way supernatural; the series thus qualifies as true science fiction.

Home Brew also bought a novelette entitled *The Lurking Fear*, which it ran as a four-part serial beginning in the January 1923 number. This extremely rococo tale tells of the degenerate descendants of a once-proud family who live in underground tunnels and venture forth every now and then to devour cannibalistically some hapless surfaceman. The story seems to derive from portions of H. G. Wells's *Time Machine*.

Before publication of this story, Lovecraft's mother, Sarah Susan, having passed some years in a Providence hospital, died, early in 1919. The knowledge that both of his parents had succumbed to maladies that left them mentally disturbed at the end is advanced by David H. Keller, M.D., in his remarkable essay *Shadows Over Lovecraft* (*Fantasy Commentator*, Summer 1938), as a possible reason for Lovecraft's preoccupation with tragic hereditary morbidity in many of his stories.

Dagon, Far Beyond, and *Beyond the Wall of Sleep* come

well within the scope of present-day science fiction but, beginning with *Herbert West* and continuing with *The Lurking Fear*, we find the science attenuated almost to the vanishing point. The extreme is reached in *The Unnamable*, published in *Weird Tales* for July 1925. The theme, clearly derived from Fitz-James O'Brien's *What Was It?*, is grave-yard investigations, which end when a nearly invisible monster streams from a pit, knocking everyone down and disappearing into the night. The story is slight in plot and fails to communicate the desired mood.

The advent of *Weird Tales* magazine, particularly the elevation of Farnsworth Wright to the editorial directorship, was the most important development in a literary sense in Lovecraft's writing career. Since 1917 he had been writing, and donating to amateur periodicals, a great many weird stories. Most of these now readily sold to *Weird Tales*.

Beginning with *Dagon*, which appeared in its October 1923 issue, *Weird Tales* published in quick succession *The Picture in the House, The Hound, The Rats in the Walls, The White Ape, Hypnos, The Festival, The Statement of Randolph Carter, The Music of Erich Zann, The Unnamable, The Temple, The Tomb, The Cats of Ulthar, The Outsider, The Lurking Fear, The Moon-Bog, The Terrible Old Man, He, The Horror at Red Hook,* and *The White Ship.*

Following the appearance of *The Rats in the Walls* in the March 1924 *Weird Tales*, readers were unrestrained in their enthusiasm. *The Rats in the Walls* certainly ranks as one of the most chillingly imaginative stories of horror ever conceived by an American writer. The atmosphere is charged with an almost supernatural horror, which is heightened by the scientific plausibility of the background.

The story tells of the discovery of a fallen underground realm beneath an old English castle, where as recently as 1600 A.D. a decadent British family raised herds of beastmen to eat. The influence of the surroundings revives the dormant urge in one of the family's present-day descendants, bringing

The Rats in the Walls to a close on a note of almost un-endurable terror.

The Outsider has frequently been referred to as Lovecraft's greatest horror tale, probably because it was used as the title story in the first major posthumous collection of his works. Unfortunately the closeness with which Lovecraft apes Poe (he begins by virtually paraphrasing *Berenice*) and the hiatuses in the build-up of horror caused by the interpolation of stretches of fantasy considerably reduce the impact of the story for many readers. But its power can hardly be denied, despite its strongly derivative aspects.

Tales like *The Rats in the Walls* and *The Outsider*, tales of horror, terror, and atmospheric beauty with undertones of scientific credibility, created Lovecraft's first reputation in the period beginning in 1923. Typical of readers' reaction was the letter of internationally famous science fiction author Ray Cummings, which appeared in *The Eyrie* of *Weird Tales* for June 1926.

> Who in blazes is H. P. Lovecraft? I never heard the name before. If he is a present-day writer—which I cannot imagine him to be—he deserves to be world-famous. I read *The Outsider* and *The Tomb*. No need of telling you they are masterful stories. Quite beside their atmosphere—all those fictional elements which go to make up a real story—I felt and still feel, looking backward upon reading of them—somehow *ennobled*, as though my mind had profited (which indeed it had) by the reading. Never have I encountered any purer, more beautiful diction. They sing; the true poetry of prose.

Who was Lovecraft, indeed? Certainly one of the strangest figures to arise in American letters. Following the death of his mother, he had somewhat emerged from his shell, traveled a bit, and seen more of the world. When *The Outsider* was published in *Weird Tales* for April 1926 he was married to an attractive, strong-willed, and extremely successful businesswoman, Sonia H. Greene, living in Brooklyn, near Prospect Park.

Nothing in his background prepared him for the role of husband and provider. For almost the entire period of their marriage, his wife was the breadwinner, while Lovecraft, away from familiar surroundings and obsessed by a detestation of anything foreign, could scarcely tolerate contact with the "alien hordes" that surrounded him in New York City. Although his wife was gracious, sympathetic, and understanding, there must have been times when her undoubted love for him was put to a severe test.

Finally, suggesting that they continue their marriage by correspondence, Lovecraft packed his bags, left his wife, and returned to his aunts in his beloved Providence.

A small weekly income of ten to fifteen dollars from a family interest in a sadly declining stone quarry provided his main source of livelihood. This minuscule sum was supplemented by occasional checks from editors, which became fewer and further apart as the years progressed.

He reverted to the living pattern of an earlier period. He worked by night and slept by day, keeping his shutters closed and the shades down. Perhaps as the aftermath of a kidney ailment, he had no tolerance for cold and scarcely ever went out of the super-heated frame house during the winter months.

Ghost writing and literary assistance to would-be writers provided another meager source of revenue. However, Lovecraft's method of revision usually consisted of discarding the client's draft completely and then rewriting the story from beginning to end. The majority of his so-called collaborations during his lifetime are almost entirely his own work and established a number of embryo reputations.

Lovecraft's most famous ghost-written story was based on an idea suggested by the famous magician Harry Houdini, who was a stockholder in *Weird Tales*. The finished story, *Imprisoned with the Pharaohs*, was featured on the cover of the May-June-July 1924 first-anniversary issue of the magazine.

Lovecraft maintained a correspondence with as many as

a hundred friends and acquaintances simultaneously, writing letters that often ran to thirty or forty pages. The warmth, brilliance, and erudition of his correspondence created fierce friendships with individuals who were never to meet him, and provided inspiration for dozens of men and women destined later to achieve literary importance. Correspondence apparently served as a consolation for the lack of human companionship in Lovecraft's life and made it possible for him to retain his stability, particularly during the final years when he became a virtual recluse. At the same time, the extraordinary volume of it prevented him from writing works of fiction that might have substantially increased his income.

Despite this, the period from 1923 to 1926 was the most successful financially of Lovecraft's life. *Weird Tales* published nineteen of his tales during those years, tales v ritten between 1917 and 1921. Already Lovecraft was outgrowing the influences of Dunsany, Machen, Blackwood, and a half-dozen other writers whose work he profoundly admired. But he would never outgrow Poe.

What was developing was something creatively original— something that in presentation and method was distinctly Lovecraft's own. But that very difference was to presage tragic and unnecessary literary problems.

The first inkling of trouble came with the writing of *The Shunned House* in 1924. Lovecraft had traveled and seen more of the world, and part of his sense of outsiderness had vanished. The early scientific interests began to reassert themselves.

This was inevitable, since Lovecraft countenanced no form of mysticism whatsoever; he embraced no religion and did not believe in the existence of a deity. He was contemptuous of the concept of the supernatural. He would not even pretend that the strange horrors he wrote about transcended natural law.

Strange lines, for a writer of supernatural fiction, appeared in *The Shunned House*: "Such a thing was surely not a physical or biochemical impossibility in the light of a newer science which includes the theories of relativity and intra-atomic action."

The Shunned House is in truth a horror science fiction story in which the denouement is the discovery and destruction of a mammoth creature buried beneath a building. Though related with documentary preciseness it did not preclude passages of truly poetic beauty. But—Farnsworth Wright rejected it.

Scarcely knowing what to do with the story, Lovecraft sent it to his old friend, W. Paul Cook, who had previously published, in his amateur periodical, *The Vagrant*, three earlier Lovecraft tales, *Dagon, The Tomb,* and *The Statement of Randolph Carter,* and had set in type but never run off *The Outsider* and *The Rats in the Wall.* In 1927 Cook had issued his legendary one-time-only publication, *The Recluse,* which contained Lovecraft's brilliant article, *Supernatural Horror in Literature.* A second issue with forty pages in proof contained *The Strange High House in the Mist,* but the number was never completed.

Cook printed *The Shunned House* as a fifty-nine-page book in 1928, with an introduction by Lovecraft's close friend Frank Belknap Long. The book was never bound and only six copies were generally circulated out of an edition that could not have exceeded one hundred. After the death of a youthful friend of Lovecraft's, R. H. Barlow, additional copies were discovered which were procured and sold by August W. Derleth.

Cool Air, a fictional account of a scientist who succeeds in sustaining mental awareness and movement in his body after it had died (slowing down physical deterioration by remaining in a refrigerated apartment), was written by Lovecraft in 1926 and graphically illustrates his growing unwillingness to explain the strange and bizarre by other than scientific means. Wright rejected this story also but Lovecraft succeeded in selling it to *Tales of Magic and Mystery,* a short-lived competitor of *Weird Tales,* in which it appeared in March 1928.

Pickman's Model, a real shudder-provoker published in the October 1927 *Weird Tales*, deals with a masterful artist of the fantastic and evil whose bizarre subject matter is discovered to have been copied from real life. This is technically a tale of science fiction aimed at creating a mood of horror. One sentence in the story served as the inspiration for Ralph Barbour Johnson's masterful science fiction horror story, *Far Below*, which elicited a strongly favorable response when *Weird Tales* published it in its issue for June-July 1939. That sentence reads:

> There was a study called *Subway Accident*, in which a flock of vile things were clambering up from some unknown catacomb through a crack in the Boylston Street subway and attacking a crowd of people on the platform.

Lovecraft's new attitude burst completely into the open with the appearance of *The Call of Cthulhu*, written in 1926 and published in *Weird Tales* for February 1928. In that story, an accident causes the undersea tomb of an ancient creature, Cthulhu, one of a group that " had come from the stars and brought their images with them," to rise to the surface. This story was a major presentation of the Cthulhu mythology couched in terms of science fiction instead of the supernatural, incorporating references to R'lyeh, great stone city under the sea and to the *Necronomicon*, the horrendous tome penned by the mad Arab, Abdul Alhazred, with its famous lines:

> That is not dead which can eternal lie,
> And with strange aeons even death may die.

Following *The Call of Cthulhu*, Lovecraft wrote what he believed to be his supreme masterpiece, *The Colour Out of Space*. This purely science fiction tale is unquestionably a great story and, if not the finest single thing composed by Lovecraft, certainly among his best three.

The story seizes the reader's interest immediately and

builds, without flagging, to its tremendous conclusion. The characterization is excellent and the dialogue possibly the best ever done by Lovecraft, who generally adhered to straight narrative. His observations on the radioactivity of the entities from space is science of a high order for the year in which the story was written.

So full of high hope for this story, Lovecraft was stunned when it was rejected by *Weird Tales*. In a letter to Frank Belknap Long, Lovecraft stormed at the shortsightedness of Farnsworth Wright. Though *Weird Tales* printed numerous science fiction stories, Wright preferred the romantic adventure so popular in *Argosy*, or even straight action stories. Lovecraft submitted the story to *Argosy*, which also rejected it as being a bit too "strong" for their readership. But the gimlet-eyed Hugo Gernsback did not let it get by him when it came his turn.

In the blurb for this windfall in the September 1927 *Amazing Stories*, Gernsback wrote:

> Here is a totally different story that we can highly recommend. We could wax rhapsodical in our praise, as the story is one of the finest pieces of literature it has been our good fortune to read. The theme is original and yet fantastic enough to make it rise head and shoulders above many contemporary scientifiction stories. You will not regret having read this marvelous tale.

This should have been the signal to Lovecraft that he no longer belonged in *Weird Tales*, especially after *The Colour Out of Space* received honorable mention in Edward J. O'Brien's *Best American Short Stories for 1928*, a distinction only two other Lovecraft stories, *The Outsider* and *Pickman's Model*, had previously received.

The chronic economic straits of *Weird Tales* also conspired against Lovecraft. According to W. Paul Cook, Farnsworth Wright paid Lovecraft a higher rate per word than most of his other authors got. Lovecraft's stories of that period tended to get longer and longer and Wright simply could not afford to pay a premium for novelettes and short novels.

The Dunwich Horror, written in 1928 and published in *Weird Tales* for April 1929, indicates by its sheer brilliance, following so closely after *The Colour Out of Space*, that Lovecraft was now at the very peak of his artistry. These stories were the beginnings of something completely original on the American scene and a major contribution to science fiction. With the deletion of a few incantations, *The Dunwich Horror*, fundamentally the story of the problems of adjustment of Wilbur Whately, offspring of a creature from outer space who has mated with an idiot human girl, becomes science fiction.

Three years were to pass before Lovecraft would see another story of his published and yet some of his finest work was being produced during this period. The weird-fantasy novel, *The Case of Charles Dexter Ward*, a precisely turned masterpiece written in 1927-28, languished in manuscript until 1941, when it was published posthumously in *Weird Tales*. The major reason for the delay was that Lovecraft was too discouraged even to prepare it for submission.

Wright wanted for his magazine, particularly from Lovecraft, weird-horror tales that were short. Lovecraft gave him only science fiction stories that were long. Finally, Wright did take *The Whisperer in Darkness*, a novelette of 28,000 words, constructed with the most fastidious detail around the idea of a colony of aliens from outer space, attempting to recruit renegades for their ill-defined purposes.

The readers went wild. The popularity of *The Whisperer in Darkness* at the time of its publication transcended that of anything Lovecraft had ever done.

Lovecraft followed it in 1931 with a 45,000-word novel— actually a modernized sequel to Poe's *Narrative of Arthur Gordon Pym*—*At the Mountains of Madness*, which, in the most detailed, scholarly fashion conceivable, outlined the history, habits, technology, and civilization of the creatures of his Cthulhu mythos. As a bible of that mythology it is indispensable to the Lovecraft fan; but as a story, it is too long by far and it should have been trimmed in half as Wright suggested upon its rejection. Most of the padding is in the first half; after that it picks up momentum and includes some of Lovecraft's best writing.

The orderly creation of background in *The Shadow Over Innsmouth*, the next story from Lovecraft's pen, written in 1932, is unsurpassed in any of his other works. Nevertheless, the story suffers from an ending of dreamlike fantasy that does not fit the projected mood. Here we find echoes of *Dagon* as the genetically altered inhabitants of Innsmouth gradually assume the shapes of civilized creatures from antiquity, still dwelling in and backoning from marvelous cities beneath the sea.

The Shadow Out of Time, written by Lovecraft in 1934, is a 30,000-word novelette, which, despite its length, retains all the fabulous imaginative qualities of good science fiction possessed by *At the Mountains of Madness*, but without that novel's tediousness.

The nature and scope of the multitude of ideas in *The Shadow Out of Time* reflect the unmistakable influence of the soaring imagination of that cosmic philosopher Olaf Stapledon, as expressed in *Last and First Men*. The plot, in which the dreams of a modern man about a civilization of the pre-human intelligences, 155,000,000 years past, are found to be probably true, is brought home to the reader with stunning impact and consummate artistry.

Neither of the remarkable science fiction excursions, *At the Mountains of Madness* and *The Shadow Out of Time*, nor the magnificent science fantasy *The Shadow Over Innsmouth*, could find a home in *Weird Tales*.

A collaboration with E. Hoffman Price, *Through the Gates of the Silver Key*, was published in *Weird Tales* for July 1934. A hybrid tale which begins as a weird story, continues as sheer fantasy, and ends as science fiction, it revolves around a powerful situation involving a human ego taking over an alien's will on a distant world, then returning to earth in his outré guise. The human drama inherent in the idea was not properly exploited, but the story is nonetheless memorable.

One by one, the Lovecraft disciples followed as he led the way to science fiction. As they did they began to sell to *Wonder Stories*, *Astounding Stories*, and *Amazing Stories*, markets that specialized in such material. Clark Ashton Smith, Donald Wandrei, Howard Wandrei, Robert Bloch, Henry Kuttner, C. L. Moore, Frank Belknap Long, Carl Jacobi, and Hazel Heald (whose work he revised) were selling easily and readily, but the near-genius Lovecraft was pathetically grateful when William Crawford, who published the semiprofessional magazine *Marvel Tales*, offered to print without royalties a 200-copy edition, in hard covers, of *The Shadow Over Innsmouth*. This project eventually materialized in 1936 as a crude little volume, selling for only one dollar and not too well at that.

Meanwhile, Lovecraft tightened his food budget to thirty cents a day and neglected his stomach to obtain postage money for his ever-growing list of correspondents, which had now become his avenue of escape from harsh reality.

Finally his friends could stand it no longer. Without his knowledge, Donald Wandrei (author of *The Red Brain* in *Weird Tales* and *Colossus* in *Astounding Stories*) secured the manuscripts of *At the Mountains of Madness* and *The Shadow Out of Time* and brought them to F. Orlin Tremaine, editor of *Astounding Stories*. Tremaine bought them both and Lovecraft received the two largest checks of his entire writing career.

Four years earlier, Hugo Gernsback had bought a Lovecraft revision of *The Man of Stone* from Hazel Heald for *Wonder Stories*. Whenever Lovecraft material was sent where it belonged, it seems to have been purchased. Yet, blinded by his outspoken disdain for the literary quality of the science fiction magazines, Lovecraft had ignored these markets to his own detriment.

For its third anniversary issue, September 1935, *Fantasy*

Magazine wanted something truly unusual. So its editor, Julius Schwartz, commissioned two round-robin stories—one of science fiction and one of weird fiction. For the weird fiction story he assigned segments to C. L. Moore, A. Merritt, H. P. Lovecraft, Robert E. Howard, and Frank Belknap Long. All went well until the story reached Lovecraft. Then the science fiction syndrome switched on and the High Priest of Cthulhu converted the story into an intergalactic tale of super-science splendor. Even more unique, if excerpted the Lovecraft portion became a complete story in itself. *Fantasy Magazine* ended up printing two science fiction tales instead of one science fiction and one weird.

One of the last things Lovecraft did in science fiction was in collaboration with Kenneth Sterling, a story called *In the Walls of Eryx*, which concerns a transparent maze on the planet Venus that traps unwary explorers.

When H. P. Lovecraft died, the morning of March 15, 1937, he was only forty-seven years old, wasted to a pitiful shadow from the effects of Bright's disease and intestinal cancer. His greatest fame was yet to come but his influence on the body of science fiction was already felt.

One of the first properly to understand and interpret his contribution was Fritz Leiber, Jr. Writing in the Fall 1944 issue of *The Acolyte*, he observed:

> Perhaps Lovecraft's most important single contribution was the adoption of science-fiction material to the purpose of supernatural terror. The decline of at least naive belief in Christian theology, resulting in an immense loss of prestige for Satan and his hosts, left the emotion of supernatural fear swinging around loose, without any well-recognized object. Lovecraft took up this loose end and tied it to the unknown but possible denizens of other planets and regions beyond the space-time continuum.

For that purpose, Lovecraft had propounded his theories on the writing of science fiction, the validity of which have been tested by time.

The characters, though they must be natural, should be subordinated to the central marvel around which they are grouped. [Lovecraft wrote in his essay on interplanetary fiction.] The true hero of a marvel tale is not any human being, but simply a *set of phenomena*. . . . All that a marvel story can ever be, in a serious way, is a vivid picture of a certain type of human mood. Since marvel tales cannot be true to the events of life, they must shift their emphasis toward something to which they can be true; namely, certain wistful or restless moods of the human spirit, wherein it seeks to weave gossamer ladders of escape from the galling tyranny of time, space and natural laws.

16

OLAF STAPLEDON:
COSMIC PHILOSOPHER

The most titanic imagination ever brought to science fiction undoubtedly belonged to W. Olaf Stapledon. His first work of fiction, *Last and First Men*, published by Methuen, London, in 1930, was an instant critical success although it caught both the literati and the science fiction devotees by surprise. Neither group had ever heard of Stapledon, nor were they prepared for the cosmic sweep and grandeur of the ideas and philosophical concepts to be found in the work. The response to this book was extraordinary.

"But far and away the best book of this kind in our time —yes, I will risk it for once, a masterpiece—is Olaf Stapledon's amazing chronicle of the next two thousand million years," wrote renowned author J. B. Priestley in *The Clarion*.

"As original as the solar system," enthused the Gothic master Hugh Walpole in *The Book Society News*.

"There have been many visions of the future, and a few fine ones. But none in my experience as strange as *Last and First Men*. Mr. Stapledon possesses a tremendous and beautiful imagination," was the evaluation of novelist Arnold Bennett, writing for *The Evening Standard*.

These reviews were not exceptions; they were typical of the book's reception on almost all levels of the literary world.

When *Last and First Men* appeared in 1930, science fiction in magazine form was already in full flower in the United States. There were seven magazines presenting highly advanced material, and most areas of the field had at least been probed, if not exhaustively mined. Development of science fiction as a form of literary art and more specifically as the well of new ideas flowered in the magazines. Little appeared in book form that was not strongly influenced by periodical science fiction.

William Olaf Stapledon was to prove not only the infrequent exception to this rule but also one of the most powerful prime movers in the history of science fiction.

Last and First Men projects the history of mankind from 1930 to the end of recorded time—two thousand million years in the future—when one of the Last Men, through a method of temporal projection, succeeds in transmitting to his distant ancestors the incredible saga of a history that is our future.

The events of the thirty years since the book was published have deprived the early chapters of validity as prophecy. Nevertheless, so skilled is the presentation that the reader can easily imagine himself on a different time track and thereby retain his willing suspension of disbelief.

The history begins with a divided and warring Europe called into conference with the president of the United States and a Chinese inventor. At the meeting, which takes place in England, the Chinese demonstrates that he has perfected an atomic bomb. At the same time as the demonstration takes place, an American air fleet, goaded by provocative incidents, has engaged the United European air fleet in combat and destroyed it.

As the victorious American air fleet sweeps upon England, it is destroyed by atomic weapons with common consent of the government heads assembled, including America's president.

In retaliation, an enraged America almost purges Europe of life through the use of gas and deadly bacteria. A later showdown with China finds America again victorious, and a world state is formed.

This is only the beginning of a rich and fertile work which widens increasingly in scope, progressing from peak to brilliantly imaginative peak. The entire panorama of mankind is spread before us. We read of the end of the Americanized era and the entrance into another dark age, eventually followed by the rise of Patagonia as a world center of culture. The rediscovery of atomic energy causes the downfall of the Patagonian civilization in a chain explosion. In the ten million years that ensue, the monkeys rise as a competitive, intelligent race, commanding subhuman slaves. Eventually the monkeys are exterminated by their own weaknesses and the revolt of their vassals. The rise of a great new human civilization follows.

The invasion of the Martians, microscopic creatures which travel in misty jelly-like floating clouds, brings on a war between Mars and Earth. All life is wiped out on Mars, but a destructive virus from the dust of Martian bodies sends mankind back to savagery.

A civilization of new men eventually arises which is in tune with nature and the wilderness. This race gradually advances to the point where it breeds stupendous brains which at first aid and then rule all mankind. Eventually, frustrated by their physical limitations in their quest for the only thing that means anything to them—knowledge—the great brains scientifically create a race of mental and physical supermen to replace them.

The approach of the time when the moon will move so close to earth that it will break apart and destroy the surface of the mother planet forces migration to Venus. There, the contemporary intelligent life forms are destroyed, the planet is reshaped, and man evolves into a race of winged creatures. Millions of years pass and it becomes necessary to migrate to Neptune when it is discovered that collision with a wandering gaseous body will cause our sun to become a nova.

On Neptune, natural and scientific progress creates a truly utopian society, but man is drastically changed, even to the point where the number of sexes required for procreation is increased. The end of all mankind occurs when the sun unaccountably accelerates the rate at which it burns up its energy and the heat dooms the last men before any scientific provision can be made to save the race.

However, before the end, the last men shoot countless artificial human spores into space, hoping eventually to seed worlds of other suns.

This simple chronology of events fails to do *Last and First Men* justice. Stapledon deals in depth with every phase of human development, covering not only the scientific but also the social, cultural, sexual, psychological, and philosophical changes. The core of this book, written as a straight narrative, with only fragmentary dialogue, is philosophy, and not philosophy on a sophomoric level but of true depth.

The events are related in a unique style of power and poetry. There is extraordinary beauty of phrasing and literally hundreds of plot ideas that have since seeded themselves in the fabric of modern science fiction.

Last and First Men made its American appearance in 1931 and the reaction here was only slightly less enthusiastic than in Great Britain. The late Elmer Davis, renowned radio commentator, author, and journalist, called it "the boldest and most imaginative book of our times."

The sensational tabloid *New York Evening Graphic*, of October 3, 1931, devoted a full page with three illustrations to the enthusiastic review of critic Lloyd Franklin, who stated, "The author out-Wells H. G. Wells, out-Shaws George J. Bernard and knocks Jules Verne for a loop."

Insurance that Stapledon's impact would be thoroughly felt in American science fiction circles was provided by Hugo Gernsback's *Wonder Stories* in 1931, which listed *Last and First Men* in a series of full-page advertisements making outstanding science fiction novels available to its readers.

Similarities were obvious in the Man Who Awoke series by Laurence Manning, which ran as five complete stories in *Wonder Stories* from March until August 1933. Manning's lead character is carried in a series of steps into a future which is very much like Stapledon's. There is, for example, an era ruled by giant brains, a period of a back-to-nature movement, and a finale ending on a Stapledonian philosophical note as the last men strive to determine the nature of life and the meaning of the universe.

More recently, the classic City series of Clifford Simak which won The International Fantasy Award as the outstanding volume of 1953 after its publication in book form, also evidenced in its form and content some influences of *Last and First Men.*

Inevitably so successful a first novel called for a sequel, and Stapledon obliged with *Last Men in London,* published in 1932 by Methuen. This fictional-philosophical tract cannot be truly appreciated without prior reading of *Last and First Men.* The title itself is completely misleading, because it does not refer to the last men alive in London after some disaster, as one might expect, but to a mental visit to our era by one of the last men who perished on Neptune in Stapledon's first book.

Through the words of this superman observer, Stapledon is enabled to present his philosophical observations on the life and times of the period from World War I to 1932. The most fascinating part of the volume from the viewpoint of the science fiction reader is the extremely substantial elaboration on the science, life, customs, and philosophy of mankind on Neptune which supplements material in *Last and*

First Men. Though the book was not as successful as Stapledon's previous work, it did see a second printing in 1934.

Meanwhile, the literary set and the science fiction readers received a trickle of information about Stapledon's background. He was born May 10, 1886, in the town of Wirral, near Liverpool, England. His childhood was spent near the Suez Canal. His parents had some means and he was educated at Abbotsholme School and then at Balliol College, Oxford, emerging with his Master of Arts degree. He taught a year at Manchester Grammar School, then worked in a shipping office in Liverpool, lecturing on history and English literature evenings for the Workers' Educational Association under the auspices of the University of Liverpool.

During World War I, Stapledon served three years with the Friends' Ambulance Unit, attached to the French Armed Forces. Prior to World War I, he had developed an interest in communism and socialism and managed to see printed two small volumes of revolutionary poetry, the first of them *Latter-Day Psalms,* published in Liverpool by Henry Young & Sons in 1914.

Following the war, he culminated a sporadic twelve-year courtship by marrying Agnes Miller, an Australian girl. Two children, a daughter and a son, resulted from the union.

He returned to the University of Liverpool and, majoring in philosophy and psychology, received his Doctor of Philosophy degree. He then lectured on these subjects at the University and elsewhere.

During this period he framed the ideas for his first philosophical effort, *A Modern Theory of Ethics,* which Methuen published in 1929. Subtitled "A study of the relations of ethics and psychology," the work, as a major part of its thesis, evaluates the Freudian theory of the origin of morality and discards it in favor of an intellectual morality which is an outgrowth of the theological "Do unto others as you would have them do unto you." This would insist on spontaneous sympathy for even "aliens" who are known to be in need. It would obligate one to extend help even if the recipient made no direct appeal, was not a friend or a close relative, and whether or not any "spontaneous sympathy" were felt— merely on the basis of the objective evidence that help was necessary.

The writing of science fiction was inspired by the works of H. G. Wells, Jules Verne, and Edgar Rice Burroughs, but Stapledon denied any reading of science fiction magazines prior to 1936. Nevertheless, it was science fiction that gave Olaf Stapledon stature as a philosopher.

Impressed by the immensity of his vision and his evident broad understanding of the philosophical and psychological structure of society as expressed in *Last and First Men* and *Last Men in London*, the book-reading public was pleased to learn that Stapledon was really an accredited philosopher and not a dilettante. They were ripe for *Waking World*, a militant philosophical and political discussion published by Methuen in 1934. Stapledon admits in this book that the bulk of his livelihood came from dividends on family investments, even while he proclaims "the system on which I live must go." *Waking World* also reveals a wide respect for H. G. Wells's social views.

Distinctly revolutionary in tone, Stapledon's *Waking World* viewed the capitalistic system as a decadent order that must be discarded. He deplored violence but could find no brief for pacifism. On religion he is a bit left of agnosticism, and politically a bit right of communism. His objectivity toward and even favorable approach to communism caused one exponent to term him sentimentally as "the last of the great bourgeois philosophers."

Stapledon was admittedly most impressed by the views of Spinoza and Hegel. He was, if anything, even more optimistic than they, expressing the thought: "Indeed it is not inconceivable that man is the living germ which is destined to vitalize the whole cosmos!"

In this period, and particularly in *Waking World*, Stapledon the philosopher is somewhat cocky, somewhat sure of himself. It is 1934 and everything is in a deplorable state. A lot of people agree with his ideas and tell him so. His patient is the world and he precisely and confidently diagnoses its illnesses and cures.

The next year, 1935, it was back to fiction again with *Odd John: A Story Between Jest and Earnest*, published by Methuen. *Odd John* is a story about a human mutant who is almost as far above men as men are above monkeys. It was not the first story of its type, nor even the first outstanding story on the theme. *The Hampdenshire Wonder* by renowned British novelist J. D. Beresford, first published in 1911, handled the idea with such consummate artistry that that novel has become a science fiction classic. Stapledon acknowledged his debt to *The Hampdenshire Wonder*. The renowned American mathematician Eric Temple Bell, writing under his pseudonym John Taine, rendered an outstanding example of the superman theme, stressing biological aspects, in *Seeds of Life*, which appeared in the Fall 1931 issue of *Amazing Stories Quarterly*. Philip Wylie scored with *Gladiator*, a hit novel of a purely physical superman, published by Knopf in 1930. *Odd John* certainly deserves to be ranked with those novels, and unquestionably brings a much more penetrating insight to focus on the possible outlook and morality of a super-being than does its predecessors.

Up to this time, Olaf Stapledon had written his science fiction with little awareness of the impact his work had had on the writers and readers of that genre. Though he had frequent contacts with H. G. Wells, it was not until Eric Frank Russell, then a beginning science fiction author, called on him during the summer of 1936, that he seriously related himself to the mainstream of fantastic literature.

"Since then I have been looking through a few of them [science fiction magazines]" Stapledon told Walter Gillings, publisher of the British science fiction fan magazine *Scientifiction*:

> and I was very surprised to find that so much work of this kind was being done. My impression was that the stories

varied greatly in quality. Some were only superficially scientific, while others contained very striking ideas, vividly treated.

On the whole, I felt that the human side was terribly crude, particularly the love interest. Also there seemed to me far too much padding in most of them, in proportion to the genuine imaginative interest.

At the time of the interview, in the spring of 1937, the proofs of his new book, *The Star Maker*, had already been corrected. Commenting on that book, Stapledon told Gillings:

> *Star Maker* is, I fear, a much wilder, more remote and philosophical work than *Last and First Men*, and may make it look rather microscopic by comparison. It will probably be my last fantastic book. I am now writing a little book on philosophy for the general public.

If any work of imaginative fiction can truly be described as *tour de force*, that effort is *The Star Maker*. Though in actual literary quality and inspired treatment of subject matter it did not surpass *Last and First Men*, the soaring magnificence of its concepts and its breath-taking scope cause it to transcend any other work of science fiction.

Where, in *Last and First Men*, Stapledon strove to unveil the future history of mankind, in *The Star Maker* he set out to relate the entire history of the universe, from its creation to its end. In that framework, the two thousand million years covered in *Last and First Men* become little more than a sentimental episode in the perspective of the cosmos.

Beginning with a view of life on planets of other star systems, utilizing the intellectual spirit of an earthman as the observer, Stapledon places special emphasis upon the symbiotic relationship of two sub-galactic races, the Echinoderms and the Nautiloids, who are to play a key role as one of the most highly developed civilizations in the universe. These chapters seem to represent the origin of modern science fiction stories based on symbiosis, including the type-story, *Symbiotica*, by Eric Frank Russell, in the October 1943 issue of *Astounding Science Fiction*.

Far more important in its profound influence on modern science fiction is Stapledon's elaborate description of galactic wars and the organization of galactic empires comprising thousands of planets. While it is possible that there may have been some passing reference to galactic empires in science fiction before this, nevertheless it is a fact that the trend can be traced precisely back to *The Star Maker*. The galactic empires so essential to many of the stories of modern science fiction writers, including Robert A. Heinlein, Clifford D. Simak, Eric Frank Russell, Isaac Asimov, Murray Leinster, and literally dozens of others, have been inspired by Olaf Stapledon and stem from the year 1937.

Similarly, placing the story on another star system and turning the plot on the psychology or philosophy of the inhabitants, instead of through direct action, is another of Olaf Stapledon's great contributions to science fiction. Such ideas do not appear before the writing of *The Star Maker*.

It follows that Stapledon may well be *the* most important influence on the plot structure of contemporary science fiction. We discover, in the final analysis, that *Last and First Men* and *The Star Maker* are the reservoir of basic ideas of modern science fiction writers and it takes very little investigation to reveal that today's science fiction has standardized its background and approach, utilizing Stapledon's works as its guide. Older writers adopted materials directly from his pages because of their need for a pilot in the imaginative immensity of island universes where formerly no guide existed. Newer writers accept the ideas on faith.

In *The Star Maker*, when finally there is an end to empire-making and peace reigns, a utopia develops in which there telepathically comes into being the Cosmic Mind—a state of existence where every mentally developed creature can share the ideas and experiences of all of the diverse and incalculably numerous intelligences of the universe. To supplement mental contact there are visits between communities that take the extreme of moving planets out of orbit and projecting them across galactic immensities.

Efforts to move entire systems with their suns result in the startling discovery that those flaming bodies are intelligent beings with a community sense. The suns, for ethical and moral reasons, attempt to destroy the parasites that disrupt their harmony with the infinite whole. Eventually, mental rapport is established between planetary life and the suns and a peaceful understanding is concluded.

Stapledon presents the nebulae as living creatures, with the stars their spawn. He delves into their lives, their thoughts, their philosophy and ambitions.

Finally he braves the question of the Star Maker, the elemental creator of the universe, observable as a prodigious star of such brightness and magnitude that it cannot be approached. The function of the Star Maker is to create. The entity, potentially omnipotent, begins with infantile experiments, then matures and learns from its mistakes. The intense strife and suffering of living creatures in the course of the development of the universe is part of its self-education, so that the next time it casts a new universe it can try a different tack to see if previous errors can be eliminated.

While great philosophers of history have searched man's past to find the answers to the riddle of life, Olaf Stapledon, with an awesome visionary probe, explores the future for the same answers. By driving his imagination to its extreme, he attempts to project the ultimate development and achievements of life forms, and from them determine the purpose of existence.

Dissatisfied with the Cosmic Mind as a unity, Stapledon is forced to devise a Star Maker, who, through mathematics, physics, and spiritual need, will fill the place that religion has reserved for God.

The paper-bound vogue was in full flower in England, and Pelican Books, a series issued by Penguin Books, had reprinted *Last and First Men* in 1937. Now, as a nonfiction original, they published in 1939 Olaf Stapledon's *Philosophy and Living*. This is Stapledon's most general work of philosophy and the one most indicative of the impressive scope of his studies and thinking on the subject. Actually, it is probably somewhat too involved for the layman; but it may prove important in the ultimate evaluation of Stapledon as a philosopher, since it is the purest of his philosophical presentations.

By contrast, *New Hope for Britain*, published the same year, is really a philosophical justification for political action and an exhortation for the adoption of socialism in England as the first step toward a world state.

Saints and Revolutionaries, still another 1939 publication, was done by William Heinemann, London, as part of the I Believe volumes, a series of personal statements by such well-known figures as J. D. Beresford, Charles Williams, Gerald Bullett, and Kenneth Ingram, as well as Olaf Stapledon. As its title implies, this book is a detailed philosophical consideration of the similarities and differences of people characterized as saints or as revolutionaries. It ends with the thought that eventually the Cosmic Mind, such as is suggested in *The Star Maker*, may be achieved and that in accomplishing this man will have created his "mythical" God image.

Olaf Stapledon clearly foresaw World War II in his preface to *The Star Maker*, which began with the words:

> At a moment when Europe is in danger of a catastrophe worse than that of 1914 a book like this may be condemned as a distraction from the desperately urgent defence of civilization against modern barbarism.

How did such a man, obviously of extraordinarily high intelligence and sensitivity, react to the second great war in his lifetime? The answer lies in his books.

During the early part of the war, he wrote *Darkness and Light*, a work of the same style as *Last and First Men*, purporting to show two different worlds and two futures, depending on whether the powers of darkness or of light won out. As far as it goes, *Darkness and Light* is certainly fascinating reading, but its prime conclusion seems to be that the great hope for mankind is the coming into being, either artificially or through mutation, of an advanced species which will possess more of godliness and less of the animal. *Darkness and Light*, thereby, swings *Odd John* more clearly into the perspective of Stapledon's philosophy and establishes his true reasons for exploring the superman concept.

The same year, 1942, Searchlight, another paper-back firm, published Olaf Stapledon's latest philosophical effort, *Beyond the 'Isms*. This work examined the major religions and political movements, and, though it found them basically wanting, it drew from them the suggestion that the development of the "spirit" was the only answer to a better future. Given as a definition of "spirit" was:

> The spirit manifests itself solely in personality-in-community. . . . We shall always recognize that both individual and society are abstractions, and neither can exist without the other. . . . And expression of the spirit, let it never be forgotten, means development in sensitive and intelligent awareness, love and creative action.

Many of Stapledon's works of fiction are prefaced by the phrase "This is not a novel," meaning that, though fiction, it does not conform to the principles generally associated with a romantic, imaginative work. No such remarks preceded *Sirius: A Fantasy of Love and Discord*, published in 1944 by Martin Secker & Warburg. As a novel this is the finest of all of Stapledon's fictional efforts. It deals with experiments in England which produce a super male dog—a dog with intelligence equal to and possibly higher than that of a human being. The methods by which this dog is trained, the problems of his adjustment to both human and canine society are brilliantly and incisively presented. The consequences of a love affair (with all of its implications) between Sirius, the dog, and Plaxy, the girl who raised him, provide adult reading with distinct allegorical applications to the world's racial situation. Within the bounds of science fiction *Sirius* is a great masterpiece, pregnant with meaning, poetic and poignant in beauty of style. With this book, Stapledon proved that regardless of the final verdict on him as a philosopher, it would be hard to dispute his stature as a skillful storyteller.

The fictional embodiment of his suggestion of worshiping the "spirit" as put forward in *Beyond the 'Isms* occurred in Stapledon's short story, *Old Man in New World*, which appeared in 1944 as a slim volume under the auspices of P.E.N., the world association of writers. A group of modern saints and revolutionaries, the "agnostic mystics," start a global strike on the eve of the third world war, resulting in an American revolution and a change in Russian policy. A world state is formed and a condition of near-utopia attained; but in the end, Stapledon predicts a human reversion to nationalism and religion which will renew, in his view, the old vicious cycle.

The final answer to how the war affected Olaf Stapledon is to be found in his novel-length prose poem, *Death Into Life*, published in 1946. Here the exploration of mysticism as an end in itself is pronounced enough to be called a retreat. The feelings of the rear gunner of a bomber going into battle are described, followed by his death and contact with the spirits of the rest of the crew and of others who have died. Finally, these merge into "the Spirit of Man," which becomes a philosophical tool for Stapledon to explore the past, the present, and the future. There are brief sections describing a tomorrow reminiscent of his past works.

A nonfiction book, *Youth and Tomorrow*, issued by the St. Botolph Publishing Co., London, in 1946, finds Stapledon repeating his thesis that personality-in-community and worship of the spirit represent the only hope for improvement of the modern world. The ultimate salvation, he reiterates, rests in future man biologically improving the species.

A brief return to the type of fantasy that had established his reputation came with *The Flames*, a 25,000-word science fiction tale published by Secker & Warburg in 1947. Writing cogently and well, Stapledon relates the efforts of flame creatures from the sun (alluded to in *The Star Maker*), who have been stranded on earth, to persuade mankind that a permanently radioactive area be established to make conditions more tolerable for them here. In return, they offer human society the spiritual guidance to help solve its dilemma. Suspicious of the motives of the Flames, their human contact rejects salvation for fear of slavery. The story is minor, however, being little more than a review of ideas Stapledon had previously presented.

Stapledon never lost his interest in the prospects of interplanetary travel. He was a member of The British Interplanetary Society and delivered an address at their London session of October 9, 1948, on "Interplanetary Man," in which he noted the irony of this world about to destroy itself on the threshold of reaching the stars. The entire 5,000-word address, discussing "the profound ethical, philosophical and religious questions which will undoubtedly arise from interplanetary exploration," was printed in the November 1948 *Journal of the British Interplanetary Society*.

Then occurred an experience which must have had a profound effect upon Olaf Stapledon. The National Council of the Arts, Sciences and Professions, labeled by newspapers a Communist-front organization, announced with great fanfare the organization of The Cultural and Scientific Conference for Peace, to be held in New York and to be followed by a country-wide tour. Outstanding figures from many nations were invited. Dmitri Shostakovich, noted Russian composer, was the star of the program and represented the caliber of delegates desired from each nation. Olaf Stapledon was one of only five invited from Great Britain. Visas to all but Stapledon were refused.

Stapledon was introduced in Newark, New Jersey, March 30, 1949, by Millard Lampell as the author of "that magnificent fantasy, *Last and First Men* . . . speaking here today because he does not want to be the last man in the world."

The answers that had once so easily flowed from Stapledon's pen were gone. "I am not a communist," he stated with emphasis, "I am not a Christian, I am just me! I am, however, a socialist, as are the majority of my countrymen. . . . Let individualism triumph over your sense of individuality. Forget one another's mistakes and for God's sake let's get together!"

He returned to Europe greatly depressed. "There may be a war at any moment," he told newspaper reporters upon his return.

One more bit of fantasy was still to appear, A Man Divided, under the Methuen imprint in 1950.

Fantasy? Autobiography is the more apt term. Ostensibly concerning a man of dual personality who seesaws between brilliant clarity of thought and action and "doltish" mass thinking, A Man Divided transparently presents the events and agonizing intellectual conflicts by which Stapledon fashioned his philosophy, and gives an intimate picture of his personality and life from 1912 to 1948.

It was as if Stapledon had a strange premonition and felt an urgent need for summing up, for within months of the publication of A Man Divided William Olaf Stapledon was dead. The end came on Septmber 6, 1950, in Cheshire, England, when he was sixty-four, and was attributed to a coronary occlusion.

The strangest was yet to come.

His widow, Agnes Z. Stapledon, painstakingly transcribed from his penciled draft, a final, unfinished book of philosophy, which was published in 1954 by Methuen and titled The Opening of the Eyes. A lifelong friend, E. V. Rieu, in a preface to the book, told of a last meeting with Stapledon after his return from America a year before his death. "He had reached the goal of his thinking," Rieu said. "He had come to terms with reality; and comprehension had been added to acceptance. There was a note of serenity in his bearing, that is a pleasure to remember now that he is gone."

This is the core of what Olaf Stapledon said in that final book:

Is this perhaps hell's most exquisite refinement, that one should be haunted by the ever-present ghost of a disbelieved-in God? . . . Illusion though you are, I prefer to act in the pretense of your reality, rather than from stark nothingness. Without the fiction of your existence, I am no more than a reflex animal and the world is dust.

He had accepted God.

Above all I spurn the subtle lure that snares the comrades [he continued], the call of brotherhood in the Revolution, and in mankind's seeming progress! There can be no progress but the lonely climbing of each solitary soul toward you.

Olaf Stapledon died with his lifelong mental anguish resolved.

He had renounced communism and socialism. He had attained The Cosmic Mind at last.

17
SPACE OPUS:
PHILIP WYLIE

In March 1930 the Book League Monthly, a paperback book club, offered its readership a selection filled with some startling situations: a man who could lift weights of four tons with ease, leap such distances that he almost seemed to fly, shed machine-gun bullets as a bridegroom sheds rice, rip bank vaults apart as though they were papier-mâché, or break a charging bull's neck with a side-handed cuff. The book was *Gladiator* by Philip Wylie. Most of today's readers will probably recognize the character: Superman, of course—the original.

A few years later, a Cleveland cartoonist Joe Schuster and his author associate Jerome Siegel would borrow the central theme from *Gladiator*, even paraphrase some of the dialogue, to create one of the most popular cartoon adventure strips of our time and no one would dream the idea had once been the basis of a serious novel.

Gladiator was the third book by Philip Wylie. It had been preceded by two novels of manners, *Heavy Laden* (1928) and *Babes and Sucklings* (1929). But in point of fact, it was the first novel he wrote, and when it was accepted by Alfred A. Knopf, the publisher agreed to hold it back for a few years until Wylie established a reputation with more general works of fiction.

There have been many types of supermen in fiction, but if we rule out Edgar Rice Burroughs' Tarzan, on the basis that it is theoretically within the realm of possibility that a properly selected, trained, and reared human being could attain comparable strength, agility, and ferocity, then *Gladiator* is probably the greatest tale of a physical superman since the Biblical story of Samson.

A Caspar Milquetoast of a professor, Abednego Danner injects his domineering wife, newly pregnant, with a chemical while she is under the effects of an opiate. The effect is the birth of a child with superhuman strength. The mother realizes she has a problem on her hands when the tiny baby displays phenomenal strength, easily smashing his crib to smithereens with a careless gesture of the hand.

The neighbors are shocked by the metal cage built for the child and the abnormality of the youthful Hugo Danner becomes the topic of conversation in the college town. The painstaking care with which the Danners train their child to hide his strength and the psychological impact upon Hugo of his growing awareness of "differentness" is superbly developed by the author.

A star football player, the boy leaves home and school after accidentally killing a member of the other team. He seeks to find a place for himself and his herculean strength in the world, at one time or another trying prize fighting, strongman acts, pearl fishing, soldiering, iron work, farming, and banking; but each career is terminated by the inability of others to accept his unparalleled physical power. A degree of verisimilitude is strengthened by Wylie's vesting Hugo Danner with only normal intelligence.

The author's purpose is simple and brutally direct—to expose the plight of a truly superior man in a world of ordinary people. As Wylie was to say years later in his *Generation of Vipers*:

> For if ever there does appear upon this planet a tightly knit minority of really superior people, it will be the end of all the rest of mankind—and mankind knows it, not having come through a billion-odd years of evolutionary struggle for nothing.

When finally a professor who understands and befriends Danner suggests the creation of a superhuman race in the wilderness, the Superman, unable to resolve his doubts, lifts his eyes to the heavens and pleads for a sign. A bolt of lightning strikes him dead.

If the book has a major flaw, it is the unconvincing ending, but excepting that, it is a rewarding, carefully written work that clearly heralded an extraordinary new talent on the science fiction scene.

Gladiator was brought to the attention of devotees by C. A. Brandt, one of the leading science fiction authorities of that period, in a thousand-word review in the June 1930 issue of *Amazing Stories*. "In spite of the obvious shortcomings of this book," Brandt concluded, alluding to its finale, "it is quite enjoyable and will not be forgotten as quickly as the average 'bestseller.'"

The science fiction world was to see much more of Philip Gordon Wylie. Born May 12, 1902, son of a Methodist minister, Philip Wylie made a case for the hereditary transmission of literary aptitude when he stated:

> I am the son of a minister of considerable eloquence and of a mother who wrote novels for magazines, the brother of a novelist, teacher and essayist, and the half-brother of as vivid a writer as death ever choked into premature silence—so I have always lived in the midst of language.

Philip's mother died while he was still a child and his father raised him. Fascinated by science, he practically memorized the children's *Book of Knowledge* by the time he was twelve. He stole books on explosives from the Montclair, New Jersey, library and successfully manufactured explosives and fireworks, somehow managing to keep from blowing his head off.

Jules Verne and H. G. Wells raised his interest in science to a fever so that in high school he favored mathematics and physics. Nevertheless, the discovery of James Joyce and other literary experimentalists of the early years of the century, plus some poetic aspirations, altered his interests sufficiently so that he registered at Princeton with the idea of majoring in English. His application was made too late and, in desperation, he pleaded wtih the dean to make an exception in his case.

The dean agreed on condition that he be permitted to lay out Wylie's curriculum. The dean was partial to science, and Wylie found himself burdened with all the higher mathematics, physics, geology, evolution, and biology he could handle. Heroically, he completed three years, then in 1923 threw in the sponge, for reasons more personal than academic.

Out of college, young Wylie veered back in the direction of a literary career, becoming a member of the staff of *The New Yorker* in 1925. His interest in science fiction had not ended with Verne and Wells and he read Edgar Rice Burroughs until the Mars series convinced him that he knew infinitely more science than John Carter's creator. When the world's first science fiction magazine, *Amazing Stories*, appeared in 1926, it could boast Philip Wylie as a charter reader.

Acceptance by Knopf of *Gladiator* in 1927 probably contributed to the brevity of his stint as advertising manager of the Cosmopolitan Book Corporation, which occupied him during parts of 1927 and 1928. In 1928, Cosmopolitan published Wright's best-seller, *Deluge*, a tale of planetary flood and disaster that was made into a motion picture by RKO in 1933. Elements in certain world catastrophe sequences in *Deluge* seem to echo in Wylie's later *When Worlds Collide*, particularly man's reversion to unreasoning savagery, a quick peeling away of the veneer of civilization.

One year after the publication of *Gladiator*, Farrar and
Rinehart issued another science fiction novel by Philip Wylie,
The Murderer Invisible, telling of a man who discovers the
secret of invisibility and seeks first to terrorize and then rule
the world. There are dramatic scenes of destruction and chaos
in Washington, D. C., and New York, but the scientist is
eventually betrayed by a girl he thought loved him. The
novel clearly reveals the paternity of H. G. Wells's *The Invisible Man* through an identical method of achieving invisibility: attaining ultimate transparency of all bone and body
tissue after neutralizing color and pigment.

Universal Studios had purchased *The Invisible Man* at the
time *The Murderer Invisible* appeared. Wylie's more sensational development of the theme attracted their attention.
They bought movie rights to Wylie's book and the picture,
The Invisible Man, which appeared in 1933, owed as much to
Wylie as to Wells in the final form. It was this film which
established Claude Rains as an American film star (even
though his face is seen only in the closing minutes).

As a novel, though fast paced and even occasionally memorable, for example the scene in which the partially invisible
professor, William Carpenter, is saved by a clergyman from
the townspeople who intend to burn him, *The Murderer
Invisible* was too melodramatic and derivative to make a
serious impact.

Just before this, Philip Wylie had made his first contact
with Hollywood on the recommendation of the editor of
The Saturday Evening Post. Paramount had purchased H. G.
Wells's *The Island of Dr. Moreau* and was looking for a man
to adapt it for the screen. They had great misgivings about
making plausible the fantastic concept of transforming animals surgically into human beings, but they took heart when
Philip Wylie, an inveterate Wells fan and science fiction
lover, assured them that the biological aspects of the story
were sound. They hired him to do the script for what became
a screen horror masterpiece, *The Island of Lost Souls*, which
starred Charles Laughton.

Wylie's adventure novel *The Savage Gentleman* was published by Farrar and Rinehart in 1932 while he was employed full-time in Hollywood. It deals with a social experiment conducted by the owner of a chain of eleven American newspapers. He takes his infant son and a few trusted aides to an uncharted island in the Pacific after an unfortunate and embittering marriage. It is his intention to raise his son away from the corrupting influences of civilization.

The island has the crumbling remains of an ancient civilization as well as types of zebu-oxen and giant lemurs that evolution forgot. After thirty-three years on the island, during which time the baby has become a physical giant capable of killing sharks with a hunting knife for sport and the equivalent of the education of a Doctor of Philosophy through the training of his father, the small group is rescued from the island by a Scandinavian freighter.

His father has died of a heart attack, but the son, Henry Stone, returns to civilization to find himself heir to an estate that has grown to twenty-two newspapers and eleven banks. He rescues his newspapers from dishonest leadership, becomes involved with women, and evolves a philosophical defense against the baser aspects of much of the world. This is an adroitly told tale whose distillation from the Edgar Rice Burroughs formula would have been obvious without the author's more than strong hint in the greeting of Henry Stone by the lawyer of his estate:

> "Stone! Good God, young man, what a surprise! And what a story!" He smiled ruefully, then. "And how we've mishandled it. We've made the young scion of our founder into a Tarzan, without any real information about him at all."

Much more significant are the lines in the book delivered by Henry Stone's father:

> "I've told him, McCobb—all about women. About women as mothers. And I've recounted their sins. Their shortcomings. Their lack of imagination and their superficiality. I've tried to educate him—prejudice him, perhaps—without lying. He understands."

This was only 1932, fully ten years before *Generation of Vipers* was to explode "Momism" on the public, but few would remember how long the idea had been in gestation. Not even Wylie seemed aware of when the concept had cropped up in his work. During a television interview with Mike Wallace on "Night Beat" in 1957, he attributed its inclusion in *Generation of Vipers* to a remark by Hervey Allen, the novelist, about a division of soldiers that had spelled out "MOM" on the drill field.

And as far as women in mass were concerned, Philip Wylie has the elder Stone leave as a legacy to his son this advice:

> "Never, never, never believe a woman. . . . Women are ruin. Love is a myth. Marry when you are over forty-five and marry someone you do not love. Love is ruin."

But *Generation of Vipers* was still a long way off and Hollywood, oblivious to "Momism" but quite aware of the popularity of Tarzan, chortled with glee at the thought that they had a screenwriter who could create a counterpart of Burroughs' apeman. Philip Wylie transferred to a movie script the Lion Man as the lead character in a thriller, *The King of the Jungle* (based on C. T. Stoneham's *The Lion's Way*, published in 1931 by Hutchinson, London), a Paramount release of 1933 that paraded the superb body of champion swimmer Buster Crabbe across the screen in his initial role.

The Island of Lost Souls had proved good box office, so Philip Wylie was assigned another horror script, which the public viewed as *Murders in the Zoo* starring Lionel Atwill, also in 1933.

But Wylie had no intention of being typed. True, during this period he was fully as handsome as many of the movie stars, a swimmer with a fine physique (maintained by a bit of weight lifting), and with a cultivated manner that contradicted the savagery of his rhetoric. Good money and good living did not diminish his interest in science. Learning that the film-makers were racking their brains for a consultant for the little-known science of radioactivity (a picture on the life of

Mme. Curie, co-discoverer of radium, was being made), Wylie assured them he knew just the man. He borrowed the script and headed for the California Institute of Technology. There he talked to Robert A. Millikan, who had won the Nobel prize in physics in 1923 for the isolation of the electron and the measurement of its charge and was then still shining up the 1932 Roosevelt Association Medal awarded him for his research in cosmic rays.

Turning the script over to a few of his associate physicists, Millikan took Philip Wylie on a guided tour around the Norman Bridges Laboratory, where crackling cyclotrons were contributing knowledge toward man's forthcoming harnessing of the atom.

Wylie was entranced and during the remainder of his stay in Hollywood spent more time at the Norman Bridges Laboratory than on the set. His scientific background at Princeton gave him a quick grasp of the subject and the information he absorbed from the leading theoreticians and experimenters at the Laboratory provided a more advanced course in physics than could have been obtained in university classrooms.

So enthusiastic and convincing did Wylie become about the wonders of future science that the studio heads decided to go ahead with a serious film to be titled *Fifty Years From Now*. They assigned him to tour the country with Milton Mackaye, visiting top scientists and experimental laboratories, to assemble authentic information suitable for the production. A marvelous portfolio was assembled and the picture about the world of 1983 was ready to go into production when the paths of H. G. Wells and Philip Wylie crossed again. Out of England came news that Alexander Korda had purchased Wells's recently published *The Shape of Things to Come* for a somewhat similar forecast of the future. This finally appeared in 1935 as *Things to Come*, starring Raymond Massey and Cedric Hardwicke, and plans for *Fifty Years From Now* were permanently shelved.

Despite his rigid Hollywood schedule, Wylie, a speedy and prolific writer, never ceased his book and magazine output.

He had been a contributor to *Redbook* magazine and had collaborated with its editor, Edwin Balmer, on a non-fantasy novel *5 Fatal Words*. Donald Kennicott, editor of *Redbook's* companion magazine, *Blue Book*, characterized Balmer as "a wizard in ideas, plot and suspenseful situation, but rather left-handed in the detail of writing. As a result, a great deal of his work was done in collaboration—for a long time with his brother-in-law William MacHarg, and later with Phil Wylie and others."

Balmer, working with MacHarg, received considerable notoriety by forecasting the lie detector. In most accurate scientific detail, they had predicted not only the method that was eventually used, but a half-dozen other approaches which might have proved equally effective, in a series of short stories published in book form by Small Maynard, Boston, in 1910 as *The Achievements of Luther Trant*. Most of the collection was reprinted by Hugo Gernsback in his science fiction magazines, *Amazing Stories* and *Scientific Detective Monthly*, in the late twenties and early thirties. Balmer also had a science fiction novel, *The Flying Death*, 1927, to his credit.

An astronomy enthusiast, Balmer had roughed out a sequence of events for a novel where two planets enter our solar system from outer space. One will strike the earth, with resultant mutual destruction. The only chance man has for survival is to build spaceships and transfer a few thousand men and women to the second invading world—which will take up an orbit around the sun—before it moves out of range. He presented this idea to Wylie and found a kindred spirit. Like a child with a new toy, Philip Wylie assembled his physicist friends at Cal Tech and mathematically mapped out the scientific elements by which this feat of spatial leap frog could be accomplished. The time lost in the advancement of atomics was unquestionably science fiction's gain.

The collaboration, written as *These Shall Not Die*, was retitled *When Worlds Collide* by Donald Kennicott and was serialized, beginning with the September 1932 issue, in *Blue Book*.

In 1932 there were not enough science fiction magazines to assuage the hunger of its thousands of avid followers. Along with *Argosy*, *Blue Book* catered heavily to this group. *Tarzan and the Leopard Men* ran almost concurrently with *When Worlds Collide*. This, together with a price reduction to fifteen cents effective with that issue, gave Balmer and Wylie's effort exposure to a readership swollen by recruits from the science fiction magazines.

"In this issue," Donald Kennicott told them, "appears one of the most remarkable novels any magazine has printed in years—'When Worlds Collide,' the collaboration of two of America's best writers . . . you have a real novelty awaiting you . . ."

The collaboration proved a sensation. There had been tales of cosmic disaster before and on a grand scale, but never one told with such scientific verisimilitude, literary facility, and focus on the individual.

The dialogue was as slick as that appearing in the best magazines, the tension mounted with every chapter, yet the author's sincerity was never in question.

When Frederick A. Stokes Co. brought out the novel in cloth covers, reviewer C. A. Brandt, who also was first reader of *Amazing Stories*, gave it an entire page in the October 1933 issue, leading off with:

> *When Worlds Collide* is easily worth twenty times that amount ($2.00) and all lovers of science fiction are urged to read it.
>
> If it had been my duty to read the manuscript and comment on it, I would have called it "super-excellent," and I am glad to say that I seldom read anything as well done as this particular book.
>
> It is an astronomical fantasy of the first magnitude, exceedingly well written.

His enthusiasm was echoed by the readers. Already, fan magazines devoted to science fiction had come into being, and one of the earliest and most famous of these, *The Time*

Traveler, polled its readers for the best magazine science fiction novel of 1932. The winner was overwhelmingly *When Worlds Collide* they announced in their Winter 1933 issue.

Any victory depends on the caliber of the competition and, by the standards of the science fiction fans of 1933, it was formidable. *Argosy* had run in the preceding year A. Merritt's *Dwellers in the Mirage*, one of his best novels; Edgar Rice Burroughs had started a new interplanetary series with *Pirates of Venus*; and Austin Hall, after more than a decade of resisting reader pressure, had finally written *The Spot of Light*, a sequel to the almost legendary *Blind Spot*, on which he had collaborated with Homer Eon Flint. *Weird Tales* had run *Buccaneers of Venus* by popular Otis Adelbert Kline; and renowned mathematician Eric Temple Bell, writing under his science fiction nom de plume, John Taine, offered *The Time Stream* in *Wonder Stories*.

If there is any conclusion to be drawn, it is the evident fact that all the above stories belonged to the old scientific romance school, long on escape and adventure and short on science. Wylie demonstrated that good science was not incompatible with gripping writing and thrilling situations.

Science fiction fans were not the only ones impressed. Paramount bought *When Worlds Collide* (keeping it on the shelf until 1951) and the novel, with the original illustrations by Austin Briggs from *Blue Book*, was syndicated to the newspapers.

A sequel was a foregone conclusion. *After Worlds Collide* began in *Blue Book* for November 1933. The first novel had ended with the landing on the new world, the discovery that the air was breathable, and evidences of alien civilization. In the sequel, the reader is led on a tour of discovery involving a chain of connected, automatically functioning cities, but with no sign of life, though paintings reveal that the original inhabitants were humanlike in appearance.

Ships from several other nations have successfully escaped from earth and their passengers have occupied another city. A grim conflict in an otherworldly setting develops between an Asiatic-held city and the Americans. Ultimately the Americans are victorious, but the prime mystery remains: What happened to the builders of the cities?

Response to *After Worlds Collide* duplicated the enthusiasm for the original story. When Stokes announced it in book form, a second printing had to be made before publication. If this does not seem very impressive, it should be remembered that the nation was in the throes of the most paralyzing depression in its history and two-dollar books were definitely on the list of luxuries.

Critic C. A. Brandt found that he had exhausted his superlatives previously and in the July 1934 *Amazing Stories* wrote:

> As I pointed out in my review published in our October, 1933, issue, I would have labeled *When Worlds Collide* "super-excellent" and if *After Worlds Collide* had been written as a first book and not as a sequel, I would likewise have been compelled to call it not only good, but excellent.

There seemed no question that a third book in the series, solving the riddle of the new planet's missing inhabitants, was next on the agenda, and indeed a plot was outlined by Balmer but vetoed by Wylie. Every word of *When Worlds Collide* had been written by Wylie and it had been published as written. Wylie had also written all of the text of the sequel, but before press time Balmer made some alterations that affected scientific plausibility. Wylie, a purist nurtured in the tradition of Jules Verne, H. G. Wells, and Hugo Gernsback, was disturbed by these changes. Balmer's plot outline of the third book would have been difficult to validate on the basis of known facts. Wylie contended that the success of the first two volumes was predicated, to a large extent, upon the high degree of respect shown for scientific accuracy. Therefore, though he continued to collaborate with Balmer on adventure and detective novels, he refused to give literary substance to the projected third book in the Worlds Collide series.

Until the publication of *Generation of Vipers* in 1942, *When Worlds Collide* was probably the best-selling of all

Wylie's books, going through dozens of printings, in standard editions as well as a low-priced Triangle printing, an Armed Services Edition, foreign translations, and eventually soft-cover printings. The novel and its sequel were collected into one volume in 1950 by Lippincott. Neither has ever been out of print in hard covers since its first publication.

Very shortly after the writing of *After Worlds Collide*, a strange thing happened. Philip Wylie sat down and began to write a novel for Philip Wylie. He had once wanted to be a poet, so there was some poetry in it. He needed to get James Joyce out of his system, so sentences started without capitals, whole pages were devoted to single words, and pointing fingers separated paragraphs. He was a slick-paper magazine specialist and a veteran at script dialogue, and it showed. He had written other novels of manners and now he placed the emphasis on morals—lack of them. He made Philip Wylie one of the characters in the book and spelled his name right. He wrote experimentally, used stream-of-consciousness and flash-backs, and seasoned it all with lots of sex.

Despite this mixture, the clarity and honesty of style so characteristic of him made the book read easily and well. He called it *Finnley Wren* and overnight he was talked of as an important mainstream writer. There was almost everything of Wylie in the book but science fiction. He corrected that by having one of his characters sit down and read two short stories, unrelated to the novel but incorporated, complete, in the text. One he called *An Epistle to the Thessalonians* and the other *Epistle to the Galatians*.

The first had the distinction of being Wylie's only fictional piece to appear in a science fiction magazine, when it ran in the December 1950 issue of *World's Beyond*. It is a brilliantly written satire involving a giant, a thousand miles in height, who appears from space, kicks the city of New York off the map, and departs as enigmatically as he arrived. The second *Epistle* is a brief but devastating vignette aimed at racism (it may have been the inspiration of Herbert Read's *The*

Green Child, 1935): a scientist discovers a drug which is a lifelong preventative for all known diseases at a cost of three-tenths of a cent per person, but no one will take it because it turns the user green.

In 1937, Wylie returned to Hollywood for two years with Metro-Goldwyn-Mayer. The motion picture *Gladiator* was released by Columbia in 1938. It was turned into a rather pointless comedy starring mammouth-mouthed Joe E. Brown, but even Brown wasn't too happy about the entire thing, since he developed a double hernia wrestling Man Mountain Dean in one of the film's sequences.

The literary world, like a fighter watching an opponent's highly-touted right hand, waited for a repetition of *Finnley Wren*. It suddenly found itself on the canvas stunned by a rhetorical left hook called *Generation of Vipers*, which Rinehart published in 1942. Wylie said in the preface:

> For many years—indeed, for all of my adult life—I have yearned far more to contribute to thought than to mere entertainment. And, while I have watched a score of men whom I considered to be the veriest charlatans attain a high degree of reputation as thinkers, my own thoughts have been almost uniformly relegated to the doghouse. . . . The urge in me to do that was unquenchable. No calumny, no ribald denunciation—not even, I have found, the burning of my books in my own country—can arrest my ambition to become that figure of more than well-paid authorship: a wise guy. That is *my* vanity.

Wylie excoriated the transgressions and lapses of his countrymen, sparing neither church, school, medicine, economics, morals, statesmen, educators, businessmen, military men, nor mothers. The last attack, epitomized under the now-generic term of "Momism," caused the greatest reaction, for mothers had previously been sacrosanct when it came to social criticism. Though some of the more direct targets yowled in dismay, and though Wylie would now be permanently stigmatized as a woman hater, his readers, with more discernment than they had been given credit for, saw that there was no meanness, viciousness, or selfish purpose behind the author's indignation, and took him to their hearts.

When *Night Unto Night* was issued in 1944, it made the best-seller list as a work of fiction. Almost mystical, touching upon life beyond our own and offering comfort and guidance to those who might have lost a loved one in the war, it represented a renunciation of the concept of the death wish. It was entirely Wylie, however, with inserted essays on morals, diatribes against inanities, and one complete science fiction story out of context titled *The Snibbs Phenomenon*, dealing with a group of Martians who gradually fitted themselves, undetected, into the pattern of the world's life during the war years, as well as an uncompleted fantasy, *The Cyfer Phenomenon*, concerning a man who awoke one morning to find that one of his legs was gone and the one in its place didn't belong to him.

Early in 1945, Philip Wylie wrote on order for the *American Magazine* a long novelette entitled *The Paradise Crater*. The story was set in 1965, and though World War II had not then ended the story presupposed that the Nazis had been defeated. A band of die-hard Nazis with headquarters in Wyoming were planning to conquer the United States by using a deadly new weapon. *American Magazine* rejected the story as too fantastic, particularly the weapon—an atomic bomb made from Uranium-237!

Harold Ober, Wylie's agent, sent the story to *Blue Book*. Though science fiction magazines were exempt, other publications were required to censor any material they felt might involve national security. Donald Kennicott decided to play safe and sent the story to Washington, D. C., for approval. Security suggested that they would be a lot happier if *Blue Book* didn't publish the story. Unaware of the storm he had raised, Kennicott returned the manuscript to a thoroughly frightened Ober, with whom Central Intelligence had already been in contact. Special agents were on their way to deal with

Wylie, who had been placed under house arrest in a West-bury, Connecticut, hotel.

At the hotel, Wylie underwent quite an experience. A major from Army Intelligence arrived with the flat announcement that he was prepared to take Wylie's life if necessary to prevent a security leak. If it were any comfort, he told a somewhat shaken Wylie, he was willing to sacrifice his own for the same cause.

Wylie, who had been doing public relations work for the government on the B-29 bomber, urged that his dossier be checked in Washington. This was done and Wylie was cleared. In response to Wylie's offer to tear up the manuscript of *Paradise Crater*, the major, mellowed by a few drinks, suggested that it be stored in a trunk until after the war.

Four months later, the atom bomb was dropped on Hiroshima and *Blue Book* asked to have the story back. It was published in the October 1945 number.

But the efforts of the military to restrict all material related to atomic research, particularly in the May-Johnson Bill, imbued Wylie with a missionary's zeal. He wrote a short story, *Blunder*, telling how the world blew itself apart by an atomic accident out of ignorance of simple experimental data. This memorable tale, which appeared in *Collier's* for January 12, 1946, is believed to have influenced opinion in favor of the McMahon Bill, which permitted a more liberal approach to the exchange of atomic data.

The crusading Wylie swung back to philosophy in *An Essay on Morals* published in 1947. In essence, he asks people to renounce the religious vanity that holds that we are animals shaped in the image of God and thereby sets us in conflict with our own instincts; and, instead, to attempt to shape ourselves into godlike animals by learning to understand our instincts and thereby our motives.

Opus 21 in 1949 was a sophisticated elaboration, in fictional form, of the material in *Generation of Vipers*, and proved to be an exceptional, if lesser, success. There is a short fantasy in the volume in which clouds form obscene words over some of the world's major cities; organized government collapses when the best efforts to dissipate them fail.

Wylie's reputation as a woman hater, earned by *Generation of Vipers*, caused the *American Scholar* to send to him for comment three articles by women intimating that the world would be a finer place if it were run by the female of the species or, better yet, if the male could be dispensed with entirely. In reply, and against the advice of his agent, who regarded the idea as uncommercial, Wylie wrote *The Disappearance*, a fantasy which set out what might happen if all men were to disappear simultaneously from the earth, and, conversely, if the same were to happen to all women. *The Disappearance*, which in superbly resourceful prose showed the interdependence of the sexes and asked for the exercise of greater understanding and love, substantiated what many readers had sensed behind the vitriolic front of Philip Wylie —that here was a fundamentally kindly and compassionate man who hoped for the best even as he exposed the worst. *The Disappearance* put Wylie's name back up on the best-seller list in 1950.

The same year *Collier's* asked Wylie to contribute to its October 27 issue, which was to be entirely built around the subject of "Preview of the War We Do Not Want" (a hypothetical nuclear struggle with Russia). In *Philadelphia Phase*, he did a slick and polished romance of Americans and Russians co-operating to clean up the rubble of an atom-bombed city.

A year later, he was warning the nation that there were other means of delivering the atom bomb besides planes or missiles in *The Smuggled Atom Bomb*, included as one of three stories in *Three To Be Read*, published by Rinehart in 1951. This story deals with foreign agents who smuggle parts of atom bombs into the United States to assemble them and blow up New York. He was unable to rescue the tale from a bit too much corn and melodrama.

Tomorrow, a novel of civil defense during an atomic war, was outdated within six months of its publication in 1954;

the development of fusion weaponry destroyed its validity.

Wylie's credo for the nuclear age was best dramatized in *The Answer*, a fantasy featured in *The Saturday Evening Post* for May 7, 1955. Both the United States and Russia find a dead angel in bomb craters after their respective atomic tests. The angels disappear, but golden books are left behind. Printed in a thousand diverse languages, many not of earth, is one message: "Love one another."

Lest his admirers feel that he was going soft, Wylie wrote for *True* for May 1958 an article whose title is self-explanatory: *To Hell With Togetherness*. But at the same time, the message of *The Answer* was still his primary sermon, as evidenced by *Jungle Journey*, an adventure story evidently originally intended for a better market, which appeared in *Jack London's Adventure Magazine* for December 1958. A first-rate thriller, it tells of the discovery in the jungle of a deserted spaceship, protected by a circle of flesh-eating plants capable of devouring a herd of elephants. When the spaceship is entered and its records are deciphered, it is found that they have been left by an alien race, thousands of years past, who check on the cultural developments of the planets and destroy races they feel are taking the wrong path: "For ours is the duty to prevent the pestilence of breeds with brains but without love from moving out into the Infinite and loving universe." They are to return in one year.

Philip Wylie addressed himself specifically to the fraternity of science fiction writers in his essay *Science Fiction and Sanity in an Age of Crisis*, which appeared in *Modern Science Fiction*, a volume published by McCann in 1953.

> We science fiction writers—most of us—have taught the people a little knowledge, but such a little and in such a blurred and reckless fashion that it constitutes true and factual information in the minds of very few. More than that, we have taught the people to be afraid—because most of *us* are afraid, and do not realize it. That man is a positive force, evolving and maturing, responsible for his acts and able if he will to deal with their consequences, we have not said.

18

DAWN OF FAME: THE CAREER
OF STANLEY G. WEINBAUM

The economic blackness of the Depression hung like a pall over the spirit of America. The year was 1934 and even though many may have desired the temporary escape which science fiction provided, they frequently could not afford to purchase more than a monthly magazine or two.

In such an atmosphere, publishers of the three surviving science fiction magazines competed desperately for a diminishing pool of readers. *Wonder Stories*, Hugo Gernsback's current venture in an exclusively science fiction magazine, gave preference to stories with new ideas and unusual approaches to the worlds of tomorrow. In this, it was joined in grim competition with *Astounding Stories*. This magazine, after a nine-month lapse in 1933, had been purchased by Street & Smith, and it also featured new and startling ideas, labeling its most unorthodox stories "thought variants."

Though harried by financial difficulties, Gernsback humored his teen-age editor, Charles D. Hornig, and took time out to read a short story which had just come in the mail. Publisher and editor, displaying remarkable restraint considering their mutual enthusiasm, wrote in the blurb for A Martian Odyssey by unknown Stanley G. Weinbaum in the July 1934 issue of Wonder Stories: "Our present author . . . has written a science fiction tale so new, so breezy, that it stands out head and shoulders over similar interplanetarian stories."

Readers were unreserved in their enthusiasm. The torrent of praise reached such proportions that Hornig, in reply to a reader's ecstatic approval, revealed: "Weinbaum's story has already received more praise than any story in the history of our publication."

This statement was no small thing, for even in 1934 Wonder Stories had a star-studded five-year history which included outstanding tales by John Taine, Jack Williamson, Clifford D. Simak, David H. Keller, Ray Cummings, John W. Campbell, Jr., Stanton A. Coblentz, Clark Ashton Smith, Edmond Hamilton, Robert Arthur, H. P. Lovecraft (a revision of the work of Hazel Heald), and dozens of other names which retain much of their magic, even across the years.

Told in one of the most difficult of narrative techniques, that of the flash-back, A Martian Odyssey was in all respects professionally adroit. The style was light and jaunty, without once becoming farcical, and the characterizations inspiredly conceived throughout. A cast of alien creatures that would have seemed bizarre for The Wizard of Oz was somehow brought into dramatic conflict on the red sands of Mars in a wholly believable manner by the stylistic magic of this new author.

It was Weinbaum's creative brilliance in making strange creatures seem as real as the characters in David Copperfield that impressed readers most. Twe-er-r-rl, the intelligent Martian, an ostrich-like alien with useful manipular appendages —obviously heir of an advanced technology—is certainly one of the truly great characters in science fiction.

The author placed great emphasis on the possibility that so alien a being would think *differently* from a human being and therefore perform actions which would seem paradoxical or completely senseless to us. This novel departure gave a new dimension to the interplanetary "strange encounter" tale.

Twe-er-r-rl was not the only creature to whom difficult-to-understand psychology was applicable. In A *Martian Odyssey* there was also the silicon monster, who lived on sand, excreting bricks as a by-product and using them to build an endless series of pyramids; round four-legged creatures, with a pattern of eyes around their circumference, who spent their entire lives wheeling rubbish to be crushed by a giant wheel which occasionally turned traitor and claimed one of them instead; and a tentacled plant which lured its prey by hypnotically conjuring up wish-fulfillment images.

How thousands of readers felt about Stanley G. Weinbaum can best be summed up by quoting H. P. Lovecraft, one of the great masters of fantasy.

> I saw with pleasure that someone had at last escaped the sickening hackneyedness in which 99.99% of all pulp interplanetary stuff is engulfed. Here, I rejoiced, was somebody who could think of another planet in terms of something besides anthropomorphic kings and beautiful princesses and battles of space ships and ray-guns and attacks from the hairy sub-men of the "dark side" or "polar cap" region, etc., etc. Somehow he had the imagination to envisage wholly alien situations and psychologies and entities, to devise consistent events from wholly alien motives and to refrain from the cheap dramatics in which almost all adventure-pulpists wallow. Now and then a touch of the *seemingly* trite would appear—but before long it would be obvious that the author had introduced it merely to satirize it. The light touch did not detract from the interest of the tales—and genuine suspense was secured without the catchpenny tricks of the majority. The tales of Mars, I think, were Weinbaum's best —those in which that curiously sympathetic being "Tweel" figure.

Too frequently, authors who cause a sensation with a single story are characterized as having come "out of nowhere." Weinbaum's ability to juggle the entire trunkful of standard science fiction gimmicks and come up with something new was not merely a matter of talent. It was grounded in high intelligence, an excellent scientific background, and, most important of all, a thorough knowledge of the field.

Weinbaum had read science fiction since the first issue of *Amazing Stories* in 1926. Before that he had devoured Mary Wollstonecraft Shelley, Edgar Allan Poe, Jules Verne, H. G. Wells, A. Conan Doyle, and Edgar Rice Burroughs, as well as many of the great utopian writers.

A graduate chemical engineer, Stanley G. Weinbaum left that field in his early twenties, to try his hand at fiction. His first successful tale was a romantic sophisticated novel, *The Lady Dances*, which was syndicated by King Features in the early 1930s under the pen name of Marge Stanley, a combination of his wife's name with his own because he felt that a woman's byline would be more acceptable on that kind of story.

Several other experimental novels were written during this period, including two that were science fiction: *The Mad Brain* and *The New Adam*. He also turned out an operetta, *Omar, the Tent Maker*, with the music written by his sister, Helen Weinbaum Kasson; a short story, *Real and Imaginary*; and a short-short, *Graph*. None of these was ever submitted to a fantasy periodical during his lifetime. The operetta has never been published or produced. A sheaf of poetry dating from this period must be in existence, judging by the manner in which he interspersed verse into the text of almost all of his novels.

Weinbaum must have turned to writing because he was a creative artist with an overwhelming urge to write, for certainly, as a means of earning a livelihood during the Depression, science fiction was not rewarding. He was thirty-two years old when *A Martian Odyssey* appeared in *Wonder*

Stories and the sum he received for the story, at the prevailing rates, could scarcely have exceeded $55.

Over at Street & Smith, Desmond Hall, as assistant to F. Orlin Tremaine, read the tale and was greatly impressed. He prevailed upon Julius Schwartz, then the only literary agent specializing in science fiction, to see what he could do about getting some Weinbaum material for *Astounding Stories*. Schwartz was also editor of *Fantasy Magazine*, a science fiction fan publication, as well as a partner in the Solar Sales Service with his close friend, Mort Weisinger. He had entry to all editorial offices. The problem now was how to obtain Weinbaum's address.

"Everyone believes that Weinbaum is a pen name for a well-known author," he ventured to Hornig of *Wonder Stories*.

"You mean Ralph Milne Farley?" Hornig queried, after checking his files and noting that both Weinbaum and Farley lived in Milwaukee. His expression was noncommittal.

"What address did Farley use?" Schwartz asked, hoping that Hornig would be reasonably co-operative. "3237 North Oakland Avenue," Hornig replied.

That was all Schwartz needed to know. He wrote Weinbaum and offered to handle his work. Weinbaum agreed and sent him a new short story, *The Circle of Zero*. It was turned down by every magazine in the field, but an agent-author relationship was formed that was to endure long after Weinbaum's death and become a major factor in the perpetuation of his fame.

Anxious to capitalize upon the popularity of *A Martian Odyssey*, Hornig urged Weinbaum to write a sequel. Weinbaum agreed and then played a strangely acceptable trick upon his readers.

An earlier draft of *A Martian Odyssey* had been titled *Valley of Dreams*. Weinbaum found that, with a few additions and a little rewriting, it would serve magnificently as a sequel. He made the changes and sent the story to *Wonder Stories*. The story appeared in the November 1934 issue and if the readers suspected they were being entertained by the same story twice you couldn't tell it from their letters.

Despite the intervention of the intrepid Julius Schwartz, *Wonder Stories* might have kept Weinbaum on an exclusive basis a while longer had it not been for an overexacting editorial policy. Weinbaum had submitted *Flight on Titan*, a novelette speckled with such strange life forms as knife kites, ice ants, whiplash trees, and threadworms. It was not up to the level of the *Odyssey* stories, but was considerably superior to the general level of fiction Hornig was running at the time.

Nevertheless, it was rejected because it did not contain a "new" idea and Schwartz, toting it like a football around end, scored a touchdown at *Astounding Stories*. The story was instantly accepted.

Parasite Planet, which appeared in *Astounding Stories* for March 1935, the month after *Flight on Titan*, was the first of a trilogy featuring Ham Hammond and Patricia Burlingame. Though this story was merely a light romantic travelogue, the slick handling of the excursion across Venus with its Jack Ketch Trees which whirled lassos to catch their food; doughpots, mindless omnivorous masses of animate cells, and the cyclops-like, semi-intelligent *triops noctivans*, charmed the readers with a spell reminiscent of *Martian Odyssey*.

In a sense, all of Weinbaum's stories were one with Homer's *Odyssey*, inasmuch as they were fundamentally alien-world travel tales. The plot of each was a perilous quest. Beginning with his tales in *Astounding Stories*, Weinbaum introduced a maturely shaded boy-meets-girl element, something brand new to the science fiction of 1935, and he handled it as well as the best of the women's-magazine specialists. The wonderful outré creatures he invented were frosting on the cake, an entirely irresistible formula.

To all this Weinbaum now added a fascinating dash of philosophy with *The Lotus Eaters*, a novelette appearing in the April 1935 *Astounding Stories* and unquestionably one of his most brilliant masterpieces. On the dark side of Venus, Ham and Pat meet a strange cavern-dwelling creature, actually a warm-blooded planet, looking like nothing so much as an inverted bushel basket, whom they dub Oscar. Intellectually almost omnipotent, Oscar is able to arrive at the most astonishingly accurate conclusions about his world and the universe by extrapolating from the elementary exchanges of information. Despite his intelligence, Oscar has no philosophical objection to being eaten by the malevolent trioptes, predatory marauders of his world.

The entire story is nothing more than a series of questions and answers between the lead characters and Oscar, yet the reader becomes so absorbed that he might very easily imagine himself to be under the influence of the narcotic spores which are responsible for the Venusian's pontifical inertia.

Economic considerations as well as loyalty to the magazine which had published his first important science fiction story required that Weinbaum continue to consider *Wonder Stories* as a market, despite its low word rates. Realizing that the magazine was reluctant to publish any story that did not feature a new concept, he gave the editors what they wanted, selling in a single month, December 1934, three short stories, *Pygmalion's Spectacles*, *The Worlds of If*, and *The Ideal*.

The first, appearing in the June 1935 *Wonder Stories*, centers about the invention of a new type of motion picture, where the viewer actually thinks he is participating in the action. The motion picture involves a delightful boy-meets-girl romance, ending when the viewer comes awake from the hypnotic effect of the film to learn that he has participated in a fantasy. All is happily resolved when he finds that the feminine lead was played by the inventor's daughter and romance is still possible.

The Worlds of If was the first of a series of three stories involving Professor van Manderpootz, an erratic bearded scientist, and young Dixon Wells, who is always late and always sorry. The plot revolves about a machine that will show the viewer what would have happened *if* he had—married a woman other than his wife; not gone to college; flunked his final exams, or taken that other job. The humor is broad and the plotting a bit too synoptic to be effective.

The second story in the series, *The Ideal*, has for its theme the building of a machine which will reveal a man's mental and emotional orientation to reality through a systematic exploration of his subconscious motives.

The final story, *The Point of View*, is based on the imaginative assumption that, through the use of an even more remarkable machine—an "attitudinizer"—one can see the world through the minds of others. The three stories are almost identical, varied only by the nature of the invention itself. There is a striking similarity in theme and characterization between this story and Erckmann-Chatrian's short story *Hans Schnap's Spy Glass*—even to the use of the term "point of view"—which appeared in the collection *The Bells; or, The Polish Jew*, published in England in 1872.

Despite their slightness, the van Manderpootz tales are important because fascinating philosophical speculations accompany each description of a mechanical gimmick. Enlivened by humor and carried easily along on a high polish, Weinbaum's style now effectively disguised the fact that a philosopher was at work.

Understandably gaining confidence with success, Weinbaum embarked on a more ambitious writing program. He began work on a short novel, the 25,000-word *Dawn of Flame*, featuring a woman of extraordinary beauty, Black Margot, and stressing human characterization and emotional conflict. A disappointment awaited him, however. The completed novel went the rounds of the magazines and was rejected as not being scientific or fantastic enough.

He altered the formula slightly, still featuring Black Margot but sacrificing some of the literary quality for the sake of action and adventure. The new and much longer version—it ran to 65,000 words—was called *The Black Flame*.

With its hero from the present awakening in the future to find himself in a divided world, its beautiful princess, its strange contrast of advanced science and medieval battle, and its fast pace and color, it should have been the answer to a pulp editor's dream. The novel was rejected a second time.

In his home city Weinbaum was invited to join a group of fiction writers who called themselves The Milwaukee Fictioneers. Members included Ralph Milne Farley, who had earned a considerable reputation as creator of The Radio Man series and other science fiction novels for *Argosy*; Raymond A. Palmer, a future editor of *Amazing Stories*; Arthur R. Tofte, an occasional contributor to the science fiction magazines, and Lawrence A. Keating, a popular Western story writer of the thirties. With his ready unaffected wit and his interest in people and the world, Stanley Grauman Weinbaum quickly won the sincere friendship of the entire group.

Within a few months, Ralph Milne Farley—the pseudonym of Roger Sherman Hoar, a former United States Senator from Wisconsin—who was doing a series of detective stories for *True Gang Life*, suggested a collaboration. Weinbaum wrote with Farley, *Yellow Slaves*, which appeared in *True Gang Life* for February 1936.

This was the first of several Weinbaum-Farley collaborations, including *Smothered Seas*, which appeared in *Astounding Stories* for January 1936 and dealt with the appearance of a strange alga which forms a scum over the surface of the seas of the world and then covers the continents, impeding transportation. It was a pleasant but undistinguished story.

The method followed by Weinbaum and Farley in collaboration was puzzling. Weinbaum would complete the entire first draft, and Farley would fill in the details and do the final polishing job. This seems strange, in view of the fact that Weinbaum was a master stylist, capable of writing the most finished prose.

The rejection of *Flame* now convinced Weinbaum that he would either have to write formula material for the pulps, a formula of his own invention, or go unpublished. Precious months had gone by in which he had written stories which satisfied him artistically but produced no income. The records of his agent, Julius Schwartz, show that Weinbaum derived not a penny from writing science fiction from the end of December 1934 until June 15, 1935, when *The Planet of Doubt* brought a check for $110 from Tremaine at *Astounding Stories*.

The final story of the Ham and Pat series, *The Planet of Doubt* suffers by comparison with *The Lotus Eaters*. It is evident now that Weinbaum was planet-hopping for immediate remuneration and not for the satisfaction of using his talent to its utmost. But by the time this story appeared, in the October 1935 issue of *Astounding*, Weinbaum could do no wrong, and this amusing tale of the animated linked sausages of Uranus was taken in stride by the readers.

It has been claimed that the pen name John Jessel, used by Weinbaum for his story *The Adaptive Ultimate*, was adopted because he feared that too many stories bearing his own name were appearing in *Astounding Stories* and that an increase in their number would not be wise.

The record of checks received at the time from his agent does not bear this out. Weinbaum had made no sales to *Astounding* for over six months. While Weinbaum may have thought that recent rejections were the result of too many appearances in *Astounding*, it seems far more likely that he had been "typed" and that Tremaine believed that the readers would look with disfavor upon any departure from his original technique.

Strengthening this possibility is the experience of John W Campbell, Jr., who gained fame as a super-science writer in the Edward E. Smith tradition with novels like *The Black Star Passes, Islands in Space,* and *The Mightiest Machine,* and found it necessary to switch to the pseudonym Don A. Stuart for his mood stories, *Twilight* and *Night,* so as not to disorient his readers.

John Jessel was the name of Weinbaum's grandfather and the first story submitted to *Astounding* under that name, *The Adaptive Ultimate,* was a complete departure from the type of science fiction which established Weinbaum as an outstanding writer in the genre.

Whereas the Martian and Venus stories had been almost plotless travelogues, made narratively diversified by ingenious inventiveness and brilliance of style, *The Adaptive Ultimate* was the most carefully plotted of all of Weinbaum's magazine stories. With possible slight overtones derived from David H. Keller's poignant *Life Everlasting*—the more likely since Weinbaum listed Keller as one of his favorite authors—*The Adaptive Ultimate* deals with a tubercular girl who is injected with a drug that makes her body instantly adaptable to any environmental change. The result is the cure of her affliction, radiant beauty, high intelligence, and the astonishing ability to defeat death by overcoming every possible obstacle, not excluding a knife thrust to the vitals. There is a concerted campaign to destroy her, led by the man she loves, who fears she will eventually rule the world. When, through treachery, he succeeds in overpowering her and changing her back to a sickly, homely girl, he is overcome with remorse. "You were right," he whispers to the unhearing girl. "Had I your courage there is nothing we might not have attained together." His punishment is the realization, even at the moment when nothing remains of her former magnificent beauty, that he still loves her and that there is nothing he can do to reverse the fact that she soon will die.

The Adaptive Ultimate was the first Weinbaum story to be anthologized, appearing in *The Other Worlds*, a fantasy volume edited by Phil Stong in 1941. It has been dramatized on the radio at least twice, the last time on *Tales of Tomorrow* in August 1952. *Studio One* produced it as a full-hour show on television under the title of *Kyra Zelas*, and it was re-enacted twice more under different titles and later released as a motion picture called *She-Devil*.

The strength of this story, so adaptable to radio, television, and motion pictures, rests in its compelling, powerful plot. It clearly showed that Weinbaum could be, when the market permitted him, considerably more than a mere literary stylist.

When Weinbaum wrote Schwartz on July 10, 1935, "I have been laid up as the result of a tonsil extraction for the past several weeks but expect to be able to send you material at a pretty steady rate from now on," there seemed to be little reason for concern. Weinbaum had already begun work on a second story under the John Jessel byline, *Proteus Island*. On August 6, 1935, he wrote to Schwartz in a somewhat more disturbing vein. "Have been laid up again with a sort of imitation pneumonia as a complication from the tonsil extraction, and as a result the John Jessel story is still in the process of being finished."

Proteus Island was a well-written 13,000-word biological tale about an island where a professor's ill-advised experiment has changed the genetic structure of all animal life and vegetation, so that no two things are alike. The tale is weakened when Weinbaum fails to take full advantage of the potentially powerful plot situation he built up, of a male visitor falling in love with a girl who he believes has been subjected to the harmful radiation of this island and therefore can never have normal children. The story found acceptance nowhere under the John Jessel name.

It was obvious now that Weinbaum was a sick man. Each of his letters spoke of heavier and heavier X-ray treatments which drained him of energy for long periods of time. Despite this, he continued to write. *The Red Peri*, sold to *Astounding Stories* on August 17, 1935, brought $190 and was featured on the cover of the November 1935 number. In an editorial in that issue, Tremaine wrote: "Stanley G. Weinbaum has been very ill. I hope he's able to sit up and enjoy this month's cover and to see *The Red Peri* in print."

The Red Peri is a woman space pirate of phenomenal cunning, daring, and beauty. The story was intended as the first of a series. Standing by itself, it proved an entertaining adventure story, barely qualifying as science fiction despite its interplanetary locale and the interesting concept that the vacuum of space would be harmless to a human being for short stretches of time.

In the same issue, *The Adaptive Ultimate* appeared as a featured novelette, with its "superwoman" heroine. Add to these the immortal Black Margot of Urbs, from the Flame novels, and the dominant characteristics of Patricia Burlingame of the Ham and Pat series and we find in Weinbaum a powerful fixation on the concept of the superwoman who is tamed by love of a man. Evidence of domination by a strong woman somewhere in his life? Evidence more probably of his subconscious wish to meet a woman who was his intellectual equal.

Despite his illness, Weinbaum continued writing, careful to turn out the kind of stories he knew the magazines would buy. *Smothered Seas*, in collaboration with Ralph Milne Farley, and *The Mad Moon* were sold on the same day, September 27, for $110 and $100 respectively.

The Mad Moon is one of the finest of his queer animal stories. It combines such novel creations as the long-necked, big-headed, giggling "loonies"; a "parcat," half cat—half parrot; and semi-intelligent, ratlike "slinkers." Bizarre as this menagerie is, Weinbaum combines them all into a delightful, straight-faced minor masterpiece with just enough pathos to lift it out of the category of ordinary adventures.

The Mad Moon was probably the last story Weinbaum ever saw in print. On November 19 he wrote Schwartz: "Lord knows I'm pleased to get your check on *Redemption Cairn*. I've been in Chicago having some X-ray treatments again, and I'm flat on my back recovering from them. I don't know when I'll be able to get some real work done.

He never stopped trying. According to Ralph Milne Farley, though pain-racked by throat cancer and barely able to speak above a whisper, he continued to work on *The Dictator's Sister*, the first draft of which he finished before he died.

Saturday, December 14, 1935, Julius Schwartz, while in the synagogue, received the following telegram from Ray Palmer: "WEINBAUM DIED EARLY THIS MORNING." Though he had never met the man, Schwartz broke down and wept. During the services he offered a prayer for Weinbaum, who was of his faith.

"Did you know that Stanley Weinbaum took off on the Last Great Journey through the galaxies in December?" F. Orlin Tremaine asked his readers in *Astounding.* "That he set his course by the stars I do not doubt. *Astounding Stories* is proud of his accomplishments in science fiction. He created a niche for himself which will be hard to fill."

"A few months before his untimely death," Charles D. Hornig, Weinbaum's discoverer, wrote in an obituary in the April 1936 *Wonder Stories,* an issue which ironically marked the end of that magazine under Gernsback's ownership, "he promised us a third tale in the 'Martian' series—but did not have time to complete it."

Fifteen months after his first science fiction story appeared, Stanley G. Weinbaum's career had ended.

Few men were as instantaneously liked as Weinbaum. He seemed to be surrounded by a sort of radiance, both mental and physical, but he was modest and unaffected, with an outgoing friendliness and a genuine interest in people. Under the sponsorship of the Milwaukee Fictioneers, a memorial volume was published soon after Weinbaum's death. Conrad H. Ruppert, who printed *Fantasy Magazine,* the fan publication edited by Julius Schwartz, played a key role in the preparation of this volume. He set the type of the 313-page *Dawn of Flame and Other Stories* by hand and ran it off two pages at a time in a limited edition of 250 copies. The sheets were sent from New York to Raymond A. Palmer in Milwaukee, who arranged with a binder to have the book bound in black leather and stamped in gold.

This was the first appearance of *Dawn of Flame* anywhere, and it revealed Stanley G. Weinbaum as a completely mature literary craftsman, tremendously talented in dialogue and superbly skilled in characterization. There is high poetry in the closing passages.

The volume contained six shorter stories—*The Mad Moon, A Martian Odyssey, The Worlds of If, The Adaptive Ultimate, The Lotus Eaters,* and *The Red Peri.* The introduction by Raymond A. Palmer was deemed too personal by Wein-

baum's widow, so another by Lawrence A. Keating was substituted. Six copies with Palmer's introduction are known
to exist.

Gernsback's *Wonder Stories* was purchased by Standard
Magazines and came under the editorial directorship of
Leo Margulies. Margulies placed Mort Weisinger, Julius
Schwartz's partner in the Solar Sales Service, in charge of the
magazine, which the Standard group retitled *Thrilling Wonder Stories*. Weisinger immediately decided to publish *The
Circle of Zero*. An "idea" story, similar in mood to the Professor van Manderpootz series, it deals with the drawing up
of memories from the past and the future. Too heavy on
theory and too light on action, it reads more like a movie
scenario than a completed work of fiction.

Learning for the first time that John Jessel was really a pen
name for Stanley G. Weinbaum, Tremaine changed his mind
about *Proteus Island* and published the novelette in the
August 1936 *Astounding Stories*.

A short story, *Shifting Seas*, which had been sold to *Amazing Stories* shortly before Weinbaum's death, eventually
appeared in the August 1937 issue. It was a minor effort dealing with a volcanic explosion that diverts the Gulf Stream,
almost freezing out Europe, and the eventual solution of the
problem by the construction of an undersea wall.

Now the search through Weinbaum's old papers began in
earnest. The first story to be rescued from obscurity was *Real
and Imagery*, a charming piece which turned on the solution
to a mathematical formula. Retitled *Brink of Infinity*, it was
greeted with enthusiasm when it appeared in *Thrilling Wonder Stories* for December 1936. No one noted that it was
actually a condensation and rewrite of George Allan England's *The Tenth Question*, which appeared in the December
18, 1915, issue of *All-Story Magazine*. Obviously *Brink of
Infinity* was an early exercise in writing, which Weinbaum
never intended to have published.

In 1938, several important changes occurred in the science
fiction field. *Amazing Stories* was sold to Ziff-Davis magazines

and Raymond A. Palmer became editor. He had Ralph Milne Farley polish Weinbaum's last story, *The Dictator's Sister*, which was published under the title of *The Revolution of 1980* in the October and November 1938 issues of *Amazing Stories*. Having for its theme a dictatorship of the United States, run by a woman who through hormone injections has changed herself into a man, the story is excellent light entertainment.

The Black Flame, purchased at a bargain price of $200 for its 65,000 words, helped insure the success of the first—January 1939—issue of *Startling Stories*. There seemed to be no end to "last" stories by Stanley G. Weinbaum. His sister, Helen Kasson, finished one, *Tidal Moon*, which was published in *Thrilling Wonder*, December 1938, but as he had written only a page and a half and had left no outline it was not significant.

Firmly entrenched at Ziff-Davis, which published books as well as periodicals, Raymond A. Palmer persuaded the publishers that it would be a good idea to consider seriously Weinbaum's early philosophical novel, *The New Adam*. It appeared in hard covers in 1939 with some rather ambiguous endorsements from Edgar Rice Burroughs, A. Merritt, Ralph Milne Farley, and Raymond A. Palmer on the jacket. The story of a superman with a dual mind who, because of his fatal passion for a woman, sacrifices the opportunity to lead the race that will replace humanity, is morbidly fascinating despite its extremely gloomy outlook. It seemed incredible that the same man who wrote with the delightfully light touch of *A Martian Odyssey*, and who was able to produce so gay a frolic as *The Mad Moon* while dying of cancer, could have been so devout a disciple of Schopenhauer in a more youthful period.

Still another very early novel, *The Mad Brain*, was condensed into novelette form and peddled by Julius Schwartz to the magazines, with no takers. Finally it was published complete as *The Dark Other* in book form by the Fantasy Publishing Co., Inc., Los Angeles, in 1950. A reworking of the Jekyll and Hyde theme, it seems hardly worthy of Weinbaum's unique talent and is of interest chiefly as a collector's item.

A clever short vignette, *Graph*, dealing with the relationship of business to blood pressure was uncovered by Julius Schwartz and published in the September 1936 issue of *Fantasy Magazine*. As late as 1957, the July issue of *Crack Detective and Mystery Stories* featured a rather second-rate detective story by Stanley G. Weinbaum, retitled *Green Glow of Death* from his original title *Murder on the High Seas*.

The true importance of Weinbaum can best be estimated by his influence. No less a master of science fiction than Eric Frank Russell quite frankly both imitated Weinbaum's style and copied his bent for queer animals to score a success with *The Saga of Pelican West*, published in *Astounding Stories* for February 1937; Henry Kuttner attracted attention in science fiction by teaming up with Arthur K. Barnes to produce the Hollywood-on-the-Moon stories, mimicking Weinbaum even down to the characters Tommy Strike and Gerry Carlyle, who were little more than carbon copies of Ham and Pat; John Russell Fearn, a very popular science fiction writer during the late thirties, invented the pen name of Polton Cross just to write stories that were parodies of Weinbaum.

More subtly, Weinbaum's methods have influenced dozens of other authors, most strikingly Philip José Farmer in his masterpiece, *The Lovers*, a tale which would have done Weinbaum no discredit.

How enduring Weinbaum's personal reputation will be depends upon a relatively small number of stories, probably *A Martian Odyssey*, *The Lotus Eaters*, *The Adaptive Ultimate*, *The Dawn of Flame*, and, paradoxically, *The Brink of Infinity*. The short span of his writing, the insistence of editors that he write to a formula, the ravages of illness, and the economic depression make it remarkable that he achieved even as much as he did. The legacy he left the science fiction world, however, is still apparent everywhere.

19

HOW SCIENCE FICTION
GOT ITS NAME

1. The Origin of the Term

No one who has followed recent literary history, and only a diminishing percentage of the general public, any longer misunderstands the term "science fiction." As a field of literature, science fiction still has not completely agreed on definition, but it docs not suffer from the absence of a name.

Since no man has ever stepped forward to claim the origin of the term science fiction, the logical thing to assume is that like Topsy, it just grew.

It grew all right, but research into its use as a separate term reveals that it also had a gardener. We have earlier indicated who this was, but now let us begin, step by step, to develop its history.

When Jules Verne started the first big wave of popularity

for scientific speculative adventure with *Five Weeks in a Balloon*, published in 1863, the French publishers and the general press created a term for such stories, *voyages extraordinaires*.

"Extraordinary voyages" became synonymous with the name Jules Verne, covering both what we consider his science fiction and his adventure-narratives of more realistic voyages. His self-acknowledged imitators, cashing in on the popularity of such tales as *Twenty Thousand Leagues Under the Sea* and *Journey to the Center of the Earth*, were forced to call their works *voyages excentriques*.

In England, Verne's stories were called "scientific romances," and the term became so entrenched that when C. A. Hinton wrote a series of semifictional scientific speculations on the nature of the fourth dimension and other imaginative subjects in 1888, they were published as scientific romances.

The rise of H. G. Wells, with *The Time Machine, The War of the Worlds*, and *When the Sleeper Wakes*, toward the end of the nineteenth century, found him inheriting that label, along with the frequent use of "scientific fantasies," frequently used to describe some of his work that seemed too scientific to be fantasy and yet not scientifically plausible. "Science fantasy" is still commonly used today to describe work of that nature.

Scientific romance, as a term, lingered to as recent a date as 1930, but it was already obsolescent at the turn of the century as "romance" began to be thought of as love and kisses first and unusual adventure second, if at all.

The need for some definite term to apply to scientific stories became increasingly acute as publications regularly featuring them became established in the United States. Frank Tousey's Frank Reade Library, begun in 1892, published stories which were referred to as "invention stories." The inventions and adventures of Frank Reade ran for 192 weekly issues until the charge was brought that they were ruining the minds of the younger generation. As a sop to the fevers of the time, Tousey discontinued the series. Even today, dime-novel collectors categorize Frank Reade and similar tales as invention stories.

Frank Munsey then picked up the torch for those who preferred their entertainment in the tradition of Jules Verne. When he changed the teen-age *Golden Argosy* into *Argosy* in 1896 and adopted a more adult formula, he began to use such stories with increasing frequency. As he subsequently launched other adventure magazines—such as *Scrap Book*, *All-Story*, *Munsey*, and *Cavalier*—fanciful tales of science became a regular part of the publishing program of each.

Since it was apparent that such fiction had a following, it soon became imperative that some term be created to let those readers know their "poison" was on tap and thereby insure their patronage. At first such tales were referred to as "off-trail stories," but this was too inclusive and could also mean anything from a story told in the second person to a Western yarn with a Christmas setting. To solve the problem, *Argosy* created the term "different stories." For years, when the simple word "different" was carried in the announcement of a story, connoisseurs knew what was coming.

Another term often found in the readers' departments of Munsey magazines was "impossible stories." That term had some currency until about 1920 when it virtually disappeared.

Still, editors of Munsey publications found that "different" was not specific enough. It was awkward to write, in every issue, that "we will continue to present 'different stories.'" Therefore they evolved a new label that received widespread use throughout the publishing world; in the early twenties it was by far the most popular single term for the genre—though everything else under the sun kept popping up as a substitute. The new term was "pseudo-scientific stories," and they might still be using it today if it hadn't been for Hugo Gernsback.

In 1908, when he was only twenty-four years old, Gernsback began publishing *Modern Electrics*, the world's first radio magazine. As the title of his publication changed from *Modern Electrics* to *Electrical Experimenter* and finally to

Science and Invention, he found himself using such stories so frequently that by 1922 he was running two or more an issue.

There was, however, a real difference between the type of science story in the Gernsback magazine and that in *Argosy.* Gernsback insisted that the basis of each story be scientifically accurate. Therefore the word so widely used at the time, "pseudo-scientific," was abhorrent to him. He was out to find some new term with a more dignified connotation.

The problem was brought to a head when it was decided to make up a cover for *Science and Invention* composed of a number of miniature magazine covers each showing a different department or regular feature of the magazine, among them Popular Astronomy, Motor Hints, Wrinkles, Recipes and Formulas, etc. Since two science stories were used in every issue, they could not be excluded. The result was "scientific fiction," probably the very first use of that particular phrase, and most certainly the first use of it prominently.

It was on this cover, in December 1922, that the science fiction magazine per se was first foreshadowed, if only in a projected cover.

From that time on all science tales in Gernsback publications were referred to as scientific fiction, with infrequent lapses to "scientific stories." The important thing to note is the use of the word "fiction" instead of the more commonly used "stories," for this is the element that gave scientific fiction as well as the later "science fiction" the distinction that won popularity.

Since its metamorphosis to an adult magazine, *Argosy* found that a large portion of its readership was made up of followers of fantastic literature. There were many other good adventure magazines on the stands, such as *Blue Book, Popular, Top Notch, Adventure, Complete Stories,* and *Short Stories,* but *Argosy,* which featured the best, and the most, "pseudo-scientific stories," enjoyed the top sales. A general fiction magazine, *Argosy* rarely ran more than one such story an issue, and occasionally it did not run any.

Gernsback's *Science and Invention* regularly ran two and

sometimes more. Its frequent references to the accuracy of the science in the stories gave them such an air of respectability and prescience as to prove irresistible to devotees. In addition, the magazine's popular science features were so speculative in character as to qualify as prophetic stories in nonfiction form.

Undoubtedly *Argosy* was losing a portion of its fantastic story following to *Science and Invention*—the more so since some of *Argosy's* top "pseudo-scientific story" authors, such as George Allan England and Ray Cummings, were being featured in *Science and Invention* as additions to its own crew of "scientific fiction" writers.

The importance Gernsback placed upon recruiting readership from science story lovers became vigorously apparent with the August 1923 issue of *Science and Invention*. That issue contained six stories, and on the cover in type an inch and a half high were the words: SCIENTIFIC FICTION NUMBER. The full-color cover, painted by Howard V. Brown, who later became a cover illustrator for Street & Smith's *Astounding Stories*, pictured a space-suited figure in a scene in G. Peyton Wertenbaker's serial, *The Man from the Atom.*

That *Argosy* was well aware of the competition it was getting, particularly the appeal of the term "scientific fiction" with its promise of scientific accuracy, was made evident when it finally reacted. The scientific novel, *The Radio Man* by Ralph Milne Farley, which began in the June 28, 1924 issue of *Argosy-All Story* magazine, was prefaced by the equivalent of a full-page editorial stressing the fact that this story marked a departure in *Argosy*, since it was written by a scientist and all the science contained therein was scientifically accurate! On the cover this story was called "a scientific adventure."

It is not precisely certain at what point *Argosy* first used Gernsback's term "scientific fiction," but in the September 14, 1929 issue, in a biography of Ray Cummings, a popular fiction writer who specialized in scientific adventures, the editor of *Argosy* used "scientific fiction" three times and other terms not at all!

Argosy and *Science and Invention* were not, however, the only magazines active on the "scientific fiction" scene at the time. *Weird Tales* magazine was founded in March 1923. Its editor, Edwin Baird, ran science stories along with tales of witches, goblins, ghouls, vampires, and werewolves. In the first anniversay issue, dated May-June-July, 1924, Mr. Baird informed his readers that *Weird Tales* was dedicated to printing two primary classifications of fiction. One was the weird tale with all its ramifications of distorted psychology and horror. The other was the "highly imaginative story," Baird's term for what Gernsback called scientific fiction. Within a few months, however, *Weird Tales* had adopted *Argosy's* term, pseudo-scientific stories, on its contents page. (It is of parenthetical stylistic interest to note that "pseudo-scientific" was often used as a single word by *Argosy*.)

Since the earliest days, a characteristic of the reader of this literature has been his enthusiasm for writing letters to the editor. He writes out of all proportion to his numbers. New publishers of science fiction magazines, accustomed to getting one or two letters a month for their other magazines, have been astonished to find their science fiction venture getting from fifty to two hundred an issue. Such letters to *Science and Invention* undoubtedly encouraged Gernsback to attempt an "all scientific fiction" magazine—as though he needed any particular encouragement.

In 1924, Hugo Gernsback mailed thousands of circulars to subscribers to *Science and Invention*, announcing that he was about to launch a new magazine dealing with the worlds of tomorrow, interplanetary travel, and scientific invention in the tradition of Jules Verne and H. G. Wells. To create a name for the new magazine Hugo Gernsback contracted scientific fiction into "Scientifiction" and projected that as the title of the publication.

The response was something less than unenthusiastic. Market research would have revealed what is generally known today: that followers of fantastic fiction are to a great extent collectors, and they dislike subscribing for fear their copy will be damaged in transit. Secondly, many magazine readers cannot bear the thought of having to wait for a publication delayed in the mails when it is plainly visible on the newsstand. Present-day publishers, aware of these facts, often induce additional subscriptions by promising that copies will be mailed flat in sturdy envelopes for delivery *ahead* of newsstand date. Gernsback had no way of knowing this.

Feeling that perhaps the magazine name *Scientifiction* lacked general appeal, Gernsback waited a bit over a year and then, without asking anyone, in April 1926 set *Amazing Stories* down on the newsstands of the United States.

Though the title of the magazine was *Amazing Stories*, the subtitle on the editorial page read: "The Magazine of Scientifiction." The editorial of the first issue was devoted to telling readers just what scientifiction was. The editorial of the third issue called the readers "scientifiction fans." Shortly, the spine of the magazine carried a dual legend: *Amazing Stories*: *Scientifiction*. A contest was sponsored to find an artistic symbol for scientifiction. The term scientifiction was used everywhere in the magazine and pushed by every promotional device at Gernsback's disposal (which included one of New York's earliest radio stations, WRNY) to popularize it as *the* term for tales of space-suits and ray guns.

The new publication was an immediate success. Within a few issues it achieved a newsstand sale of 100,000. This figure, for a twenty-five-cent publication of specialized appeal, was considered quite a respectable one in the twenties. So fine a response indicated that a ready-made audience existed for scientifiction. Where did it come from?

Some of it was from the ranks of the readers of *Science and Invention*. Most were recruited at the expense of *Argosy*, and a sizable number from *Weird Tales*.

The latter publication, now edited by Farnsworth Wright, who had purchased a controlling interest in the company, recognized the threat instantly. Though afflicted with a form

of cerebral palsy as an aftereffect of sleeping sickness contracted during World War I—an illness which left him with
an involuntary shake and shiver which could have made him
the butt of grim humor, since he edited a magazine calculated
to scare the daylights out of its readers—Wright brilliantly
managed his publication through trying times. He discovered
and encouraged dozens of authors who are today great names
in the literary world, including Tennessee Williams, and
eventually became one of the most beloved and respected
figures in pulp-magazine circles.

He recognized that Gernsback's *Amazing Stories* was directly competing with him, since it could easily siphon off
readers that read *Weird Tales* primarily for its scientific
stories. A still greater threat was the term scientifiction, with
its connotation of literary respectability, that by implication
wooed the reader with the thought: "If it isn't scientifiction
it can't be scientifically accurate."

The first issue of *Amazing Stories* was dated April 1926.
The June 1926 issue of *Weird Tales* carried a two-page editorial by Wright informing his readers that pseudo-scientific
stories was a misnomer for the tales of science carried in his
magazine. He stressed the point that there was a strong basis
of science in all the science stories published in his magazine.

Wright knew he had to find a new term, fast. The term had
to have the word *science* in it, but it would not be prefaced
by *pseudo*, which meant fake. Nor could the new term be
scientific fiction or science stories alone, because his readership was divided into two factions. One wanted pseudo-
science stories eliminated and only weird material published.
The other group bemoaned the fact that too few stories of
this type were being published. To make them both happy,
Wright hit upon the combination "weird-scientific stories."
This he used for the first time in the July 1926 issue, announcing a forthcoming "weird-scientific story" by Marion
Heidt Mimms, to be called *The Chair*. Pseudo-scientific
stories, as a term, was dropped for good. The idea to get
across was that, while the magazine would continue to print

bigger and better science stories, in which the science would be accurate, they would be weird to boot.

This was the status of the terms up to the end of the decade. Gernsback used scientifiction in all of his publications, which included *Amazing Stories, Amazing Stories Quarterly, Science and Invention,* and *Radio News. Argosy* gradually discarded different stories and pseudo-scientific stories and after serious discussion adopted Gernsback's earlier scientific fiction. *Weird Tales* grimly held to its own weird-scientific.

Oddly enough, the last use of the term created by *Argosy,* different stories, may not have been by *Argosy* at all, since *Mind Magic Magazine,* in its June 1931 issue, announced a Ralph Milne Farley story scheduled for its next number as a *different* story.

In 1929, Hugo Gernsback lost control of the Experimenter Publishing Corp. and of *Amazing Stories.* Though the editor-in-chief was nominally Arthur H. Lynch, editorial supervision of the publication passed into the hands of Dr. T. O'Connor Sloane, son-in-law of Thomas A. Edison, and a bearded octogenarian whose major claim to fame was the invention of the self-recording photometer, a device for recording the illuminating power of gas. His imagination also remained to some degree in the gas-lit era, for one of his favorite pastimes was to chide his readers for their childish notions that space travel would ever be possible.

Sloane had formerly been employed by Gernsback as associate editor of *Amazing Stories.* In his first editorial in the May 1929 issue, Sloane went back to the use of the original Gernsback term, scientific fiction. The editorial page still bore the subtitle "The Magazine of Scientifiction" and the word scientifiction stayed on the spine of the magazine, but the spell was broken—for the first time a term other than scientifiction was used in an all-science-story magazine.

Between leaving his old company and organizing a new one, Gernsback left scarcely a thirty-day lapse. The first publication of his new company was *Science Wonder Stories,* dated June 1929.

The great distinction of *Science Wonder Stories* is that it was the first publication in history to use the term *science fiction* in its pages.

The term was first used in Gernsback's editorial, "Science Wonder Stories," in the first issue, dated June, but published in May, 1929. In fact, it is used as a matter of policy throughout the entire magazine, even down to letters in the readers' columns.

Though this was the first use of science fiction in a publication, it was not literally the first use of the term. The distinction of first using it, however, also goes to Gernsback, who wrote a form letter over his signature in 1929, which was mailed to former subscribers of *Amazing Stories* and *Science and Invention*, announcing the new magazine and offering fifty dollars for the best letter on the subject: "What Science Fiction Means to Me."

Among those receiving honorable mention for replying to that letter were today's famous science fiction authors Edward E. Smith, Ph.D., and Jack Williamson. They were certainly unaware of the fact that they were among the first people ever to use the term science fiction in any manner.

A careful search of the six-point type of the readers' letters in all the issues of *Amazing Stories* before that date, and careful combing of every other publication in any way connected with the publication of fantastic literature, fails to reveal the use of the words science fiction anywhere before the June 1929 issue of *Science Wonder Stories*.

When these facts were presented to him, Gernsback recalled that he had invented the new term to have something different from his former publication. Scientifiction, as a result of his own efforts, was inextricably associated with *Amazing Stories* (which he no longer published) and with no other publication.

Thus, the term science fiction came into existence so quietly that its origin was hardly noted at the time and had been almost forgotten even by the man who created it.

2. The Adoption of the Term

When Hugo Gernsback used "science fiction" for the first time, it was unaccompanied by the fanfare and promotion that were accorded his word "scientifiction" three years earlier. Since Gernsback, the principal publisher in the field, did not beat the drums for the general adoption of the term, how did it come to be universally accepted?

First, science fiction (without the hyphen) was used throughout all of Gernsback's science fiction magazines as a matter of policy. At that time he had had more such magazines than any other publisher: *Science Wonder Stories*, *Air Wonder Stories*, *Science Wonder Quarterly*, *Scientific Detective Monthly*, in addition to a group of booklets called *Science Fiction Series* and an attempt at paper-bound books known as *Science Fiction Classics*.

In department headings, announcements, flyers, readers' columns, book reviews, and editorials, all references to the genre were standardized as science fiction, with one exception. Apparently there was a member of Gernsback's promotional staff who had not been fully indoctrinated. Research has not fully unmasked the culprit, but in the house ads which *Science Wonder Stories* ran for its companion magazine *Air Wonder Stories*, the term scientific fiction was *always* used. But the ads run in *Air Wonder Stories* for *Science Wonder Stories* always used the approved term science fiction.

Inventing new terms was all very well, but dissemination and popularization of the term was up to the readers. What was their line of thinking?

The most vocal of the readers were the active letter writers and fans. Therefore, the appearance of the first true science fiction fan magazine in history, *The Planet*, published in New York in July 1930 by The Scienceers could be expected to reflect their sentiments. Allen Glasser, editor of *The Planet*, primarily used science fiction throughout his journal, with an occasional lapse into scientific fiction in the text of the articles, apparently under the impression that it was grammatically more precise. Gernsback's old scientifiction was sometimes used, and it was not uncommon to have all three terms in the same article. To add to the confusion, science fiction was at times hyphenated and at other times not. Since science fiction was the newest of the terms, its preference was of great significance.

His former brain-children continued to live with Gernsback, however. Farnsworth Wright, editor and publisher of *Weird Tales*, contracted to run a series of ads in Gernsback's *Science Wonder Stories* emphasizing the fact that he published good interplanetary yarns as well as weird stories. Then, as now, advertisers' copy was sacrosanct. If Gernsback noticed the fact that the advertisement which *Weird Tales* ran in the April 1930 issue of *Science Wonder Stories* appealed to readers of the "*scientifiction* type of stories," he must have chalked it down to a belated victory and an educational job too well done.

In 1929, another magazine entered the field of tales of space and time. This was *Astounding Stories of Super Science*, the first issue of which was dated January 1930. Here was recorded the first major use of the term *super science* as a title for the genre. Would *Astounding* now attempt to popularize it?

The fourth, April 1930, issue of *Astounding* supplied the answer. In the first readers' column in that magazine, Harry Bates, *Astounding's* first editor and the man who later went on to write the story upon which the motion picture *The Day the Earth Stood Still* was based, used "science fiction" exclusively in his introductory notes.

But it was a pyrrhic victory for Gernsback. Virtually every letter in the "Readers' Corner" also used the words science fiction. Since most of the readers in the other important periodical of the type, *Amazing Stories*, were still using scientifiction, only one conclusion could be drawn. While *Astounding Stories* was the first non-Gernsback magazine to adopt the term science fiction, it was also adopting a good many of Gernsback's readers.

Amazing Stories, which since Gernsback's departure had shown, under the guidance of its editor, T. O'Connor Sloane, a tendency to swing away from scientifiction, the term that had become synonymous with it, toward scientific fiction, continued this trend. A new column, "In the Realm of Books," began in the September 1929 issue of *Amazing Stories*, run by science fiction collector C. A. Brandt, and carrying the subtitle, "Mostly Scientific Fiction."

Though "scientifiction" still appeared on the spine of *Amazing Stories*, in blurbs for a few of the stories, and on the editorial page, where *Amazing Stories* still referred to itself as "The Magazine of Scientifiction," there was decided movement away from its use. A full-page advertisement which ran in the September 1929 issue of that magazine offering six issues for a dollar, subtitled the publication "The Magazine of Scientific Fiction." In its readers' columns, letters continued to refer to scientifiction. It is possible that the letters were edited to read that way, but this is to be doubted for two primary reasons. First, *Amazing* itself was already pulling away from the editorial use of the term. Second, the first use of science fiction in the pages of *Amazing Stories* was by editor Sloane himself, in the heading to a letter in the Discussions column (page 568 of the September 1930 issue). This innovation was repeated in the heading of another letter, from author R. F. Starzl in the following number, with the slight difference that this time the term was hyphenated. The November number of *Amazing Stories* found the expression in the body of a reader's letter. From that point forth, its appearance in the readers' columns of *Amazing Stories* became increasingly frequent.

Though the onset of the Depression and the conservatism of its editor, Sloane, had put *Amazing Stories* together with its companion *Amazing Stories Quarterly* into a steady decline, they still represented the ranking publications in the field, partly because they were the first of all science fiction magazines and partly because the majority of leading science fiction writers of the day continued to write for them. Therefore, their adoption of the term science fiction was of considerable consequence. This process, however, was a gradual one. The July 1930 issue saw the subtitle "Scientific Fiction" added to *Amazing Stories* on the contents page. Oddly enough, the editorial page, which faced it, still bore the legend "The Magazine of Scientifiction." The August 1930 number had the words "And Other Scientific Fiction" tacked onto the "In Our Next Issue" notice on the contents page.

Throughout 1930 and 1931, the terms scientific fiction and scientifiction were used indiscriminately on the cover and in story blurbs. Then, abruptly, for the blurb of the story *The Stone from the Green Star* by Jack Williamson in the September 1931 issue, Sloane used science fiction for the first time in any story heading. In addition, "In Our Next Issue" ended with the line: "And Other Science Fiction." This became "And Other Scientific Fiction" again with the next number, but only temporarily. With the February 1932 issue it was "And Other Science Fiction" and remained that way.

The September 1931 *Amazing Stories* used "science fiction" on its cover for the very first time, as did the Fall–Winter 1932 edition of *Amazing Stories Quarterly*. The book review department, "In the Realm of Books," jettisoned the subtitle "And Other Scientific Fiction" for good with the February 1932 number of *Amazing Stories*. The really major change came when the November 1932 editorial page of *Amazing Stories* bore the subtitle "The Magazine of Science Fiction" in place of "The Magazine of Scientifiction"—which it had carried since its very first number in 1926. The contents page, which sometimes faced the editorial page, still carried the words "Scientific Fiction" beneath the title of the magazine. Scientifiction was used on the spine of the magazine for the last time the next month. This upset another tradition, since it had shared the limelight with the magazine's title in that spot since the third issue.

With its January 1933 number, *Amazing Stories* commenced a series of symbolic and impressionistic covers by Sigmund. Some modern editors of science fiction could have saved themselves a lot of grief if they managed a way to commune with the spirit of T. O'Connor Sloane and found out what happens to a science fiction magazine's circulation when it puts abstract art on the cover too many issues in a row. To balance the new, natty title logotype, the words scientific fiction were carried on the cover in very large letters. The March 1933 issue, however, found the artist in tune with the times, and science fiction was substituted for the duration of the disastrous experiment of "futuristic art for a futuristic magazine."

Dr. Sloane finally got around to the subtitle on the contents page, with the May 1933 issue, changing that to "Science Fiction," and then lived happily with the term ever after.

Weird Tales, however, had its own problems. The magazine was in danger of becoming as ghostly as some of its stories. It needed new readers desperately and the only conceivable source was from the science fiction magazines. Fearful of factionalism, Farnsworth Wright had through the years clung tenaciously to his own invention, weird-scientific, to describe his tales of galactic exploration and future invention. Now, with every other science fiction magazine using science fiction, he realized that while the term weird-scientific might be sop to his more mystical minded readers, it was frightening off would-be science fiction purchasers.

When *Argosy* turned down Otis Adelbert Kline's *Buccaneers of Venus* because Edgar Rice Burroughs had submitted *Pirates of Venus* to them, Wright was offered a chance at the story.

A contributor to *Weird Tales* since its first, March 1923, number, where he had *The Thing of a Thousand Shapes*, Kline was partial to Wright. For *Weird Tales* the story *Buccaneers of Venus* was to be the lure to attract thousands of science fiction readers, but to attract them Kline's story had to be called science fiction. Breaking precedent, Wright did just that, announcing *Buccaneers of Venus* in a ludicrous face-saving bit of double talk on page 573 of the October 1932 issue as "a stupendous weird-scientific story by a master of science fiction." This appears to be the earliest editorial use of science fiction in what was then America's oldest fantasy magazine.

Weird-scientific was subsequently used in *Weird Tales*, but it was as if Farnsworth Wright had tacitly agreed that though the genre was known as science fiction, he reserved the right to call it something else if the spirit so moved him.

Farnsworth Wright left *Weird Tales* in 1939 and died a short time later following an experimental brain operation to which he had agreed in the forlorn hope of correcting his worsening palsy due to Parkinson's disease.

When he left, the term weird-scientific was completely discarded by *Weird Tales*, except for a house ad which had been running for over fifteen years, offering the book *The Moon Doom* by A. G. Birch as a subscription premium.

Clayton Publications, publishers of *Astounding Stories*, foundered early in 1933, and *Astounding Stories*, along with several other titles, was purchased and revived by Street & Smith later the same year. As a leading publisher, adequately financed, Street & Smith could have pioneered a new term and possibly made it stick. However, F. Orlin Tremaine, the new editor of *Astounding Stories*, decided to stay with science-fiction, using it in the November 1933 issue of the magazine, and continuing to use it in hyphenated form for his entire term as editor.

But though the term science fiction had obtained recognition, no magazine carried it as a title or as part of a title. The first publications to use the term were not professional journals, but semiprofessional efforts published by the fans of science fiction themselves.

Among those fans were Jerry Siegel and Joe Schuster, who were to rise from their initial humble efforts to become the author and the artist, and the creators, of the comic strip character Superman. They published, out of Cleveland, a mimeographed fiction magazine titled, pure and simple, *Science Fiction*. The October 1932 date of the first issue (the magazine lasted five numbers) lost them the distinction of being the first publication to use science fiction in the title—by one month. That honor belongs to *Science Fiction Digest*, a printed, monthly combination science fiction fan magazine and trade journal, whose first issue was dated September 1932.

To add a dash of irony, two of the original publishers of *Science Fiction Digest*, Julius Schwartz and Mort Weisinger, now edit the Superman comic group, while Superman's originators, Siegel and Schuster, no longer have any connection with it.

Long years were to pass before science fiction publishers could shake off the idea that to call a spade a spade might frighten off prospective readers. Eventually, *Astounding Stories*, with John W. Campbell, Jr., in editorial control, changed its title to *Astounding Science-Fiction* with its March 1938 number and became the first newsstand publication to use science-fiction in its title. The hyphen was kept until November 1946, when it was unceremoniously dropped.

In 1939, Blue Ribbon Magazines rang up another "first" by publishing the initial newsstand magazine called simply *Science Fiction*. That number was dated March 1939. Though there was a long hiatus during and after World War II, publication was eventually resumed under the slightly altered title *Science Fiction Stories*.

It is far from unlikely that Blue Ribbon's use of the naked term science fiction as the full title for their entry may have been inspired by Hugo Gernsback. Louis Silberkleit, publisher of Blue Ribbon, was a friend of Gernsback's. The first issue of *Science Fiction* carried a full-page guest editorial by Gernsback.

To add credence to the possibility that Gernsback may have influenced Silberkleit to make bold use of the *Science Fiction* title was the fact that Charles D. Hornig, who had worked under Gernsback on *Wonder Stories*, was employed to edit the publication, possibly upon recommendation of his former boss. As a dyed-in-the-wool science fiction fan thoroughly sold on the use of the term science fiction, Hornig would have been in favor of the idea.

Today science fiction is so commonly used as part of the title of science fiction periodicals that when Blue Ribbon Magazines, now Columbia Publications, revived the magazine title *Science Fiction*, and put a blurb at the top of the cover, "The Original," active science fiction fans as well as casual readers referred to the magazine as "The Original Science Fiction Stories," believing that this meant no reprints. It came as a shock to many that what the line actually meant was that it was the first fantasy periodical to be titled simply *Science Fiction*.

Primary credit for the spread of the term to non-science fiction media belongs to the writers' magazines such as *The Author & Journalist*, *Writer's Digest*, *The Writer*, etc. Editors publishing in the tradition of Verne and Wells called their medium science fiction when sending editorial requirements to the writers' magazines. These listings were published as received, and that is the way the entire publishing field learned to refer to this new branch of magazine publishing.

A typical early use of "science fiction" in an article outside the science fiction field was Allen Glasser's *The Wane of Science Fiction*, which appeared in the June 1933 number of *The Author & Journalist*, written at a time when the Depression had almost swamped the science fiction periodical field. The same number carried an article by science fiction writer Ralph Milne Farley, which used the words science fiction in its text. To add to the old-home-week atmosphere Willard E. Hawkins, editor of *The Author & Journalist*, had written science fiction himself.

Even earlier was the January-February 1933 issue of an amateur publication dealing with dime novels and other nostalgic literature, published by Ralph P. Smith of Lawrence, Massachusetts, and called *Happy Hours Magazine*. That little periodical featured an article titled *Science Fiction in the Dime Novels*.

Acceptance of the term, let alone publication of any quantity of science fiction material, was much slower in the book world. Pocket Books, Inc., broke the ice when they permitted Donald A. Wollheim, an editor and writer of science fiction, to persuade them to publish *The Pocket Book of Science Fiction* in 1943.

A similar welcome to hard-cover book publishing had to wait until after the war, when Crown issued *The Best in Science Fiction*, edited by Groff Conklin, a real estate expert who took to science fiction as an avocation. The words science fiction had not been used in a cloth-bound book before that time, 1946.

The virility of the term science fiction is no better illustrated than by the manner in which it has taken hold in foreign nations. In England, Scotland, Canada, and Australia, science fiction is quite frequently part of the title of fantasy magazines. The expression is equally popular in France where one publication was titled simply *Science Fiction Magazine* and where *Fiction* continues to spread the gospel by drawing for the main part from *The Magazine of Fantasy and Science Fiction* for its content. That science fiction will remain the approved designation of space literature in France seems to have been assured by the publication for several years of a magazine titled *Satellite Science Fiction*, no direct kin of its American namesake. The ill-fated Dutch magazine *Planeet* carried the subtitle "Science Fiction," as the Swedish periodical *Hapna* still does. The German usage *"Utopische Romane"* (utopian novels) to describe tales of space and time has bowed to science fiction, due largely to the missionary work of the fan groups of that country.

There seems no question that science fiction is today the approved name for tales of space and time all over the world.

The other terms died slowly. They died hard, but they died.

Phil Stong, author of *State Fair*, edited a mixed collection of weird, fantasy, and science fiction tales which appeared in hard covers in 1941 under the title of *The Other Worlds*.

In his voluminous notes preceding the stories, he used "scientifiction" throughout in quotes.

Walter Gillings, a British enthusiast, produced a fan magazine titled *Scientifiction, The British Fantasy Review*, which
began in January 1937, and ran for seven issues.

After purchasing *Wonder Stories* from Gernsback, Standard Magazines changed the title to *Thrilling Wonder Stories*
and slanted it toward a younger group of readers. This policy
bore fruit so that in time *Thrilling Wonder Stories* begat
Startling Stories, which in its first issue, dated January 1939,
ran on its spine the slogan: "The Best In Scientifiction."
This it continued to do until January 1953, when smooth-
trimming the edges necessitated redesigning the publication
and the slogan was dropped.

That marked the end of the prominent usage of scientifiction anywhere, except for one technical point. An abbreviation of scientifiction had achieved widespread usage: "STF"
(pronounced *stef*). The peak of its prominence came in 1940
and 1941 when F. Orlin Tremaine, then editing *Comet* magazine, sprinkled the term liberally throughout the magazine,
both cover and interior. It has remained in use, though declining, among science fiction lovers until today.

However, the abbreviation of science fiction, "SF," is beginning to make inroads and may eventually supplant it. This
trend received impetus when Dell Publications brought out,
during the first half of 1956, the first of an annual series of
paper-backed anthologies of the best science fiction of the
past year, edited by Judith Merrill, and titled simply *SF*.
Beginning in 1955 England saw the publication of the first of
a number of hard-cover anthologies entitled "*sf*" (lower case).

"Super science" as an appellation for science fiction was
never a strong contender as "the" term. However, it has
established itself as a permanent reference for the more far-
fetched forms of "space opera" dealing with movements of
entire solar systems and disruptions on a galactic scale in the
grand tradition of Edward E. Smith. A brief period of prominence was inaugurated when Popular Publications, fetching

about for new titles during a boom in science fiction, turned out *Super Science Stories* for a number of years under the editorship of Frederik Pohl, starting in March 1940. Later, Crestwood published *Super Science Fiction* for several years.

"Fantascience stories," as a term, can be traced back no further than Williams and Wilkins, Baltimore publishers, who in the jacket blurb of John Taine's novel *Before the Dawn*, published in 1934, referred to that book as a work of "fantascience."

Science fiction fans used it frequently, as in the heading of feature columns entitled "Fantascience Filmart," in the fan magazine *Imagination*, and as the title of another prominent science fiction fan magazine, *Fantascience Digest*, which expired in 1941. Its publisher, Robert A. Madle, for a number of years wrote "Inside Science Fiction," a popular column which appeared in *Science Fiction Stories*.

The term scientific fiction, like an old soldier, merely faded away, until today its user, as well as the term, assumes an antiquarian aspect.

If there is anything left to argue about it is probably whether science fiction should be spelled with a hyphen. When Hugo Gernsback re-entered the science fiction field briefly with *Science-Fiction Plus* in 1953, the hyphen was deliberately inserted in "science-fiction" everywhere in the magazine to establish a different style. But production costs on this slick paper experiment with five-color covers and no ads sank it after only seven issues. As recently as its May 12, 1956, number, *Saturday Review* was still hyphenating "science-fiction."

From time to time, particularly during periods of slack sales, the suggestion arises that the term "science fiction" be changed to something more accurately descriptive of what the genre includes. These suggestions can no longer be taken seriously. The term has become generic and is now part of the vocabulary of both the general public and the in-group of readers. It has world-wide usage as identification for this category of literature.

20

THE FUTURE
IN PRESENT TENSE

The story has been retold many times of the U. S. military
agents who walked into the editorial offices of *Astounding
Science-Fiction* the spring of 1944 and demanded that its
editor, John W. Campbell, Jr., reveal the "leak" in the Manhattan Project. They were searching for the "obvious" source
of the atomic energy ideas in *Deadline* by Cleve Cartmill
(*Astounding Science-Fiction*, March 1944). The story has a
point because it anticipated a new, more serious attitude
toward science fiction. The following year the first atomic
bomb dropped on Hiroshima focused all eyes on the prophecies of this all-but-ignored literature. With this examination
of a hitherto neglected if not derided field came respect it
had not previously enjoyed. This chapter is intended briefly
to bring the story up to date. Only the major influences in
science fiction since 1938 are discussed at all.

It would have seemed, with the end of World War II, with atomic energy, rockets, jet planes, and scores of other fictional dreams transformed into reality, that 1945 would have marked the logical time for a science fiction renaissance. Unfortunately for logic, the renaissance had occurred before the outbreak of the war and had taken a sociological and literary direction, with prophecy a declining and minor part of the literature.

Therefore, curiosity seekers sampling science fiction for the first time and looking for some stimulating scientific predictions found instead that the futuristic devices present in most stories were stereotyped to facilitate either a psychological or philosophical study, as in the leading magazines, or a straight action adventure, as in those with more juvenile appeal.

Science fiction, like any other kind of literature, is an evolving art. Publishers and editors could not be expected to know that some day prophecy would be in great popular demand and that they should build toward that end. For them, survival in terms of continued reader interest meant a constantly changing policy to give the feel of freshness to the product. In terms of quantity, a revival of interest was in full swing in science fiction by the end of 1938. That was the year that *Amazing Stories*, the oldest magazine in the field but an unprofitable venture for at least the previous four years, was sold to Ziff-Davis Publications. As early as 1934, that magazine inadvertently revealed in its annual statement of ownership an average monthly circulation of only 19,000. Even in the era of soup kitchens and apple vendors, so low a figure could scarcely yield a profit. Within a few issues under the new ownership, word got out in the trade that *Amazing Stories*, with better distribution, new window dressing, and a price reduction, was climbing toward 50,000 sales.

Almost concurrently, the first new science fiction magazine in nearly seven years made its appearance, issued by Red Circle Publications and named *Marvel Science Stories*. The editor, Robert O. Erisman, made no secret of the fact that the first issue of the magazine, dated August 1938, had sold 60,000 copies. To publishers in the pulp magazine field, working on the theory that a few hundred dollars an issue was an acceptable profit, the tempting possibility of the $2,000 an issue inherent in a readership of 60,000 could not be overlooked. As a result, virtually overnight, science fiction became a regular part of most pulp publishers' strings.

There is a school of thought that holds that the dramatic Orson Welles *War of the Worlds* scare, on the evening of October 30, 1938, provided the real basis of the science fiction magazine boom of that period. That the program may have helped give impetus to the spate of new publications is quite possible, but that it inspired them is impossible, since four new magazines—*Startling Stories, Fantastic Adventures, Strange Stories,* and *Dynamic Science Stories*—all had been publicly announced as forthcoming *before* the date of the program.

Until wartime paper shortages curtailed publishers' optimism *Unknown, Science Fiction, Science Fiction Quarterly, Future Fiction, Famous Fantastic Mysteries, Fantastic Novels, Planet Stories, Captain Future, Astonishing Stories, Super Science Stories, Stirring Science Stories, Cosmic Stories, Comet, Uncanny Tales,* and *Uncanny Stories* would be added to the list. By contrast, before the boom there had been but four magazines in publication, and one of them was predominantly supernatural—*Astounding Science-Fiction, Thrilling Wonder Stories, Amazing Stories,* and *Weird Tales.*

The demands of this widening market naturally attracted to the field many authors who had never written science fiction, as well as lured back others who had been absent for a long period. Most important, it encouraged the development of new talent, writers destined to remake the form of science fiction.

The key figure in this process is John W. Campbell, editor of *Astounding Science-Fiction.* Campbell, a big man with hawklike features, who for years permitted the rumor to circulate that he had flunked out of Massachusetts Institute of

Technology because of failing grades in English (actually it was due to his inability to master German), had become the editor of *Astounding Stories* in 1937. Though only twenty-eight, he was regarded then as one of the half-dozen greatest living writers of science fiction. He had established his first reputation by composing great super-science epics which involved action on a galactic scale and which he laced through with hundreds of provocative ideas. When the popularity of that type of story began to ebb, he adopted the pseudonym Don A. Stuart and specialized in delicate mood pieces directing sympathy toward the works of man, displaying the creations of the human mind and the manifestations of research and discovery as fundamentally benevolent and trustworthy. He also underscored the need for incorporating some cementing philosophy as an ingredient of science fiction, in the process engaging in a high degree of experimentalism in presentation of ideas which had a substantial influence on the writers who followed him.

The magazine he edited was stable, profitable, and the accepted leader in its field. It paid top rates and was regarded as a prestige publication. The editor of such a magazine was in a position to assume literary leadership and shape the direction of the entire field. This Campbell proceeded to do.

It was a peculiarity of Campbell's outlook that he was forever mentally hypothesizing his own universes, philosophies, "natural" laws, to fit whatever tidbits of information intrigued him at the moment. If he ran across a seeming paradox, he fabricated his own train of highly imaginative logic to explain it. Frequently, some relatively minor research would have revealed that the answers were already known and documented, but Campbell was always suspicious of pat theories and, besides, he found them rarely as fascinating as his own.

This was an attitude made to order for a successful science fiction writer. Campbell, as a result, was a fount of ideas that never ran dry. These ideas he fed to his authors at such a prodigal rate that it can be truthfully said most of them owed as much of their success to him as they did to their own talent.

A relatively new author he inherited when he took over the magazine was Eric Frank Russell, an iconoclastic Britisher who first came to the attention of the readers by trading on Stanley G. Weinbaum's method in *The Saga of Pelican West* (*Astounding Stories*, February 1937). Russell gained considerable notoriety when a novel he submitted gave Campbell the idea of launching a new fantasy magazine, composed of "fairy tales for grownups," to be called *Unknown*. The novel, *Sinister Barrier*, led off the first (March 1939) number of the new publication and was based on the ideas of Charles Fort, suggesting that the earth was "property" owned by aliens, and that humanity was being "raised" by them, much as we breed cattle.

Besides acting as the apostle of Fortean concepts, Russell eventually developed into one of the finest craftsmen in the field; his short story *Allamogoosa* won the "Hugo" Award in 1955 as the best science fiction short story of the year.

Another favorite of Campbell's during that early period was that rarity among science fiction authors, a bona fide satirist stylistically competent enough to pull off the jibes which are the lifeblood of such work. This was L. Sprague de Camp, a tall, handsome man whose light fantasies were based on a rare degree of scholarship. De Camp pointed the way to a lighter, less self-conscious tone in science fiction. Few of the writers who later tried to emulate him anticipated the labor that went into attaining that "easy" style and they soon deserted it for a less strenuous line.

The discovery and rise to popularity of Lester Del Rey, a small, almost delicate youth with a powerful voice and equally powerful mind, came in 1938. Del Rey wrote with a sentimentality that would have dissolved into bathos if he had not been gifted with a style of near poetry. His short story *Helen O'Loy* (*Astounding Science-Fiction*, December 1938), about a "female" robot who falls in love with her owner, is regarded as a classic in the restricting but fascinating art of the robot story. In vivid contrast, his story *Nerves* (*Astounding Science-Fiction*, December 1942, later expanded into a novel), which employed brittle hard prose to relate the drama resulting from an accident in an atomic energy plant, is regarded as a milestone in science fiction realism.

Recruited from the ranks of the more prolific pulpsters was L. Ron Hubbard, a real professional down to the electric typewriter, whose flaming red hair accurately indicated the spirit of a true adventurer. He first tried science fiction and fantasy in a farcical vein but really scored when he wrote *Final Blackout* (*Astounding Science-Fiction*, April, May, June, 1940), the most powerful antiwar novel in future tense up until then, with characterization memorable by any standards, but almost transcendental in science fiction.

"We rather suspect the name of A. E. van Vogt will be among those of top favorites a year or so from now," Campbell predicted in forecasting *Black Destroyer* by that author, the cover story of the July 1939 issue of *Astounding Science-Fiction*. It was quite a safe prediction. Van Vogt, a near-sighted Canadian with a penchant for championing offbeat self-improvement cults, was a born storyteller capable of translating his personal obsessions into excellent entertainment. He created numerous talented monsters in his early stories; but he is best known for an entirely new approach to the exceptional individual or "mutant" in *Slan* (*Astounding Science-Fiction*, October, November, December, 1940; published in book form in 1946 by Arkham House), which inspired literally hundreds of stories on the theme. He popularized semantics, the science of the meaning of words, as a basis for science fiction stories and championed monarchies (see *The Weapon Makers*) as the government of the future so engrossingly it almost evolved into a trend.

The very same, July 1939, issue, a Brooklyn candy store owner's son, aspiring chemist Isaac Asimov appeared with *Trends*, a story which evaluated the mass psychology and politics that would enter into national participation in space travel. Asimov went on to revolutionize robot stories by introducing, in *Runaround* (March 1942, in *Astounding Science-Fiction*) The Three Rules of Robotics which would circumscribe the behavior of the pseudo-men, and thus charted a rich vein of plot exploitation. He dramatized the Machiavellian, behind-the-scenes political maneuvers that prompted action, rather than action itself, popularizing in the process the concept of galactic empires with most inhabitable planets populated by human beings rather than alien creatures. While Asimov was not discovered by Campbell, a good part of his most effective contributions to the field owed some debt to that editor.

Robert A. Heinlein, Annapolis graduate and practicing engineer, who made his debut in science fiction with a short story, *Life Line*, in the August 1939 issue of *Astounding Science-Fiction*, would thereafter become possibly the single most important figure in modern science fiction. In ideas, he pioneered in the magazine's exploration of the role of religion in the world of the future, particularly the part it might play in government. His novel *Sixth Column*, first published in 1940, broke the long-standing taboo against religion in science fiction and opened the path for a string of memorable novels including *Gather Darkness* by Fritz Leiber, Jr., *A Canticle for Leibowitz* by Walter M. Miller, and *A Case of Conscience* by James Blish.

He outlined a "History of the Future" for himself and generally fitted his writings into that framework, which made for greater internal consistency, and increased enjoyment on the part of the readers. Other authors, including figures as prominent as Isaac Asimov and Clifford D. Simak, to a greater or lesser degree adopted this method of an imposed consistency in their own writing.

The concept of a gigantic spaceship on its way to the distant stars, a self-contained world in which new generations were born and died without ever setting foot on a planet, was delineated so effectively by Heinlein in his novelette *Universe* (1941) that it thereafter became a standard and frequent plot in science fiction.

Heinlein's most important influence on science fiction, however, has been stylistic. He told his stories in a matter-of-fact manner which gave the impression that his characters accepted the marvels about them as a matter of course. Equally adept at straight narrative or dialogue he adroitly wove an extraordinary amount of background concerning the science of the future into his imaginative explorations, giving them the ring of authenticity.

Dozens of young writers imitated his casual, almost sophisticated approach, giving science fiction thereby a polish it had rarely hitherto possessed; but they were unable or unwilling to weave the substance of the world of tomorrow into their narratives. The result was ultimately harmful to the main body of science fiction, since the fascinating scientific speculations which were the wellspring of the genre were replaced by standardized symbols, and science fiction gained a veneer of literary sheen at the expense of part of its substance.

As if it were not enough to garner van Vogt, Asimov, and Heinlein in a two-month period, Campbell, in the September 1939 *Astounding Science-Fiction*, presented Theodore Sturgeon with *Ether Breather*, a light tale of electronic gremlins playing hob with television performances at a hypothetical future date when great networks would be operating across the nation just like 1939's radio. Sturgeon was a literary phenomenon. In every one of his stories he strove not only for originality of idea or approach, but for a style to fit the story line as well. No two stories were even remotely alike. He was forever experimenting. There were a certain number of duds, but every now and then all elements of his abilities came into focus and he produced landmarks in science fiction. The climax came in his novel *More Than Human* (1953), which so successfully utilized Gestalt psychology as the basis of the plot that it won the International Fantasy Award as the best novel of the year. Sturgeon made science fiction's writers aware that changing the style of writing to fit the mood and nature of the material could be most effective in achieving story impact.

With such a plethora of rich talent, John Campbell easily outdistanced his competition. Old stand-bys seemed to blossom under his direction. Clifford D. Simak, news editor of the *Minneapolis Star*, a dreamer with his heart still pledged to the farmland where he had been raised but with his eyes lifted to the stars, projected a vast future history of mankind in the manner of a more kindly Olaf Stapledon, in a series of stories collectively titled *City*, which also won the 1953 International Fantasy Award as a book.

With the events following Pearl Harbor, Campbell found most of his brilliant crew recruited by the armed services. He began to develop "newcomers" to replace them. The two best of these were generally conceded to be Lewis Padgett and Lawrence O'Donnell. Reader interest in the activities of this duo of promising authors forced an admission that they were actually Henry Kuttner and Catherine L. Moore, a married couple who had been writing fantasy together since 1938.

Kuttner was a retiring little man with a tremendous sense of humor. Previously his writing career had been undistinguished. He had been versatile and prolific but largely imitative. Under the Lewis Padgett disguise he perfected technical writing skills that were the envy of his contemporaries and, though his most successful work was based on adapting the methods of John Collier's fantasies to science fiction, he added enough novelty to win a loyal following.

To what degree his wife deserves credit for his transformation from a second-line hack to a top-drawer pro may never be completely resolved, since they wrote in relays, each taking over where the other left off. C. L. Moore had established a reputation as a veritable giant in the field of fantasy as far back as 1933. She was without question one of the most able women ever to contribute to the science fiction magazines. Her strong points were beauty of style, excellence of characterization, and a considerable ability to create and sustain a mood even over a relatively long piece of work.

Kuttner was better at the mechanics of plotting and had a

light touch foreign to the very serious and self-conscious efforts of Moore; nevertheless, the milestones appear to have been those works definitely attributed almost entirely to Moore. From her early famous series about the interplanetary adventurer Northwest Smith (*Weird Tales*, 1933–1939) to the esthetic nuances of *Vintage Season* (*Astounding Science Fiction*, September 1946), under the cloak of Lawrence O'Donnell), in which men of the future run tourist trips to the past, there is more that is distinguished and permanent about her work.

From all of the foregoing it would appear that Campbell's magazine was science fiction and science fiction was Campbell in the period following 1938. While it is true that his influence was monumental, he was not the only source of progress, nor were his instincts always correct.

Certainly one of the most famous writers to emerge from the science fiction magazines has been Ray Bradbury, who owes virtually nothing to Campbell. He began writing as a teen-age science fiction fan, publishing his efforts under aliases in his own mimeographed publication, *Futuria Fantasia*. Literally a self-made writer, he wrote tirelessly, endlessly piling up mountains of rejection slips years on end. Finally, drawing upon psychological horrors from the fears of his childhood, which he transformed into chilling episodes for *Weird Tales* magazine, he began to win recognition.

Studying mainstream writers, he wrote science fiction in an unlikely synthesis of the styles of Hemingway and Wolfe and surprisingly sold his stories to action magazines like *Planet Stories*, *Thrilling Wonder Stories*, and *Amazing Stories*. Employing this technique he approached the themes of the future and exploration of other worlds entirely from the emotional standpoint. He raged against throwing beer cans in Martian canals, projected today's commercialism in describing hot-dog stands on Mars, predicted attempts to convert the Martians to Christianity, and provocatively asked what would happen if the Negroes got to Mars first and arranged to segregate the whites. A group of these artistically

done literary protestations were collected into a loosely inte-
grated book called *The Martian Chronicles* (1950). The
result was a critical success and the blossoming of a bright
literary career, but even before this Bradbury was already
serving as a model for a number of science fiction writers, the
most prominent of whom was Richard Matheson, who went
on to make his mark in—and out—of the science fiction
world.

An illustrious figure in science fiction, who made an international reputation without entering the Campbell circle, is
British author Arthur C. Clarke. Clarke was mightily impressed by Campbell the writer even during his early attempts
at science fiction writing, which included *Against the Fall of
Night*, a novel in the mood of the stories of Don A. Stuart—
who was Campbell. Nevertheless, Clarke never broke with
the old tradition of science fiction. Possessing an excellent
technical background he was one with the Gernsback conception that scientists are the best source for science fiction.
A joint Book-of-the-Month-Club selection, his work of nonfiction *Exploration of Space* served as the springboard for
securing serious critical attention for his science fiction. The
result was international renown as a writer of science fiction,
particularly for *Childhood's End, The City and the Stars,
The Deep Range,* and *A Fall of Moon Dust,* the last of
which managed financially and critically to eclipse most of its
predecessors.

Yet essentially Clarke does not belong in the modern
tradition. The sophisticated dialogue, the scientific explanation through inference which has become the stock in trade
of so many of the modern writers, contrast with his traditional, straightforward prose, which is occasionally illumined
with flashes of poetry. A very real and very deep scientific
knowledge lends to his stories a note of authenticity which
few of his contemporaries can match. Like Bradbury, he has
achieved recognition on his own terms and remains an independent spirit.

Virtually unknown outside science fiction, but one of the

few original voices to arise in the past decade, is Philip José Farmer. Ever since its beginnings, science fiction had disdained sex and to a lesser degree even love interest as a part of its make-up. The few efforts to incorporate sexuality into science fiction were miserable failures. Farmer was the great exception. His short novel *The Lovers*, which appeared in 1952, was a landmark in the history of science fiction. Every word of the 40,000-word story was keyed to the basic theme of sex, but it was sex treated as a scientific base of the story, not for its own sake or for titillation. Undisciplined and uneven in style, Farmer nevertheless distilled into his thematic variations on scientific sex a note of freshness and originality that denoted a major shaper of the field. His novelette *The Mother*, involving the symbiotic sexual relationship of an earthman with a monstrous otherworldly life form, does things with Freud that the *avant-garde* never thought of, and belongs in the roster of important modern American short stories.

His appearance and popularity were regarded as a signal for the breaking of taboos by a bevy of science fiction writers who treated sex as phenomenon rather than science. After a brief flurry, sex is again rare in science fiction, except when written by Farmer.

In previous decades, science fiction pulp writers had borrowed much from men outside the field. Since 1940, writers have been few who are divorced from the magazines and who contribute meaningfully to science fiction. The most noteworthy among this handful were C. S. Lewis of *Screwtape Letters* fame; H. F. Heard, a graduate from detective thrillers who first attracted attention with *A Taste for Honey*; and George Orwell, who set the stage for his big performance with a satiric fantasy on communism, *Animal Farm*.

The use of science fiction to promote theological concepts is as old as the literature, though in general the magazines have steered clear of religion, but C. S. Lewis in his conception of planets where the human race has not fallen from grace and where there was no original sin, as unfolded in the trilogy *Out of the Silent Planet* (1943), *Perelandra* (1944), and *That Hideous Strength* (1945), uncovered the potential psychological drama in science fiction of plots which put religious dogma to the test.

The conscious use of religion as an essential plot theme in the modern science fiction magazines began with *If This Goes On——* by Robert A. Heinlein (*Astounding Science-Fiction*, February 1940) and is continuing. Lewis did succeed, however, in placing the subject more tightly in focus, particularly as far as the precepts of Catholicism were concerned and he therefore can be termed an important influence.

George Orwell in *1984* (published in 1949) put his very great faculties to work to write a novel of unusual power warning about the ruthlessness, decadence, and tyranny of the absolute state. The idea of a utopia in reverse is very old in science fiction, but Orwell's handling is considered classic.

A very skillfully developed, slightly earlier novel by H. F. Heard, *Doppelgangers* (1947), deserves to be discussed whenever Orwell's book is, because it ingeniously shows how man can be as hopelessly enslaved and deprived of all his rights by lavishing him with all the comfort and kindness that modern science and psychology can devise. The iron hand is necessary for relatively few.

The "warning" story as exemplified by Orwell and Heard had been a constant part of science fiction throughout its entire existence. Heinlein's *If This Goes On——* (1940) quite literally presents all the elements contained in Orwell's *1984*, which came nine years later. Without denying the fact that *1984* is the superior work, Orwell deserves no medals for farsightedness or originality. He is reacting to a danger after it has become crystal-clear, in 1949. This is hindsight not foresight. On the other hand, the freedom of thought and unfettered imagination traditional in science fiction magazines outlined the pattern before it had fairly emerged—in 1940.

Orwell may never have read a science fiction magazine, but Heard clearly reveals both in the style and the context of *Doppelgangers* that he was thoroughly familiar with the field. His story could have been published in a leading science fiction magazine without being out of place and would have been applauded as an original twist on an old theme.

It is in no way intended to detract from the efforts of Lewis, Heard, and Orwell to say that they lagged behind the pulp magazines. In the past, this was not necessarily true of outside writers who attempted science fiction. Men like Aldous Huxley, Olaf Stapledon, Karel Čapek, and Philip Wylie were by and large ahead of the pulpsters, if only because they were not bound by magazine taboos. As limitations were removed from the plot spectrum of magazine science fiction by its editors, "mainstream" authors who attempted science fiction borrowed much and returned little to the advancement of the literary form.

Two editors who contributed strongly to a wider freedom of expression in science fiction were Anthony Boucher (pen name of William Anthony Parker White), who, as H. H. Holme, established his first reputation as a novelist in the detective field, and Horace L. Gold, who began writing science fiction in 1934 as Clyde Crane Campbell and had put in a stint as a pulp editor with Standard Magazines in the forties.

With Lawrence E. Spivak as publisher, Boucher thought up what was to become *The Magazine of Fantasy and Science Fiction*, the first issue dated Fall 1949. A digest-size publication, with type set straight across the page like a book rather that in the two columns of the pulp magazines, its early intent appeared to be to establish a prestige publication in the fantasy field comparable to what *Ellery Queen's Mystery Magazine* (also published by Spivak) had become in the detective.

The Magazine of Fantasy and Science Fiction became the repository of the "cute" story with good writing in the modern vein and of anything that was off-trail. As a respected critic of detective stories Anthony Boucher was listened to when he urged newspaper and magazine reviewers to give increased coverage to science fiction books (which had begun to pour out at an unprecedented rate, spearheaded by science fiction fans going into the publishing business). Boucher also established a fantasy and science fiction review column in the book section of the Sunday New York *Herald-Tribune*. He gave his own magazine literary tone with comprehensive book coverage and the inclusion of articles of literary quarterly quality on diverse aspects of the field.

Critical recognition of his magazine was phenomenal. There were some years when all but a half-dozen of the magazine's stories were anthologized or collected in hard covers. Particularly notable was the editor's discovery of Richard Matheson. Another milestone was the publication of the novel *Bring the Jubilee* by Ward Moore, widely acknowledged as the best story produced to that time or what would have happened if the South had won the Civil War. Even more important was the first publication of a series of novelettes that later made up the heart of *A Canticle for Leibowitz*, by Walter M. Miller, possibly the finest science fiction novel on a theological theme to come out of the magazines. The magazine's influence in presenting a new image of science fiction to the public succeeded far out of proportion to its circulation.

Horace L. Gold was responsible for conceiving and for ten years editing *Galaxy Science Fiction*, which, with its first issue, dated October 1950, took up exploration of an aspect of science fiction in which John Campbell of *Astounding Science Fiction* was losing interest: the investigation of the psychological and sociological effects of tomorrow's world on human beings. Gold underscored the importance of slick, even arch writing in the modern vein. He would give short shrift to the most original concept if it were not placed in the frame he considered most appropriate.

The result was an exceptional refinement and sophistication of a narrow area of science fiction (which came to be called "psychological science fiction") for a period of about four years, followed by a steady and uninterrupted decline due to the strait-jacket approach, until the editorship finally passed into the hands of Frederik Pohl in 1960.

Nevertheless, the record of achievement was considerable: Ray Bradbury's first short novel *The Fireman* (reissued in book form as *Fahrenheit 451* in February 1951); *The Demolished Man* (January, February, March, 1952), a pyrotechnic display of the type of fiction Gold championed, an achievement which catapulted Alfred Bester into the top ranks of science fiction writers: *Gravy Planet* (June, July, August, 1952), a satirically grim foreboding of advertising agencies in control of the world, which caused the science fiction world to upgrade their estimates of its authors, Frederik Pohl and Cyril Kornbluth; *The Caves of Steel* (October, November, December, 1953), a novel accomplishing the impossible by successfully amalgamating detective stories with science fiction, an achievement of Isaac Asimov —as well as an impressive roster of outstanding stories in the shorter lengths.

Throughout the 1940s and the early 1950s, a number of specialized magazines featuring reprints of science fiction and fantasy from a wide variety of sources enjoyed popularity. Catering to the collecting instincts of a sizable portion of the readership, the best of them, *Famous Fantastic Mysteries,* was published from 1939 to 1953 and enjoyed years when it was voted in impartial national polls as the most popular magazine in the field, eclipsing those publishing all-new stories. Another, *Avon Fantasy Reader,* contributed toward popularizing the digest-size periodical which eventually replaced the larger pulp format.

The reprint magazines undoubtedly served as a balance against the increasing sophistication and "in"-ness of the literature. Their demise was in good part attributable to the rising popularity of paperback books, which furnished an increasing quantity and a selection of reprints in editions priced no higher than the magazines.

The preoccupation with how things were said instead of what was said resulted in a relatively static condition in the field as far as new concepts were concerned. This situation was aggravated by a drastic reversion to stark simplicity of theme as new discoveries in atomic energy and space presented themselves. Fictional "documentaries," many written by the top names in the field, began to appear. Their subjects: the preparation for the first moon flight, the first moon flight, the first earth satellite, the first nuclear war, the psychological impact on the first man in orbit. Magazine covers showed nothing more thrilling than a Vanguard rocket rising from its pad.

Suave writing had diluted most of the "sense of wonder" in science fiction. The "documentary," too close to the present to allow for any imagination, rinsed out most of what remained.

Despite its loss of direction and cessation of evolution as a literary type during the early 1950s, a significant number of excellent practitioners produced a substantial body of outstanding stories under the broad and generalized classification of "modern science fiction."

Its writers have been floundering, but veterans of the field feel confident that science fiction will right itself, take direction, and assume the role it is best suited for: the dramatic presentation of *new* scientific concepts and the social, psychological, and philosophical consequences of those ideas.

INDEX

About the Author

SAM MOSKOWITZ is widely recognized as the leading authority on the history of science fiction. His library of science fiction works, both magazines and books, encompasses what is probably the most complete collection in the world. He published a history of science fiction fandom, *The Immortal Storm*, in 1954, shortly after he served as editor of *Science-Fiction Plus*, a notable experiment in science fiction magazine publishing. Mr. Moskowitz has taught college extension courses in science fiction writing and was a literary agent in the field for a number of years. He has edited several anthologies and collections, both hard- and soft-cover, has published scores of articles in the principal magazines on the history of science fiction, in addition to some dozen stories, was an organizer in 1939 of The First World Science Fiction Convention—so successful that world conventions have been held every year since—and is also founder of the Eastern Science Fiction Association, the principal group of science fiction enthusiasts in the eastern states.